Certificate in Corporate Finance

Corporate Finance Technical Foundations

Edition 7, January 2016

This learning manual relates to syllabus version 11.0 and will cover examinations from **11 April 2016 to 10 April 2017**

APPROVED WORKBOOK

Welcome to the Chartered Institute for Securities & Investment's Corporate Finance Technical Foundations study material.

This workbook has been written to prepare you for the Chartered Institute for Securities & Investment's Corporate Finance Technical Foundations examination.

Published by:
Chartered Institute for Securities & Investment
© Chartered Institute for Securities & Investment 2016
8 Eastcheap
London
EC3M 1AE
Tel: +44 20 7645 0600
Fax: +44 20 7645 0601

Email: customersupport@cisi.org
www.cisi.org/qualifications

Author:
Kate Creighton, Chartered MCSI

Reviewers:
Jon Beckett, Chartered MCSI
Nick Harriss, Chartered FCSI

This is an educational manual only and the Chartered Institute for Securities & Investment accepts no responsibility for persons undertaking trading or investments in whatever form.

While every effort has been made to ensure its accuracy, no responsibility for loss occasioned to any person acting or refraining from action as a result of any material in this publication can be accepted by the publisher or authors.

A learning map, which contains the full syllabus, appears at the end of this manual. The syllabus can also be viewed on cisi.org and is also available by contacting the Customer Support Centre on +44 20 7645 0777. Please note that the examination is based upon the syllabus. Candidates are reminded to check the Candidate Update area details (cisi.org/candidateupdate) on a regular basis for updates as a result of industry change(s) that could affect their examination.

The questions contained in this manual are designed as an aid to revision of different areas of the syllabus and to help you consolidate your learning chapter by chapter.

Learning manual version: 7.1 (January 2016)

Learning and Professional Development with the CISI

The Chartered Institute for Securities & Investment is the leading professional body for those who work in, or aspire to work in, the investment sector, and we are passionately committed to enhancing knowledge, skills and integrity – the three pillars of professionalism at the heart of our Chartered body.

CISI examinations are used extensively by firms to meet the requirements of government regulators. Besides the regulators in the UK, where the CISI head office is based, CISI examinations are recognised by a wide range of governments and their regulators, from Singapore to Dubai and the US. Around 50,000 examinations are taken each year, and it is compulsory for candidates to use CISI learning manuals to prepare for CISI examinations so that they have the best chance of success. Our learning manuals are normally revised every year by experts who themselves work in the industry and also by our Accredited Training Partners, who offer training and elearning to help prepare candidates for the examinations. Information for candidates is also posted on a special area of our website: cisi.org/candidateupdate.

This learning manual not only provides a thorough preparation for the examination it refers to, it is also a valuable desktop reference for practitioners, and studying from it counts towards your Continuing Professional Development (CPD). Mock examination papers, for most of our titles, will be made available on our website, as an additional revision tool.

CISI examination candidates are automatically registered, without additional charge, as student members for one year (should they not be members of the CISI already), and this enables you to use a vast range of online resources, including CISI TV, free of any additional charge. The CISI has more than 40,000 members, and nearly half of them have already completed relevant qualifications and transferred to a core membership grade. You will find more information about the next steps for this at the end of this manual.

With best wishes for your studies.

Lydia Romero, Global Director of Learning

It is estimated that this manual will require approximately 80 hours of study time.

What next?
See the back of this book for details of CISI membership.

Need more support to pass your exam?
See our section on Accredited Training Providers.

Want to leave feedback?
Please email your comments to learningresources@cisi.org

Chapter One

Quantitative Methods for Corporate Finance

This syllabus area will provide approximately 6 of the 50 examination questions

1. Introduction

The key principles of financial mathematics (or quantitative methods) can be summarised in the following three aphorisms:

1. Don't put all your eggs in one basket.
2. A bird in the hand is worth two in the bush.
3. There's no such thing as a free lunch.

These are reflected in the following fundamental financial principles:

1. A portfolio with many different types of investment is less risky than a portfolio with only one type – the principle of diversification.
2. A pound (or euro or dollar) today is worth more than the promise of a pound tomorrow – the principle of the time value of money.
3. To earn a higher return on an investment, you have to accept a higher level of risk – the principle of risk versus reward.

Each of these principles can be applied using a quantitative methodology, or series of formulae, to derive conclusions on investment decisions. The main quantitative tools for corporate finance are:

1. Correlation and covariance – measuring the degree and strength of the relationship between the returns on two different investments.
2. Discounting – to calculate the value in today's terms of cash flows expected in the future.
3. Variance and standard deviation – to calculate the variability of returns on investments based on historical data.

2. Financial Mathematics

Learning Objective

1.1.1   Understand how to measure the risk and return of investments

2.1   Risk and Return of Investments

Some investments are riskier than others. A short-term loan issued by a government is more likely to generate its promised return on investment than an equity stake in a small mineral exploration company searching for gold in a politically sensitive emerging economy. However, while there is limited risk to the returns on the government loan, there is also limited potential. The equity investment, albeit carrying more risk to both income and capital, could also generate theoretically unlimited returns.

Understanding how to measure risk, and ensure that the potential returns compensate investors adequately for this risk, is key to investment decision-making.

In this context, risk is defined as **the possibility that actual returns will be different from expected returns**.

The greater the variability of returns, the greater the risk. Risk encompasses both downside potential (the possibility of lower income, or erosion of capital invested) and upside potential (the possibility of higher income, or capital growth). Therefore, we need to understand potential returns in order to understand risk.

Different asset classes are expected to have different risk/return profiles. (An asset class is a group of investments that share the same general characteristics, for example, gilts, shares of FTSE 100 companies, property, or AAA-rated corporate bonds.)

A graphical depiction of the main UK asset classes, showing their different risk/return profiles, is as follows:

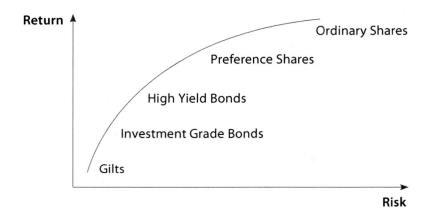

2.2 Holding Period Return

Investors need to be able to compare the returns of different asset classes, and different investments within an asset class, in a consistent way.

The most common way of measuring return on investment is called the **holding period return (HPR)**, which is the total return on an investment over a specified time period, typically a year. The HPR incorporates both the change in price over the specified time period **AND** the income earned from that investment (interest, dividends, or other cash receipts).

The formula for HPR is:

$$\frac{((\text{Price at end of period } P_1 - \text{Price at start of period } P_0) + \text{Cash flow from investment CF})}{\text{Price at start of period } P_0}$$

or,

$$\text{Return} = \frac{((P_1 - P_0) + CF)}{P_0}$$

Example

1.   Purchase of a bond with exactly one year remaining until maturity when the face value is repaid. The bond's purchase price is £98 and its face value is £100. During the year, you received £5 in interest.

2.   Purchase of a share in Comeback plc on 1 April 2015 for 79.8p. It was then sold on 30 June 2015 for 101.5p. The company's final dividend of 1.1p was paid to all shareholders in May 2015.

What are the holding period returns?

1.   (($100 – £98) + £5) / £98 = £7 / £98 = 0.07143 or 7.14% per annum.
2.   ((101.5p – 79.8p) + 1.1p) / 79.8p = 22.8p / 79.8p = 0.2857 or 28.57% during the quarter.

Note that the second example presents the return on Comeback shares on a 'per quarter' basis. It is more helpful to calculate annual returns, as these can be compared with other investments more easily. Therefore, we use a formula that will 'annualise' returns for a shorter period:

$$(1 + HPR)^n - 1$$

where:

n = the number of periods per year.

On an annualised basis, the Comeback return would be:

$$(1.2857)^4 - 1 = 2.732 - 1 = 1.732 = 173.2\%$$

On the face of it, this is an impressive return for a three-month investment. However, although this figure is useful for comparing returns on investments with different terms, it is not the same as the investor's actual annual return; this depends on how he or she manages to reinvest the share sale proceeds.

2.3   Measuring Average Return

Learning Objective

1.1.2   Be able to calculate the expected return/arithmetic mean of investments

2.3.1   Arithmetic Mean

In the section above, we examined the annualised returns for a single period. However, it is more common to examine the annualised return of an investment over a longer period.

The simplest way of measuring longer-term returns is to calculate the arithmetic mean (the average) of the single-period returns. The average of a group of returns is the sum of the returns divided by the number of returns. In a mathematical format, this is presented as:

$$Mean = \frac{\Sigma HPR}{n}$$

where:

$\sum$HPR = the sum of all holding period returns.

n = the number of returns being measured.

So, for example, let us examine the returns on a portfolio of shares over five years:

Year	Annual Return/HPR
1	16%
2	–32%
3	18%
4	4%
5	6%
Mean	2.4%

ie, (16% – 32% + 18% + 4% + 6%) / 5 = 2.4%.

2.3.2 Historic Returns and Expected Returns

Stock market analysts often use long-term historical arithmetic means (averages) for different assets as a proxy for expected returns in the future. This tends to work well enough with entire asset classes (all gilts, for example), but less well when predicting the expected return of a single asset, for example an individual company share, or short-term market direction.

As can be seen in the table above, the portfolio's returns averaged 2.4%. However, this masks a wide range of returns, from an impressive 18% in Year 3, to a disappointing minus 32% in Year 2. When measured over the past 50 years, UK equities have had a mean annual real return of about 6%. Given that this length of time covers recessions, wars, market booms and a wide range of differing economic conditions in between, it is a reasonable assumption that the result is representative of general economic conditions in the long run, so that the future long-term real return on a broad portfolio of shares will be approximately 6%. This does not mean that you can expect 6% every year, but only that, over the long term, the average expected real return is likely to be at around that level[1].

One approach for an investor to establish the **expected return** on an investment for a single period is to calculate a range of possible outcomes, and use these to calculate the expected return, as the arithmetic mean of the possible outcomes. This approach is mathematically simple, but does require some initial qualitative analysis.

For example, let's assume that Company A achieved a return last year of 10%. We might assume that there is a 50% chance that, this year, Company A will achieve a return of 11%; a 30% chance that it will achieve a return at the same level as last year; and a 20% chance that it will achieve a return of just 9%.

---

1 Recently, there has been an extended period of low interest rates and nominal returns, and some observers suggest that this 'new normal' is a better guide to longer-term future returns than estimations based on more historic data.

The expected return is calculated as follows:

Expected Return	% Probability	Weighted Probability
11%	50%	5.5%
10%	30%	3.0%
9%	20%	1.8%

The expected return is the **weighted average probability**, ie, the sum of 5.5%+3.0%+1.8% = 10.3%.

2.4   Measuring Risk

Learning Objective

1.1.3   Be able to calculate the degree of variability of investments using the variance and standard deviation of returns

As mentioned in Section 2.1, in a financial context, risk is **the possibility that an investment's actual future return will differ from its expected return**. The difference could be due either to lower returns than expected or to higher returns than expected. Financial risk measures the **variability of investment returns**.

There are two main tools for measuring financial risk: **variance** and **standard deviation**. Both are very common statistical parameters.

2.4.1   Variance

Given that we can calculate the average return for a particular asset class or asset, it will also be helpful to establish how widely different actual individual returns have been compared with this average, ie, what the variance from the average has been. The greater the range of possible returns, the greater the financial risk.

In summary, to calculate variance, we start by calculating the deviation from the arithmetic mean of each of the investments. We then square these, before calculating the arithmetic mean of these squared deviations.

The formula for calculating variance is shown below:

$$\text{Variance} = \sigma^2 = \frac{\Sigma(x - \mu)^2}{n}$$

where:

σ^2 = the symbol for the population variance (called sigma squared).
Σ = sum of all $(x - \mu)$ observations (called sigma).
x = the value of one observation in the population.
μ = (pronounced mu) the arithmetic mean of the population.
n = the number of observations in the population.

In these calculations, the term 'population' means the group of data points being analysed, and the term 'observation' means an individual data point being analysed. 'Population variance', therefore, means the degree of variance found within the population.

There are five steps to calculate the population variance:

1. Calculate the mean of the population of observations (μ).
2. Calculate the difference between each observation and the mean result ($x - \mu$).
3. Square the difference of each value found in step 2.
4. Add up the total of all the squared differences (Σ).
5. Divide the total by the number of observations (n).

Example

Step 1

We have already calculated the mean return as 2.4% (see Section 2.3).

Step 2

Calculate the difference between each annual return and the population mean, as below. We have done this below expressed first as a percentage, and then in numerical format.

Year	Annual Return	Mean	Difference	Annual Return	Mean	Difference
	Percentage			Numerical		
1	16%	2.4%	13.6%	0.16	0.024	0.136
2	−32%	2.4%	−34.4%	−0.32	0.024	−0.344
3	18%	2.4%	15.6%	0.18	0.024	0.156
4	4%	2.4%	1.6%	0.04	0.024	0.016
5	6%	2.4%	3.6%	0.06	0.024	0.036

Note that using the numerical format may be easier than using the percentage format. Thus, $(13.6\%)^2$ is 0.136 x 0.136, ie, 0.0185 or 1.85%. The numerical format is more intuitive but using percentages throughout avoids making mistakes through mixing percentages and decimals.

Step 3

Squaring the difference is easily achieved with a calculator.

Year	Difference	Difference Squared
1	13.6%	$1.85\%^2$
2	−34.4%	$11.83\%^2$
3	15.6%	$2.43\%^2$
4	1.6%	$0.03\%^2$
5	3.6%	$0.13\%^2$

Step 4

The sum of the differences squared is 16.27%^{2}, or 16.27 per cent squared.

Step 5

Finally, dividing 16.27%^{2} by five (the number of items in the population) gives the variance as 3.25%^{2}.

Overview

The same information presented in the formula format is shown below:

$$\text{Variance} = \sigma^2 = \frac{(16\% - 2.4\%)^2 + (-32\% - 2.4\%)^2 + (18\% - 2.4\%)^2 + (4\% - 2.4\%)^2 + (6\% - 2.4\%)^2}{5}$$

$$\text{Variance} = \sigma^2 = 3.25\%^2$$

Understanding Variance

So what is the significance of this number? This is the degree of potential variability from the expected returns from an investment. Very broadly, a high variance suggests higher risk than a low variance.

However, whether the risk is acceptable or not depends on the actual level of expected return, as well as the risk appetite of the individual investor. An investment which has the potential to generate a return of 30%, with a variance of 3.25%^{2}, may still be a 'good' investment, as 3.25%^{2} is fairly low compared to the high expected return. However, for an investment with the potential to generate only, say, 5.5% return, a variance of 3.25%^{2} is much more significant.

2.4.2   Standard Deviation

The final stage in the process is to apply the variance to the arithmetic mean. This will enable us to calculate the range of potential returns from the investment, above and below the arithmetic mean.

In calculating variance, the results are expressed in units of per cent squared. However, to apply the variation to the arithmetic mean it is far more helpful to bring the variance into the same units of measurement as the mean – ie, into a simple percentage. To do this, we convert the variance into the standard deviation.

The standard deviation is simply the **square root of the variance**, and is calculated as:

$$\text{Standard deviation} = \sigma = \sqrt{\frac{\Sigma(x - \mu)^2}{n}}$$

To continue with the earlier example, the standard deviation of the population of investment returns is the square root of 3.25%^{2}, which is 18.03%. (Note in numerical format, the square root of 0.0325 = 0.1803.) This end result now uses the same measure – per cent – as does the mean return of 2.4%.

The standard deviation is a mathematical measure derived from variance of the spread or dispersion of the individual observations of data around the mean result. We can say that the mean return is 2.4%, plus or minus 18.03%, or, in numerical format, 0.024 ± 0.1803. Thus, the expected return can be as high as 20.43% (2.4% + 18.03%), or as low as –15.63% (2.4% – 18.03%), based on the standard deviation.

The lower the standard deviation, the lower the variability in the average result. When this process is applied to investment returns, we note that low standard deviation returns are referred to as being less risky (having lower variability) than returns with high standard deviations.

2.4.3   Population Variance and Sample Variance

When dealing with data, you must be able to distinguish whether the information relates to an entire population or a sample of a population.

If an entire population is being considered, every member or constituent of a particular group will be included in the analysis: all companies contained in the FTSE All-Share Index, for instance. A sample of this population, however, as its name suggests, will only contain a selection of UK company shares from this index.

For example, one can measure the mean and variance of all the FTSE 100 shares over a period of five years. If the sole purpose is to measure the FTSE 100, then those shares constitute the entire population with which one is concerned. However, if one intends the returns on the FTSE 100 to represent returns on all shares quoted on the UK stock market over five years (or a longer period), the original data (FTSE 100 shares) clearly represents only a sample of all quoted shares on the London Stock Exchange (LSE).

It is often the case that populations become so large and cumbersome that using and making inferences from samples is the only viable and cost-effective means of analysing the population. With all samples, the larger the sample used, the more representative it is of the population. For example, the market capitalisation of the FTSE 100 constituent companies is over 80% of the market capitalisation of the FTSE All-Share Index and is a very good representative sample for the All-Share Index.

Samples can be either:

- **Random** – that is, they are selected randomly so that each constituent has an equal chance or probability of being included by using a table of random numbers to ensure that the selection is free from any bias.
- **Non-random** – the alternative is to employ a non-random method of selection that it is believed will select a more representative sample.

The formula for variance differs depending on whether we are calculating variance for an entire population or for a sample.

Mathematically, the variance formula when working with a sample is modified by changing the denominator from n to n – 1, and the revised formula is as shown below:

$$\text{Variance (sample)} = s^2 = \frac{\sum (x - \mu)^2}{n - 1}$$

where:

s^2 =   sample variance.

Σ =   sum of all $(x - \mu)$ observations.

x   =   the value of one observation in the population sample.

μ =   the arithmetic mean of the population sample.

n – 1   =   the number of observations in the population sample minus one.

While the example above is not actually using a population, but a sample drawn from that population, we adjust step 5 of the calculation as follows (steps 1 through 4 remain the same):

Step 5

Finally, dividing $16.27\%^2$ by four (n – 1), gives the variance as $4.07\%^2$.

In the earlier example, we measured the standard deviation of a population. If the data set were, instead, a sample drawn from the population, we could adjust the result (by making the (n – 1) correction as we did for variance of samples above). Thus, the standard deviation of a population where only a sample was drawn becomes:

$$\text{Standard Deviation} = s = \sqrt{\frac{\Sigma(x - \mu)^2}{n - 1}}$$

With a sample variance of $4.07\%^2$, we take the square root to find that the sample standard deviation is 20.17%, showing that historic returns have been 2.4% ± 20.17%. This latter result has higher variability because it represents only a sampling from a larger population and so is less accurate than taking and measuring the results for the whole population.

Whether you are using a population or a sample, the key point to take from this section is that **higher variance or standard deviation implies higher risk**, while **lower variance or standard deviation implies lower risk**.

3. Correlation and Covariance

Learning Objective

1.1.4 Be able to calculate the covariance of investments

1.1.5 Understand the impact of correlation on diversification

1.1.6 Be able to calculate the correlation of investments

As we have seen above, the risk of holding individual securities in isolation is given by their standard deviation.

However, when combining two or more securities in a portfolio, the portfolio's standard deviation of return will often be lower than the weighted average of the standard deviations of these individual securities. (The weightings are given by the proportion of the portfolio held in security A and that held in security B.)

This reduction in risk for a given level of expected return is the benefit of diversification.

To quantify the diversification potential of combining securities in a portfolio, two concepts are used:

- correlation; and
- covariance.

Both of these involve analysing the relationships between the movements of different assets – do they move in line with each other or against each other, and by what degree?

3.1   Correlation

Intuitively, the reader will understand that the macroeconomic factors influencing equity prices in the US and UK are influenced by many similar factors: when one market is doing well, it is very likely that the other is performing in a similar manner. There is much less reason, however, to expect any particular relationship between US equities and those of the emerging market areas, since prevailing economic conditions will be widely different.

Correlation is the name given to the measure of how two asset returns may be related (or move together, or correlate), and covariance is the measure of the strength of the correlation. For instance, in general, people who study harder for exams tend to do better than those who do not. Thus, if we plotted a graph showing study time compared with exam results, we would expect to find that exam scores increase in line with the amount of time spent studying. The two variables are said to be positively correlated. As one variable increases, so does the other; if they were to increase exactly in line with each other then they would be said to be perfectly correlated.

Globalisation has increased correlation between markets but, generally, markets are most closely correlated with those in their own geographic area. For example, Australia's markets move closely in line with those in Hong Kong, Singapore and Malaysia, but have limited correlation with the US. Correlation also changes over time – markets are most closely correlated at times of global economic or political crisis whereas, in times of stability, this correlation tends to decrease.

The **correlation coefficient (CORR)** is simply a mathematical measure of the strength of the correlation. It is measured on a scale of −1 to +1, where a CORR of between 0 and +1 means that both variables move in the same direction; if the CORR is +1, they have moved exactly in line and there is therefore a perfect positive correlation. If the CORR is between 0 and −1, there is a negative correlation, and the variables have not moved in line. If it is −1, the variables have moved in exactly opposite directions. A CORR of zero means there is absolutely no relationship between the returns of the two assets. You may also see CORR referred to by the symbol 'r'.

Correlation is calculated using the following formula:

$$\text{CORR X,Y} = \frac{\Sigma XY - \frac{(\Sigma X)(\Sigma Y)}{n}}{\sqrt{\left(\Sigma X^2 - \frac{(\Sigma X)^2}{n}\right)\left(\Sigma Y^2 - \frac{(\Sigma Y)^2}{n}\right)}}$$

where:

X = variable x.

Y = variable y.

n = number of measurements.

To calculate correlation, you need to follow the steps below.

Step 1 – draw up a table of the variables, including extra columns which we will use later. For this example, our variables are the returns on stock X and stock Y, and we will use returns over three years, as follows:

Return on Stock X	X^2	Return on Stock Y	Y^2	XY
80		45		
150		60		
200		90		

Step 2 – now calculate X^2, Y^2 and XY (ie, X times Y) and enter these in the table:

Return on Stock X	X^2	Return on Stock Y	Y^2	XY
80	6,400	45	2,025	3,600
150	22,500	60	3,600	9,000
200	40,000	90	8,100	18,000

Step 3 – now calculate the sums of each column and enter these in the final row:

Return on Stock X	X²	Return on Stock Y	Y²	XY
80	6,400	45	2,025	3,600
150	22,500	60	3,600	9,000
200	40,000	90	8,100	18,000
ΣX: 430	ΣX2: 68,900	ΣY: 195	ΣY2: 13,725	ΣXY: 30,600

Step 4 – next, enter the data into the formula shown above:

$$\text{CORR X,Y} = \frac{\Sigma XY - \dfrac{(\Sigma X)(\Sigma Y)}{n}}{\sqrt{\dfrac{(\Sigma X^2 - (\Sigma X)^2)}{n} \dfrac{(\Sigma Y^2 - (\Sigma Y)^2)}{n}}}$$

$$\text{CORR X,Y} = \frac{30,600 - \dfrac{(430 \times 195)}{3}}{\sqrt{\dfrac{(68,900 - (430)^2)}{3} \dfrac{(13,725 - (195)^2)}{3}}}$$

$$\text{CORR X,Y} = \frac{2,650}{2,762} = 0.96$$

Step 5 – the conclusion is that the returns on the two stocks, X and Y, are very closely correlated, as the correlation coefficient is close to 1.

3.2   Covariance

Covariance is another statistical measure of the relationship between two variables, such as share prices. It measures how changes in one variable are related to changes in a second variable.

A positive covariance between the returns of A and B means they have moved in the same direction, while a negative covariance means they have moved inversely. The larger the covariance, the greater the historic joint movements of the two securities in the same direction.

The covariance between two shares can be calculated in a similar way to variance; simply by multiplying the standard deviation of the first share by both the standard deviation of the second share and the correlation coefficient.

The covariance of the returns of two assets, A and B, is written as COV(A,B) and is calculated as follows:

$$\text{COV(A,B)} = \text{SD}_A \times \text{SD}_B \times \text{CORR(A,B)}$$

where:

SD$_A$ = standard deviation of asset A.
SD$_B$ = standard deviation of asset B.

CORR(A,B)   =   correlation coefficient between asset A and asset B.

From this equation, the following conclusions can be drawn:

1. Although it is possible for two combinations of two different securities to have the same correlation coefficient as one another, each may have a different covariance, owing to the differences in the individual standard deviations of the constituent securities.
2. A security with a high standard deviation in isolation does not necessarily have a high covariance with other shares. If it has a low correlation with the other shares in a portfolio then, despite its high standard deviation, its inclusion in the portfolio may reduce overall portfolio risk.
3. Portfolios designed to minimise risk should contain securities as negatively correlated with each other as possible and with low standard deviations to minimise the covariance.

Example

Consider the case of an investor who attempts to minimise risk. The investor has a choice of investing in two out of three portfolios (assuming, for this example, that the investment will be 50/50 in each portfolio). The possibilities are:

Portfolio A – invest in large, blue chip UK companies; standard deviation is 14%.

Portfolio B – invest in large, blue chip US companies; standard deviation is 12%.

Portfolio C – invest in emerging market companies; standard deviation is 29%.

At first glance, one would assume that mixing the two portfolios with the lowest standard deviations would produce least risk. After all, portfolio A and portfolio B have standard deviations less than half that of portfolio C.

But, given that the correlation coefficients work out to be:

CORR(A,B)   =   0.81

CORR(A,C)   =   0.13

CORR(B,C)   =   −0.05

the covariance of each of the three possible portfolios will be:

COV(A,B)   =   (0.14) x (0.12) x (0.81)

            =   0.0136

COV(A,C)   =   (0.14) x (0.29) x (0.13)

            =   0.0053

COV(B,C)   =   (0.12) x (0.29) x (−0.05)

            =   −0.0017

Thus, the covariance is least between portfolios B and C. There is very little covariance between the annual returns of portfolios A and C, and the covariance is highest between portfolios A and B.

Example

This example demonstrates how to calculate covariance of a population with two variables and three observations, as follows:

Year	A	B
1	4%	15%
2	11%	12%
3	12%	9%

The formula to use is:

$$COV(A,B) = \frac{\Sigma\,(A - \mu)(B - \mu)}{n}$$

where:

Σ = sum of all $(A - \mu) \times (B - \mu)$ observations.

A,B = the value of one observation in the population.

μ = the arithmetic mean of the population (to be calculated for A and B separately).

n = the number of observations in the population.

Year	A	A – μ	B	B – μ	(A – μ)(B – μ)
1	4	–5	15	3	–15
2	11	2	12	0	0
3	12	3	9	–3	–9
	μ = 9		μ = 12		Σ = –24

$$COV(A,B) = \frac{-24}{3} = -8$$

3.3   Investment Conclusions

At the beginning of this chapter, we stated that a portfolio with many different types of investment is less risky than a portfolio with only one type – the principle of diversification.

However, we can further reduce risk within a diversified portfolio by ensuring that investments are not positively correlated, so that they move in different directions, thus reducing the covariance of the portfolio. This negative correlation of investments reduces the exposure of the portfolio to any one stock price movement, or market trend, or economic event.

4. Discounted Cash Flows

4.1 Present Value

Learning Objective

1.2.1   Be able to calculate the present value (PV) and net present value (NPV) of future multiple cash flows using the discounting formula

Most people intuitively understand that cash in the hand now is worth more than the promise of cash received in the future. There are two main reasons for this. The first is risk – there is always some degree of uncertainty as to whether you will actually receive that cash in a year's time (this is referred to as 'credit risk'). The second is the 'opportunity cost'. That is, if you have cash today, you can do something with it, whether it is to consume something that you desire, or to invest in something that will deliver greater value in the future.

The amount of required return for any asset relates to the level of risk involved. If you are 100% certain that the UK government will repay your investment in a 90-day Treasury bill, you will not require a high return. However, if you are investing in a company with a brand new, unproven technology, the rate of potential return you require in order to take this risk will be significantly greater.

4.1.1   Present Value of One Payment in the Future

The starting point for understanding discounted cash flow is to calculate the present value of a single one-off sum, to be paid or received at a specified time in the future.

To illustrate this, we will use the example of a bond, which will be redeemed at the end of five years for £1,000. There are no interest payments (ie, it is a zero coupon bond). Our question is: what is the present value of this bond? Or, to put it differently, what are investors prepared to pay today, in exchange for this promise of £1,000 in five years' time?

The present value takes into account three things: the cash flow, the delay to receiving the maturity value; and the required rate of return of the investors. In this example, we will assume that the required rate of return is 10%.

The price is calculated using the following formula:

$$PV = \frac{CF}{(1 + r)^n}$$

where:

PV = present value (in this case, the price of the bond).
CF = cash flow; in this case, the maturity value (redemption amount).
r   = rate of return (in bond terminology this is equivalent to the yield-to-maturity).
n   = number of years to maturity (some sources use 't' instead of 'n').

First, the investor must determine the appropriate rate of return ('r') that will compensate him for giving up his cash for five years. The rate of return is the rate that investors will receive on investments of similar risk and duration (maturity).

Assuming that an investor determines 10% to be the appropriate annual rate of return, the formula yields:

CF = £1,000.
r   = 10%.
n   = five years.

$$PV = \frac{£1,000}{(1 + 0.10)^5}$$

$$PV = \frac{£1,000}{1.61051}$$

$$PV = Price = £620.92$$

Thus, the present value of a five-year zero coupon bond with a 10% annual return rate is £620.92. In other words, given £620.92 cash in hand now, the investor could earn a compound 10% yearly and the sum would grow to £1,000 in five years' time.

So, the investor earns 10% compounded annually on purchasing the bond. At the same time, we can see that it costs the company 10% per year to have use of the investor's loan. We will return to this concept of cost in Chapter 3.

4.1.2   Present Value of Multiple Future Payments

For most bonds, the price takes into account both the maturity value and the sum of the interest payments over the duration of the bond. In this case the formula to calculate the price of a bond is as follows:

$$PV \text{ (price)} = \sum \frac{CF_n}{(1+r)^n}$$

where:

$\sum$ = sum of cash flows discounted for each year.
CF_n = cash flow received in period n (coupon payments and principal repayment).
r   = rate of return (yield-to-maturity).

As an example, we shall assume that a company decides to issue a traditional coupon bond, that is, bonds paying an annual coupon and repaying the face value on maturity. Consider two alternatives.

Alternative One

Assume the investor's required annual rate of return is 10% and the principal or face value of the bond is £1,000. Also, assume the company pays an annual coupon of 10% (£100) at the end of each year.

Using the formula above, we find that the price equals:

$$\text{Price} = \frac{£100}{(1+0.10)^1} + \frac{£100}{(1+0.10)^2} + \frac{£100}{(1+0.10)^3} + \frac{£100}{(1+0.10)^4} + \frac{£100}{(1+0.10)^5} + \frac{£1,000}{(1+0.10)^5}$$

$$\text{Price} = 90.9091 + 82.6446 + 75.1315 + 68.3013 + 62.0921 + 620.9213$$

$$\text{Price} = £1,000.00$$

(Note that this illustration does not calculate an exact figure of £1,000 due to rounding. Using a calculator or Excel would do so.)

Each individual interest payment, as well as the repayment of principal, has been discounted by a factor which recognises both the discount rate (required rate of return) and the date when the payment will be received.

In this case the price = £1,000.00. This is because the bond is paying a coupon (interest payment) of exactly 10%, the required rate of return. If the bond paid interest below the required rate of return, the price would be less than £1,000.00. If it paid interest above the required rate of return, the price would be higher than £1,000.00.

Alternative Two

Now, assume that the company only pays a coupon of £80 per £1,000 annually, or 8%. Since 8% is below the investor's required return rate, he will be unwilling to pay £1,000 per bond, as illustrated below:

$$\text{Price} = \frac{£80}{(1+0.10)^1} + \frac{£80}{(1+0.10)^2} + \frac{£80}{(1+0.10)^3} + \frac{£80}{(1+0.10)^4} + \frac{£80}{(1+0.10)^5} + \frac{£1,000}{(1+0.10)^5}$$

$$\text{Price} = 72.7273 + 66.1157 + 60.1052 + 54.6411 + 49.6737 + 620.9213$$

$$\text{Price} = £924.18$$

Here, the investor is only willing to pay £924.18 because he is receiving £20.00 per year less in income than he could earn elsewhere for similar risk. The price he is prepared to pay is the price which generates a holding period return of 10%.

This approach can be used to value a wide range of investments. Bonds and other fixed interest securities are relatively easy to value, because they promise a fixed stream of interest payments on specified dates in the future. Equities, by contrast, have much more uncertainty regarding future dividend receipts and capital appreciation. However, discounted cash flow (DCF) is one of the most important business valuation methods, and will be discussed in Chapter 4.

4.2 Net Present Value

Learning Objective

1.2.1 Be able to calculate the present value (PV) and net present value (NPV) of future multiple cash flows using the discounting formula

The concept of net present value is central to the valuation of companies and evaluation of investments and, therefore, key to the practice of corporate finance. Simply put, the formula determines whether the future cash inflows from an investment are worth more in 'present-day values' than the cash outflows invested. For example, it does not make sense to pay £15 million for a company whose cumulative future cash flows only total £12 million in present-day values.

Discounted cash flow (DCF) techniques seek to discount a project's expected cash outflows in order to compare them against the present value of the expected cash inflows. In other words, it seeks to discount the costs of the investment made and then to compare this to the present value of the revenue it expects to derive from the project.

The difference between the present value of the inflows and the present value of the outflows is known as the net present value (NPV).

The NPV formula is shown below:

$$NPV = CF_0 + \sum \frac{CF_n}{(1+r)^n}$$

where:

CF_0 = the initial investment (note that this is an OUTflow, and, therefore, negative).
CF_n = cash inflow in period n.
r = required rate of return.
n = period (usually year).

Example

A company is considering undertaking an investment project that will require it to spend £75,000 this year and which, in return, it expects to generate revenues of £20,000 in the first year and the same amount in each of years two, three, four and five. The discount rate it uses is 10%.

Year	Cash Flow	Discounting	Present Value of Cash Flow
0	−75,000.00		−75,000.00
1	20,000.00	$\dfrac{CF}{(1+10\%)^1}$	18,181.82
2	20,000.00	$\dfrac{CF}{(1+10\%)^2}$	16,528.93
3	20,000.00	$\dfrac{CF}{(1+10\%)^3}$	15,026.30
4	20,000.00	$\dfrac{CF}{(1+10\%)^4}$	13,660.27
5	20,000.00	$\dfrac{CF}{(1+10\%)^5}$	12,418.43
Net Present Value			£815.75

In the above table, the first column denotes the year the cash flow is received (made). Time (year) '0' represents today, which is the beginning of year one, while '1' represents the end of year one.

The cash flow column sets out the cash flows in nominal terms (ie, the value to be received at the end of each year). The present value column shows the value of the cash flows, discounted at 10% annually.

Since the NPV of this project is above zero, it should be accepted.

If the discount rate used were lower, the NPV would be higher as illustrated in the following table. The only thing changed in the following table is that the discount rate is 8%, not 10%.

Year	Cash Flow	Discounting	Present Value of Cash Flow
0	−75,000.00		−75,000.00
1	20,000.00	$\dfrac{CF}{(1+8\%)^1}$	18,518.52
2	20,000.00	$\dfrac{CF}{(1+8\%)^2}$	17,146.78
3	20,000.00	$\dfrac{CF}{(1+8\%)^3}$	15,876.64
4	20,000.00	$\dfrac{CF}{(1+8\%)^4}$	14,700.60
5	20,000.00	$\dfrac{CF}{(1+8\%)^5}$	13,611.66
Net Present Value			£4,854.20

4.3 Internal Rate of Return

Learning Objective

1.2.2 Understand the internal rate of return (IRR) for a series of multiple cash flows

By applying a discount rate to a project's anticipated cash flows, we can determine that, if the result is a positive NPV, then this implies that the project should return in excess of the discount rate over the term of the project. If the result is a negative NPV, this tells us that the project will return less than the discount rate, and the project should not be undertaken.

There is an alternative method of analysing the cash flows, which is to calculate the expected return of the project relative to the cost of the investment. This approach establishes what the break-even rate of return is. In other words, it calculates the discount rate which implies an NPV of zero, where the percentage return is exactly equal to the percentage discount rate. This rate of return is called the **internal rate of return (IRR)**.

Thus, the NPV formula can be rewritten as follows:

$$0 = CF_0 + \sum \frac{CF_n}{(1+IRR)^n}$$

where:

CF_0 = the initial investment. Note that this is an outflow, and, therefore, negative.

CF_n = cash inflow in period n.

IRR = internal rate of return.

n = period (usually year).

The only accurate way to establish this IRR is through a lengthy process of trial and error using a range of discount rates: this is easily carried out by a scientific calculator or spreadsheet. However, an approximate IRR can be derived through a short-cut methodology known as **interpolation**. Interpolation takes a lower discount rate that produces a positive NPV and a higher discount rate that results in a negative NPV and then finds the rate between them that produces a zero NPV. The formula for estimating IRR by this method is:

$$IRR = \text{Lower rate} + \left(\frac{\text{NPV at lower rate}}{\text{NPV at lower rate} - \text{NPV at higher rate}} \right) \times (\text{higher rate} - \text{lower rate})$$

To illustrate this, return to the example in Section 4.2. The NPV of the five-year project is £815.75 when using a discount rate of 10%. If we calculate the NPV using an 11% discount rate, the result is –£1,082.05 as illustrated below.

Year	Cash Flow	Present Value of Cash Flow
0	−75,000.00	−75,000.00
1	20,000.00	18,018.02
2	20,000.00	16,232.45
3	20,000.00	14,623.83
4	20,000.00	13,174.62
5	20,000.00	11,869.03
Net Present Value		−£1,082.05

Therefore, we know that the discount rate (IRR) that leads to a zero NPV lies somewhere between 10% (0.10) and 11% (0.11). Using the interpolation formula results in the following:

$$IRR = 0.10 + \frac{(815.75)}{(815.75 - (-1{,}082.05))} \times (0.11 - 0.10)$$

(Remember, when subtracting a negative number, the presence of two negative signs means that you add the two numbers.)

$$IRR = 0.10 + \frac{815.75}{1{,}897.80} \times 0.01$$

$$IRR = 0.10 + (0.430 \times 0.01)$$

$$IRR = 0.10 + 0.00430$$

$$IRR = 0.10430 \text{ or } 10.43\%$$

The interpolation method shown here is useful but not exact; the accuracy depends on how close to IRR the discount rates used are (ie, how close to zero the NPVs in the formula are). In practice, corporate finance practitioners use spreadsheet models or financial calculators to calculate IRR as these provide complete accuracy. For example, if you used 10.430% in a financial calculator or spreadsheet to calculate NPV, the NPV will equal −£9.81, which is very close to zero, but not exact. The precise IRR according to a spreadsheet is 10.424844%.

Competing projects are usually ranked in ascending order of their respective NPVs rather than their IRRs, as the NPV provides a superior means of ranking. The IRR, instead, should only be used as a way of establishing the break-even rate of return for investment projects, and setting a hurdle rate for evaluating investments. It is widely used by private equity investors in this way.

4.4   DCF: Conclusion

Further considerations that should be borne in mind when using DCF techniques include:

- **Forecasting errors** – the initial investment and any subsequent costs and/or the anticipated revenues may be incorrectly forecast.
- **Inflation** – the effect of inflation has been ignored here. However, if the project cash flows take inflation into account, the discount rate applied must also take inflation into account. If cash flows are expressed in real terms, the same must be true of the discount rate.
- **Project risk** – depending on its exact nature, acceptance of a project can increase or, indeed, reduce the risk attached to a company's existing operations. This must be taken into account when choosing the discount rate.

The **rate of interest** or **discount rate** used to calculate the net present value of a project is one of the most important factors in investment appraisal.

For a project to be viable, the return needs to be greater than a company's **cost of capital**. A company's cost of capital depends upon the sources of that capital which will typically be either equity or debt. If it is equity, then this involves the use of share capital and reserves and the cost of capital is equal to the return expected by shareholders. If debt is used, the cost of capital is the interest payments on any debt less any corporation tax relief. Most projects undertaken by companies involve financing by a mixture of both debt and equity. In this case, the **weighted average cost of capital (WACC)** is the appropriate discount rate to use for investment appraisal. It is often known as the **hurdle rate**, in that it represents the minimum return that must be achieved from a project to be worthwhile.

A further discussion of WACC and DCF valuations follows in Chapters 3 and 4.

End of Chapter Questions

Think of an answer for each question and refer to the appropriate workbook section for confirmation.

1. What is the definition of risk?
   Answer reference: Section 2.1

2. What are the components of holding period return?
   Answer reference: Section 2.2

3. What is the purpose of calculating variance?
   Answer reference: Section 2.4.1

4. How do you calculate standard deviation?
   Answer reference: Section 2.4.2

5. What is the effect of correlation on diversification?
   Answer reference: Section 3

6. What is a correlation coefficient?
   Answer reference: Section 3.1

7. Explain why money has a time value.
   Answer reference: Section 4.1

8. What is NPV and what is its main purpose?
   Answer reference: Section 4.2

9. How is interpolation used to achieve an approximate IRR and why is it less accurate than calculating an investment's NPV?
   Answer reference: Section 4.3

10. What considerations should be taken into account when using DCF techniques?
    Answer reference: Section 4.4

Chapter Two
Financial Statements Analysis

This syllabus area will provide approximately 10 of the 50 examination questions

1. Basic Principles

Learning Objective

2.1.1   Understand the purpose of financial statements

1.1   Financial Statements

In the UK, both public and private companies are required under the Companies Act 2006 to publish their financial results, in the form of annual financial statements. Financial statements may also be referred to as the company's report and accounts. In addition, publicly quoted companies are required to publish shorter half-yearly financial statements (also referred to as interim financial statements) and to update their shareholders and the market on material changes in their financial performance or position on an *ad hoc* basis as required. Until November 2014, companies listed on the Main Market of the London Stock Exchange were required to provide an interim management statement for those quarters when full and half-yearly financials were not due. This requirement has now been abolished, but many UK-listed companies do produce an interim management statement or quarterly accounts on a voluntary basis.

Larger companies are required to include within their financial statements a significant degree of explanation and background information. They are also required to have their annual accounts independently audited: that is, tested for accuracy and compliance with the applicable rules by appropriately qualified accountants (auditors) who provide an audit report for inclusion within the financial statements.

Financial statements have a number of functions:

- Directors are required to report to the company's shareholders on how they have managed the company's funds and assets over the course of the year, and the value of those funds and assets at the year-end.
- The financial statements provide bankers and other lenders with an independently verified confirmation of the company's compliance with any lending covenants, and therefore its continuing suitability as a borrower.
- The financial statements form the basis of the detailed analysis carried out by equity analysts, who use them as a guide to their investment recommendations.
- Shareholders use the financial statements to assess the quality of corporate governance and commercial management provided by the directors, and to understand the quality of their investment.
- Directors and managers use the financial statements to confirm and evaluate their own performance over the past financial year.

1.2 Contents of the Financial Statements

A company's annual report and accounts contain the following main items:

- The **financial statements**, comprising:
  - the **statement of comprehensive income** (also referred to as the 'profit and loss account') – this may be shown as one single document, or it may be divided into two parts (the income statement and the statement of comprehensive income). Either way, this is the statement showing the company's total income and expenses for the last financial year, and its profit or loss for that year;
  - the **statement of financial position** (also referred to as the balance sheet) – the statement of the company's assets and liabilities as at the end of the financial year;
  - the **statement of cash flows** – the statement showing the sources and uses of cash during the financial year and the net cash position at the end of that year;
  - the **statement of changes in equity** – a breakdown of the different elements contributing to changes in the company's equity over the year; and
  - **notes to the financial statements** – which provide breakdowns of the more complex items, as well as explanations and additional information, such as the company's accounting policies.
- **Narrative reporting**, which includes:
  - the **chairman's statement** – highlighting key issues in the company's development and current position;
  - **reports by the CEO and other directors**, as appropriate;
  - a **strategic report** containing a fair review of the company's business, the principal risks and uncertainties facing the company and an analysis of its development and performance during the year;
  - an **audit report**, stating that '...*the company's financial statements as presented give a true and fair view of its balance sheet and income statement for the period ended.....[date]*' . When the auditors have been unable to provide this 'clean' audit report, their report is said to be 'qualified', and it must indicate the reasons for this qualification.
- **Corporate governance statements**, which include:
  - the **directors' remuneration report**, showing a breakdown of the salary and other benefits paid to the directors;
  - a **corporate governance report**, with details of how far the company has complied with the UK Corporate Governance Code and explanations of any departures from this Code.

Quoted companies are required to include the most extensive information, whereas small companies may have exemptions including some of the detail listed above.

As stated above, directors of all UK companies must prepare financial statements and file them in accordance with the Companies Act 2006 at Companies House (an agency of the Department for Business, Innovation & Skills), where they will remain on file and are available for inspection by the public indefinitely.

- Companies that are traded on a stock exchange must publish these accounts by the deadline specified by that exchange – for companies listed on the main market of the London Stock Exchange, this is within four months of the year-end, and for companies trading on AIM it is six months after the year-end (although this is typically reduced to five months for UK-incorporated companies. This is due to the requirement under the Companies Act for public limited companies to hold their annual general meeting within six months of their financial year-end; this requires 21 days' notice, which is usually sent out with the company's annual reports and accounts).

- Private companies must generally file their accounts in accordance with the deadline provided in the Companies Act, which is within nine months of their year-end.

Financial statements are prepared on a 'going concern' basis. This means that the directors assume that the business will continue in operation for the foreseeable future and that there is no intention (or necessity) to liquidate it or cease to trade.

1.3 Accounting Standards

Learning Objective

2.1.2 Understand the requirements for companies and groups to prepare accounts in accordance with applicable accounting standards

2.1.3 Know the purpose of, and major differences between: International Financial Reporting Standards (IFRS); Statements of Standard Accounting Practice (SSAP); UK Financial Reporting Standards (FRS); US Generally Acceptable Accounting Principles (GAAP)

Directors must draw up their financial statements in accordance with the accounting standards applicable for the country and type of company concerned. This is important to ensure that the accounts can be readily understood and evaluated, that they are prepared with the minimum of distortion, and that they can be compared on a like-for-like basis with other similar companies.

Historically, all countries evolved their own **generally accepted accounting principles (GAAP)** over time, as a means of providing a common standard for the preparation and analysis of financial statements in their own countries. In the UK the national standard is UK GAAP (now used only by private companies) and, in the US, US GAAP.

UK GAAP is the term used for the overall standards used for the preparation of private company accounts in the UK. However, within this overall framework are a number of individual standards, setting out the recommended accounting treatment for individual items in the accounts. These individual standards are issued by the accounting bodies. The original accounting body, the Accounting Standards Committee (ASC), issued standards between 1970 and 1990, referred to as **Statements of Standard Accounting Practice (SSAPs)**. The ASC became the Accounting Standards Board (ASB) in 1990, and subsequent accounting standards were known as **Financial Reporting Standards (FRSs)**. In 2015, the introduction of a single reporting standard, FRS 102, replaced all existing FRSs and SSAPs in providing a 'New GAAP' which is applicable to the majority of UK private companies. This provides detailed guidance for directors on how certain items should be stated or calculated and provides the benchmark for auditors in determining whether the accounts have been properly prepared.

Over the last fifteen years, the International Accounting Standards Board (IASB) has developed **International Financial Reporting Standards (IFRS)**, which have been adopted by an increasingly wide number of countries and markets. This has meant that, across Europe in particular, companies increasingly prepare their accounts to a common standard. In the UK, quoted companies must in most cases prepare their accounts under IFRS, although private companies may still use UK GAAP; however, over the years, changes to UK GAAP have brought this largely in line with the main features of IFRS, reducing the differences.

The principal driver for this is the **International Organization of Securities Commissions (IOSCO)**, which represents the interests of securities regulatory bodies worldwide. Thus, public companies requiring listing in several different continents find it easier to produce one version of their worldwide accounting information compliant with one international standard rather than having to comply with a multitude of differing local standards. IOSCO accepts this point and, in general, IFRS (and their forerunner IAS) are usually stricter than local standards.

In the US, SEC-registered companies must prepare their accounts under US GAAP, unless they are non-US registered companies. In this case, they can choose between US GAAP, IFRS or (providing that they include a reconciliation to US GAAP) its national GAAP. Over recent years, the US Financial Accounting Standards Board (FASB) has been working with the IASB on reducing the differences between US GAAP and IFRS.

A number of differences still remain, and some of the more significant of these are as follows:

- The US GAAP classification of debt as compared to equity differs from the IFRS classification.
- Under US GAAP, revaluation of property, plant and equipment is not permitted. Under IFRS, these assets may be revalued, providing that a fair value can be reliably measured.
- There are further differences in the approach to the valuation of intangible assets and investment property.
- Under US GAAP, inventory is measured at the lower of cost and market value, with cost taken at either first in, first out (FIFO) or last in, first out (LIFO); under IFRS it is measured at the lower of cost and net realisable value, and LIFO is prohibited.

In summary:

- US (domestic) SEC companies must prepare their accounts under US GAAP, while non-US SEC companies may choose between US GAAP, local GAAP and IFRS.
- UK private companies and unquoted public companies may prepare their accounts under UK GAAP or choose to prepare them under IFRS.
- UK quoted companies (main market and AIM) must prepare their accounts under IFRS.
- UK GAAP includes a number of detailed provisions set out in SSAPs and their successor, FRSs.
- IFRS includes detailed provisions, each individually called an IFRS.

2.   Group Accounts and Company Accounts

Learning Objective

2.1.4   Understand the differences between group accounts and company accounts and why companies are required to prepare group accounts (candidates should understand the concept of goodwill and minority interests but will not be required to calculate these)

2.1   Introduction

The Companies Act 2006 requires UK companies to publish consolidated financial statements if they comprise a 'group'. A group structure arises when a parent or holding company controls one or more companies through direct share ownership or other methods of control. A company controlled by another is called a subsidiary. In addition to including the parent company and all subsidiaries, group accounts are also required to include associates (companies where the parent or a subsidiary owns a significant shareholding).

2.1.1   Subsidiaries

Generally, a parent will be treated as controlling its subsidiary if it owns more than 50% of the subsidiary's shares (a 'simple majority'), which gives it the right to pass an ordinary resolution at a general meeting. However, it may also be said to control a subsidiary if it has dominant or significant influence and the ability to influence the composition and actions of the board of directors.

As the parent effectively controls all of the assets, activities and management of the subsidiary (irrespective of the fact that it does not necessarily own 100% of these), it is allowed to include 100% of the assets, liabilities, income and expenses of the subsidiaries in the group accounts. This is referred to as 'consolidation'.

2.1.2   Associate Companies

A company may instead be treated as an 'associate company' if the parent company owns or controls a significant shareholding (generally, 20–49.9%). Since the parent does not actually control the associate company, it is not allowed to consolidate 100% of the assets, liabilities, income and expenses of the associate. Instead, it includes just the proportion of the associate's net assets and net profit/loss that is represented by its shareholding: ie, if it owns a 25% stake in the associate, it includes 25% of the associate's net assets and net profit/loss in its group accounts.

2.1.3   Investments

One final category of company to be found within a group is one where the parent does not have a significant shareholding. Instead, the parent is a passive minority shareholder, with only the right to receive dividends. The company is classified as an 'investment' and, in this case, the group accounts show only the actual income received from the investment and a valuation of its shareholding on the balance sheet.

2.2 Group Accounts

The parent company of a group of companies must produce both **consolidated financial statements**, showing the contribution of its subsidiaries, associates and investments, and **company accounts**, which simply show its stand-alone position and performance. Consolidated accounts show a much more complete picture of the performance and financial position of the group, and are generally more useful and relevant to investors.

As stated above, consolidated accounts include 100% of the income, expenditure, assets and liabilities of a group's subsidiaries, even when these are not wholly owned, to reflect the fact that the group has control of these subsidiaries, and access to their assets and liabilities. However, the reality is that in many cases a third party also owns shares in these subsidiaries and this fact must be properly reflected in the accounts. This is done by way of a final deduction of a **minority interest** from the consolidated income statement. This minority interest represents the proportion of the subsidiary's earnings which 'belong' to the third party owning the minority interest in the subsidiary.

In addition, the balance sheet includes the deduction of a minority interest, again representing the proportion of the subsidiary's net assets belonging to the third party. Under IFRS, this minority interest is referred to as a **non-controlling interest (NCI)**.

The purpose of these consolidated accounts is to show shareholders both the 'big picture' of the entire economic group controlled by the parent, and the 'clean picture' of the proportion of that group which actually belongs to the parent company's shareholders.

Example

Company M owns 90% of the shares in its subsidiary, Company T. Company M has profit after tax of £100,000; Company T has profit after tax of £50,000. In summary, Company M's profit will be shown in the consolidated accounts as follows:

Consolidated profits	£150,000
Less: minority interest*	(£5,000)
Profit attributable to Company M's ordinary shareholders	£145,000

* 10% of Company T's profits of £50,000, being those which do not belong to Company M's shareholders.

3. Financial Statements

For the remainder of this chapter, the financial statements of ExampleCo plc (a major manufacturer) will be used to illustrate the principal accounting classifications and performance ratios commonly used in corporate finance appraisals. Extracts from ExampleCo plc's accounts are shown below.

ExampleCo plc Income Statement (in £ millions)		
	2015	2014
Revenue	**3,453.7**	**3,406.5**
Cost of sales	(2,445.0)	(2,409.6)
Gross profit	**1,008.7**	**996.9**
Distribution costs	(223.2)	(232.1)
Administrative expenses	(214.7)	(236.6)
Other gains	2.2	0.7
Trading profit	**573.0**	**528.9**
Share of results of associates	1.8	0.9
Operating profit (EBIT)	**574.8**	**529.8**
Finance income	0.9	0.8
Finance costs	(24.3)	(25.3)
Profit before taxation	**551.4**	**505.3**
Taxation	(150.5)	(141.3)
Profit for the year	**400.9**	**364.0**
Attributable to equity holders of parent	401.1	364.1
Attributable to non-controlling interest	(0.2)	(0.1)
Profit for the year	**400.9**	**364.0**
Basic EPS	221.9	188.5
Diluted EPS	216.5	185.6

ExampleCo plc Statement of Financial Position as at 31 December (in £ millions)		
	2015	**2014**
Non-current assets		
Property, plant and equipment	592.4	577.2
Intangible assets	46.5	47.4
Investments in associates	5.1	4.0
Financial investments	25.3	23.7
Retirement benefit surplus	55.7	0.0
	725	**652.3**
Current assets		
Inventories	368.3	309.0
Trade and other receivables	645.6	616.6
Other financial assets	4.1	8.6
Cash and cash equivalents	49.3	107.0
	1,067.3	**1,041.2**
Total assets	**1,792.3**	**1,693.5**
Current liabilities		
Bank overdrafts	(10.2)	(4.7)
Bank loans	(115.0)	(0.0)
Trade and other payables	(544.6)	(550.3)
Other financial liabilities	(54.7)	(93.6)
Current tax	(108.4)	(109.5)
	(832.9)	**(758.1)**
Net current assets	**234.4**	**283.1**
Non-current liabilities		
Borrowings	(471.2)	(520.9)
Deferred income	(0.0)	(49.5)
Financial instruments	(13.3)	(13.4)
Deferred tax liabilities	(239.9)	(213.8)
Retirement benefit obligations	(2.6)	(4.4)
	(727.0)	**(802.0)**

Total liabilities	(1,559.9)	(1,560.1)
Net assets	**232.4**	**133.4**
Capital and reserves attributable to equity holders		
Called-up share capital	18.1	19.1
Share premium account	0.8	0.7
Capital redemption reserve	11.8	10.8
Share options reserve	(138.6)	(78.2)
Other reserves	(1,442.4)	(1,434.0)
Retained earnings	1,782.6	1,615.2
Shareholders' equity	**232.3**	**133.6**
Non-controlling interest	0.1	(0.2)
Total equity	**232.4**	**133.4**

ExampleCo plc Statement of Cash Flows (in £ millions)		
	2015	**2014**
Cash flows from operating activities		
Operating profit	574.8	529.8
Depreciation and amortisation	119.3	123.1
Impairment	2.3	6.4
Loss on disposal of property	6.9	5.5
Other non-cash items	(32.8)	(24.9)
(Increase)/decrease in inventories	(59.3)	9.7
(Increase)/decrease in trade receivables	(29.0)	6.0
(Decrease)/increase in payables	11.7	31.1
Cash generated from operations	**593.9**	**686.7**
Corporation tax paid	(141.9)	(115.2)
	452.0	**571.5**
Cash flows from investing activities		
Proceeds from sale of property	1.9	0.4
Purchase of property, plant and equipment	(120.6)	(98.6)
Payment of deferred consideration	(19.4)	0.0
Interest received	0.9	0.9
	(137.2)	**(97.3)**
Cash flows from financing activities		
Repurchase of own shares	(221.6)	(101.8)
Employee share scheme	(68.7)	(5.5)
Proceeds/(repayment) of bank loans	115.0	(75.0)
Repurchase of corporate bonds	(51.3)	(46.6)
Interest paid	(21.6)	(32.1)
Payment of finance lease charges	(0.3)	(0.4)
Dividends paid	(129.6)	(108.5)
	(378.1)	**(369.9)**
Net decrease/increase in cash and cash equivalents (63.3)		104.3
Opening cash/cash equivalents	102.3	1.5
Effect of exchange rate movements	0.1	(3.5)
Closing cash/cash equivalents	**39.1**	**102.3**

3.1   Statement of Financial Position/Balance Sheet

Learning Objective

2.2.1   Know the purpose of the statement of financial position, its format and main contents (including off-balance sheet items)

2.2.2   Understand the concept of depreciation and amortisation

2.2.3   Understand the difference between authorised and issued share capital, capital reserves and retained earnings

2.2.4   Know how loans and indebtedness are included within a statement of financial position

The statement of financial position provides a snapshot of the company's financial position at a particular date, by showing the value of its assets and the sum of its liabilities at that date. This statement may also be referred to as a balance sheet.

The statement of financial position has five main items:

1.   Non-current assets (historically referred to as fixed assets).
2.   Current assets.
3.   Current liabilities.
4.   Non-current liabilities (historically referred to as long-term liabilities).
5.   Capital and reserves.

3.1.1   Non-Current Assets

Non-current Assets	2015 (£ millions)	2014 (£ millions)
Property, plant and equipment	592.4	577.2
Intangible assets	46.5	47.4
Investments in associates	5.1	4.0
Financial investments	25.3	23.7
Retirement benefit surplus	55.7	0.0
	725.0	**652.3**

Non-current assets are assets which are held long term, and which generally are expected to last over several accounting periods. They fall into three categories: tangible; intangible; and financial.

- **Tangible assets** – assets which are capable of being touched and observed, such as buildings, machinery, plant, vehicles, office equipment and computers. Generally, the accounts will show these in a single category of 'property plant and equipment', with a more detailed breakdown in the notes to the accounts. In the UK, all tangible fixed assets with a limited economic life must be **depreciated** (or written down) over their expected life. The balance sheet reflects the depreciated value of these assets, rather than the original cost or any estimate of market value. This depreciated value is referred to as **net book value (NBV)**. The subject of depreciation is discussed in more detail in Section 3.1.8.

- **Intangible assets** – assets which cannot be touched or observed such as patents, trademarks, licences and other intellectual property. One very common kind of intangible asset is **goodwill**. Goodwill arises when the parent company acquires a subsidiary for a price which is greater than the value of the subsidiary's net tangible assets. The excess price is said to be payable in return for the goodwill in the subsidiary – effectively, for the expectation of future profits and growth. Intangible assets may also be written down over time, although the term used is amortisation rather than depreciation.
- **Financial assets** – assets of a financial nature, such as investments in shares or bonds, intended to be held long term. This may include investments in associate companies.

Additionally, if the company has a surplus on a retirement benefit scheme, this surplus may be shown in non-current assets (as is the case with ExampleCo).

3.1.2 Current Assets

Current Assets	2015 (£ millions)	2014 (£ millions)
Inventories	368.3	309.0
Trade and other receivables	645.6	616.6
Other financial assets	4.1	8.6
Cash and cash equivalents	49.3	107.0
	1,067.3	**1,041.2**

Current assets are short term in nature and include all those assets which are used in the company's trading cycle. The main types of current asset are inventory, trade receivables and cash.

Inventory (historically referred to as stock) consists of three items:

- **Raw materials** which have been bought but, as at the balance sheet date, not yet used in producing goods.
- **Work in progress** – products in the process of being manufactured, or services being provided, which are part-finished at the year-end.
- **Finished goods** – products which have been made, but not yet sold as at the year-end.

As raw materials are converted into work in progress, and then into finished goods, they are expected to increase in value. However, for IFRS accounting purposes, all inventory must be valued at the lower of cost and net realisable value, so that there is no risk of overstating the value of current assets.

Receivables (historically called debtors) represent amounts owing from customers for goods provided or services rendered. When a customer has bought goods, and been supplied with them, but has not paid for them at the year-end, the customer's obligation to pay is recognised in the accounts as a trade receivable. It is a current asset, because the company is entitled to receive this amount within the next year.

The figure shown in the statement of financial position does not usually represent the total amount owing to the company from its customers. Most companies experience some bad debts – when a customer does not pay all, or part, of its bills. In order to be prudent, companies must analyse how far their receivables book is impaired (in that there is the possibility or likelihood of non-payment), and then deduct a provision for this impairment from the total. This is referred to as a 'provision for bad or doubtful debts'. The receivables figure is, therefore, shown net of provisions, but the amount of the provision must be shown in the notes to the accounts.

Cash refers to the cash balances in the company's bank account(s) and cash registers at the financial period end. The phrase 'cash or near-cash' or 'cash equivalents' is sometimes used and reflects the fact that, included with cash, there are often other items, such as outstanding money market deposits, banker's drafts and short-term securities, which are invested to generate interest income but can be realised and turned into cash very quickly.

It may be helpful to clarify the relationship between inventory, receivables and cash.

- **Inventory** – raw materials, unfinished goods, and finished goods which are unsold. These will be turned into receivables.
- **Receivables** – finished goods which have been sold but not paid for. These will be sold later for cash.
- **Cash** – received in exchange for finished goods, sold and paid for.

In addition, the statement of financial position may include other assets of a short-term nature, such as assets which are intended to be sold, or short-term financial investments.

3.1.3   Current Liabilities

Current Liabilities	2015 (£ millions)	2014 (£ millions)
Bank overdrafts	(10.2)	(4.7)
Bank loans	(115.0)	0.0
Trade and other payables	(544.6)	(550.3)
Other financial liabilities	(54.7)	(93.6)
Current tax	(108.4)	(109.5)
	(832.9)	(758.1)

Current liabilities represent obligations that the company must settle within one year and therefore represent the company's more pressing obligations. They include the following:

- **Trade and other payables** – these are amounts due to be paid to the company's suppliers or other parties. Typically, when the company buys its raw materials, distribution and administration services, it pays for these on agreed terms of, say, 30 days from the date of invoice. Trade payables represents the total of any invoices received by the company, but not yet paid, at the financial period end.
- **Short-term loans**, or the current portion of long-term debt. This includes any amount that falls due for repayment during the next year. It also includes any overdraft balance at the financial period end.
- **Other items**, such as corporation tax due, dividends declared but as yet unpaid, or amounts due to be paid to the pension fund. These are amounts when an obligation has arisen, but which are still unpaid at the financial period end.

3.1.4 Net Current Assets

As stated above:

- **Current assets** are those assets which are short term in nature, and used in the company's trading cycle. They are also those assets that can be turned into cash relatively quickly, compared with non-current assets.
- **Current liabilities** are those liabilities which have to be repaid within one year.

If a company has more short-term assets than it has short-term liabilities, it is likely to be able to meet its obligations as they fall due in the next year. If it has more immediate liabilities than it has assets capable of being converted into cash, then it may have difficulty paying its debts and is said to have 'net current liabilities'.

Net current assets is calculated as **current assets less current liabilities**.

For ExampleCo, net current assets is:

	2015	2014
Current assets	1,067.3	1,041.2
Current liabilities	(832.9)	(758.1)
Net current assets	234.4	283.1

3.1.5 Non-Current Liabilities

Non-current Liabilities	2015 (£ millions)	2014 (£ millions)
Borrowings	(471.2)	(520.9)
Deferred income	0.0	(49.5)
Financial instruments	(13.3)	(13.4)
Deferred tax liabilities	(239.9)	(213.8)
Retirement benefit obligations	(2.6)	(4.4)
	(727.0)	**(802.0)**

Non-current liabilities are obligations falling due beyond one year. These include the following:

- **Borrowings (debt)** – this includes bank loans, bonds, debentures or mortgages due for repayment in more than a year. These liabilities generally decrease yearly in amount as the company makes its scheduled repayments. Any portion of the borrowings falling due for repayment in less than 12 months is allocated to current liabilities.
- **Provisions** – this refers to situations when the company anticipates an expense arising in the future, but when the amount and timing of that expense is not yet certain. This could relate to restructuring, bad debts, or some other expense. In this case, the company makes an estimate of the expense and includes it in the accounts as a provision. One example of a provision is **deferred tax**. This arises when the company has a potential obligation to pay tax in the future as a result of differences between the tax and accounting treatment of the value of assets.

- **Retirement benefit obligations** – when a company has a deficit on its pension scheme (ie, its future liabilities outweigh the value of the assets in the scheme), this is shown in long-term liabilities.

At any given period-end, the company will review the long-term obligations and split the current portion (the amount falling due with 12 months) from the deferred portion (owing beyond 12 months). The current portion is then included in current liabilities (see above).

Take the example of a £100 million ten-year loan, repayable in equal instalments over the life of the loan. At the beginning of the year, one instalment is due to be paid by the year-end, and is thus a current liability. The statement of financial position will show:

Current liability: £10 million
Non-current liability: £90 million.

3.1.6 Off-Balance-Sheet Items

Not all the company's assets and future obligations may be shown on the statement of financial position. If a company does not have a definite legal liability for a sum, or does not have full legal ownership of assets that it uses, it may exclude these items from its accounts. These items are then referred to as off-balance-sheet items.

For example, contingent liabilities (potential, rather than certain, obligations when the amount and timing are unknown). They are not recorded on the statement of financial position. Instead, explanatory information is disclosed in the notes to the accounts. Other examples include operating leases (assets which are leased, and when the lessee does not have a legal obligation to insure and maintain them) and funding through certain investment vehicles.

3.1.7 Shareholders' Equity

	2015 (£ millions)	2014 (£ millions)
Net assets	232.4	133.4
Capital and reserves attributable to equity holders		
Called-up share capital	18.1	19.1
Share premium account	0.8	0.7
Capital redemption reserve	11.8	10.8
Share options reserve	(138.6)	(78.2)
Other reserves	(1,442.4)	(1,434.0)
Retained earnings	1,782.6	1,615.2
Shareholders' equity	232.3	133.6
Non-controlling interest	0.1	(0.2)
Total equity	232.4	133.4

The company's net assets are the total of all its assets, minus all its liabilities. This number is always equal to value of the equity in the company; this is because the value of the company's assets, net of all liabilities, must be equal to the amount of a shareholder's equity investment plus/minus all retained reserves. If you look at the extract from the statement of financial position shown above, you will see that ExampleCo's net assets in 2015 were £232.4 million; and its total equity was also £232.4 million.

This 'total equity' may also be referred to as **shareholders' funds** or **shareholders' equity**. Shareholders' funds is made up of a mixture of equity capital subscribed by shareholders over the years, and value created by the company over the years.

Reserves

You will note that the term used in the statement of financial position is 'capital and reserves.' This is because all of the profits created and retained by the company are allocated across a number of reserves, and the nature of the reserve determines what directors are allowed to do with that value.

Reserves may be capital reserves or revenue reserves.

A **revenue reserve** is created when the company has made a profit from its trading activities, and retained some or all of this profit within the business. In general, revenue reserves can be used to pay dividends to shareholders. The most common revenue reserve is the **profit and loss reserve**, also called the **retained earnings reserve**. If a company has accumulated losses (so that it has a deficit on the retained earnings reserve) it is not allowed to pay dividends until it has accumulated enough profits to create a positive balance.

Capital reserves generally represent wealth created for the company out of some change to the company's capital base. In general, capital reserves cannot be used to pay dividends to shareholders.

For example, a company may have a **revaluation reserve**. This might arise because the company's assets have been revalued upwards. It would be unwise to see this uplift in value as part of the company's profits – after all, no cash will be realised until the assets are actually sold, and property values could go down again. However, the value of the assets has been increased in the statement of financial position, and, to make sure that net assets remains equal to shareholders' funds, the value of shareholders' funds is increased, by creating a revaluation reserve which shows the unrealised gain on the revaluation. This reserve cannot be used to pay dividends. However, if the assets are finally sold, and the company makes a profit on the sale, then the gain in the revaluation reserve is transferred into the profit and loss/retained earnings reserve, and (if there is a positive balance) can then be used to pay a dividend.

Another very common capital reserve is the **share premium account**. This arises when shares are issued to shareholders at a price in excess of the nominal value of the shares. For example, a company might have £1 nominal value shares in issue, and be preparing to issue 1,000,000 shares. The appetite in the market for the shares is strong, and the company has a good track record, so investors are prepared to pay a premium of, say, £1.50 for the shares, bringing the price to £2.50 per share. The total funds raised will be £2,500,000.

The accounts will record the effect of the share issue as follows:

	Assets	Liabilities
Increase cash	£2,500,000	
Increase share capital		£1,000,000
Increase share premium reserve		£1,500,000
Total	**£2,500,000**	**£2,500,000**

This provides shareholders with clarity as to the nominal value of the capital (ie, number of shares x face value) as well as information on the premium paid.

Issued and Authorised Share Capital

The share capital shown in the statement of financial position comprises the **issued share capital** of the company; that is, the shares which are currently in issue and owned by shareholders. Directors may increase the issued share capital by issuing new shares to raise capital, providing that they have the approval of shareholders to do so. In many countries, the number of shares that can be issued is also restricted by the provisions of a company's Articles of Association, which sets out its total **authorised share capital**. This is the maximum number of shares that can be issued at any point. It may be significantly higher than the issued share capital. In the UK, however, the concept of authorised share capital was abolished in 2009 under the Companies Act 2006.

3.1.8 Depreciation and Amortisation

At the point of purchase, a non-current asset appears on the statement of financial position at its original cost. In subsequent years, the asset reduces in value until, in due course, it has no useful economic life left; as it has no financial value it is then not shown in the statement of financial position any more.

This reduction in value is referred to as **depreciation** – the asset is said to depreciate over its useful economic life. This depreciation in value could be due to physical wear-and-tear, technical obsolescence, or depletion (in the case of minerals).

Non-current assets are shown in the statement of financial position at **net book value (NBV)**. NBV is simply the cost of the asset less the accumulated depreciation to date.

In the accounts, we can see depreciation in two places. The first of these is in the statement of financial position, where we can see the value of assets reducing in value in consecutive periods. The second place is in the company's income statement, where the depreciation is shown as an expense. This treatment reflects the fact that the purchase of assets is one of the company's operating costs, in the same way as wages and marketing expenses. Rather than simply recognise the whole cost in the year that an asset is acquired, it makes more sense to allocate the cost over the whole of the asset's useful economic life, so that in each year we can see the amount of that asset's value that is being depreciated, and also see clearly the full costs that are incurred in generating each year's revenue.

Amortisation is similar, but it is the name reserved for certain kinds of intangible assets, such as patents or licences. These intangibles are said to be 'amortised over their useful lives'.

Straight-Line Method

Some assets, such as aircraft engines, may be used for 50 years before they are worn out, and therefore the annual depreciation charge will be $1/50$ of their original cost. Other assets, such as computer equipment, may be depreciated over, say, three years, reflecting how quickly they become obsolete. Here the annual depreciation charge is $1/3$ of the original cost. In both these cases we have assumed that the asset depreciates by an equal amount in each year. This method of calculating the depreciation charge is known as the 'straight-line method'.

Example

Smithson purchases a new item of plant costing £20,000. The company expects the plant will have a scrap value of £5,000 at the end of a ten-year asset life. Company policy is to depreciate the asset in equal annual amounts (straight-line).

Over its life, the asset will fall in value from £20,000 to £5,000 – a drop of £15,000. This equates to an annual fall in value of £1,500 (£15,000 divided by 10 years). In each year, the income statement will show a depreciation charge of £1,500, and a reduction of the NBV of the asset by £1,500.

Year	Asset Cost	Annual Depreciation Charge* (to Income Statement)	Accumulated Depreciation (to Statement of Financial Position)	Final NBV (Cost less Depreciation) (to Statement of Financial Position)
Year 1	£20,000	£1,500	£1,500	£18,500
Year 2	£20,000	£1,500	£3,000	£17,000
Year 3	£20,000	£1,500	£4,500	£15,500
Year 4	£20,000	£1,500	£6,000	£14,000
Year 5	£20,000	£1,500	£7,500	£12,500
Year 6	£20,000	£1,500	£9,000	£11,000
Year 7	£20,000	£1,500	£10,500	£9,500
Year 8	£20,000	£1,500	£12,000	£8,000
Year 9	£20,000	£1,500	£13,500	£6,500
Year 10	£20,000	£1,500	£15,000	£5,000

* The annual depreciation charge is calculated as follows:

$$\frac{\text{Asset value} - \text{scrap value}}{\text{Expected useful life of asset}} = \frac{£20,000 - £5,000}{10 \text{ years}} = £1,500 \text{ per year}$$

Reducing Balance Depreciation

An alternative method of calculating depreciation is known as the 'reducing balance method'. This method reduces the book value of the asset by a set percentage each year (rather than by an equal amount). This results in a higher depreciation charge in the early years of the asset's life but a lower charge in the later years, compared with the straight-line method. The total amount written off over the asset's useful economic life will be the same in both cases.

Which of the depreciation methods is the more appropriate depends on the type of asset being depreciated and its use in the business. The argument in favour of using the reducing balance method is that, as tangible non-current assets tend to confer the greatest benefits in the earliest years of their use, these should be matched by a higher depreciation charge.

Non-current assets are always shown on the statement of financial position at NBV. Details of the depreciation policy, the original cost and the accumulated depreciation are summarised in the notes to the accounts.

Depreciation and Cash Flow

Although depreciation is shown as an expense in the income statement, you should be clear that it is not a cash expense. Cash leaves the company's bank account when the asset is first acquired, not in instalments over the life of the asset. This will be discussed in more detail when we look at the statement of cash flows in Section 3.3.

3.2   Statement of Comprehensive Income

Learning Objective

2.3.1   Know the purpose of the statement of comprehensive income, its format and main contents

2.3.2   Understand the difference between income from ordinary activities and other items included in comprehensive income

2.3.3   Understand the difference between capital and revenue expenditure

3.2.1   Purpose of the Statement of Comprehensive Income

The statement of comprehensive income (also known as the 'profit and loss account') is intended to provide a formal record of the company's performance over a particular accounting period. This can be used:

- To provide a comparison with previous accounting years: has the company improved its efficiency and profitability, or not?
- To provide information to shareholders: has the company generated enough profit to pay a dividend in the year?
- To provide a guide as to the company's creditworthiness: has it historically generated sufficient profits to pay interest and make capital repayments, with a reasonable margin? And is it generating enough profit to provide suppliers with confidence that their invoices can be paid?
- As a guide to value; this is discussed in more detail in Chapter 4.

Under IAS 1, a company may choose to present its statement of comprehensive income in one of two ways:

- As two separate documents – in this case, the first shows all the components of profit or loss (broadly, from revenue down to profit/loss for the year), and is named the 'income statement'. The second starts at profit/loss for the year, and shows all other, non-regular elements of comprehensive income, such as exchange rate movements and revaluations. This is then named the 'statement of comprehensive income'. This dual-statement approach is more common for UK companies.
- Alternatively, the company is permitted to present all of this information in a single document; this is then named the 'statement of comprehensive income'.

The examples in this text focus on the information contained in the income statement.

3.2.2 Contents of the Income Statement

	2015 (£ millions)	2014 (£ millions)
Revenue	3,453.7	3,406.5
Cost of sales	(2,445.0)	(2,409.6)
Gross profit	**1,008.7**	**996.9**
Distribution costs	(223.2)	(232.1)
Administrative expenses	(214.7)	(236.6)
Other gains	2.2	0.7
Trading profit	**573.0**	**528.9**

The income statement contains the following key items:

Turnover (or **sales** or **revenue**) is the total value of goods and/or services that the company has supplied and invoiced during the accounting period. The company may additionally earn other income such as bank interest or dividend receipts; however, this is not included in turnover for a trading company as it is not related to the company's principal business activity, which is the supply of goods or services. Turnover is recognised (entered into the accounting process) at the point of sale and not when the goods or services are paid for.

Cost of goods sold (or **cost of sales**) refers to the direct costs associated with the production of goods and/or services supplied by the company. This includes such items as the cost of raw materials, manufacturing wages and factory expenses. Cost of sales does not normally include indirect expenses such as marketing, administration costs or directors' remuneration.

Gross profit (turnover less cost of sales) represents the profitability of the principal activity alone, and thus is a useful indicator of the basic efficiency of the company's core trading process.

Operating (indirect) expenses represent the remaining ongoing costs of running the business. Some companies divide operating expenses into separate categories, such as distribution and administrative expenses. This is the case with ExampleCo plc. Operating costs include general overheads, such as selling, marketing, administration, depreciation and amortisation and all necessary business costs not directly related to producing goods and services. They do not include interest expenses or taxation, nor do they include the cost of purchasing non-current assets, such as plant and machinery, which is included within capital expenditure.

To summarise, only **revenue expenses** are recorded on the income statement. The difference between capital expenditure and the company's revenue expenditure is as follows:

- **Capital expenditure** is money spent to buy non-current assets, such as plant, property and equipment. This is not shown in the income statement, which instead shows depreciation over the life of the asset. Capital expenditure is shown instead in the cash flow statement, and its effects (ie, increase in assets and capital) are reflected in the income statement.
- **Revenue expenditure** is money spent in order to generate revenue, and is therefore shown both in the income statement and the cash flow statement. Examples of revenue expenditure include purchase of raw materials, wages paid to staff, rent paid on property, advertising and professional fees (such as audit fees). Note that it includes both operating expenses and cost of goods sold.

Operating expenses may include **exceptional items**. These are generally costs which are unusual, either in terms of the amount or the occurrence. For example, a customer may collapse, leaving the company with a large bad debt. If this is not disclosed separately, it will create a misleading impression of an increased level of normal operating expense.

Trading profit (gross profit less operating expenses) represents a key measure of profitability that shows the company's performance after deduction of all business-related costs and other indirect expenses.

	2015 (£ millions)	2014 (£ millions)
Trading profit	573.0	528.9
Share of results of associates	1.8	0.9
Operating profit (EBIT)	**574.8**	**529.8**
Finance income	0.9	0.8
Finance costs	(24.3)	(25.3)
Profit before taxation	**551.4**	**505.3**
Taxation	(150.5)	(141.3)
Profit for the year	**400.9**	**364.0**

Operating profit is also commonly expressed as **earnings before interest and tax (EBIT)**. It represents trading profit plus/less income and expense from non-core business-related activities. In many cases trading profit and operating profit are the same or very similar. Some of the additional items included in operating profit might be a share of the profits or losses of associated companies, or a profit on the sale of assets.

Finance income and finance costs show the cost of borrowing money, and the income from financial investments including cash deposits. These may also be referred to as **interest cost** and **interest income**, and should be shown separately rather than netted off against each other. Interest charges are normally tax-deductible.

Profit before taxation is the company's profit after all deductions except taxation and dividends.

Taxation is the corporation tax arising in respect of the relevant accounting period. Some of this will already have been paid in advance by the company during the year, and some of this will still be due to be paid after the year-end. Any corporation tax still unpaid at the year-end will appear on the statement of financial position as a current liability.

Profit for the year is profit after all deductions, except dividends. This profit may be used to pay dividends, or it may be retained in the business, and transferred to the retained earnings reserve. It represents the consolidated profit generated by the group of companies (see Section 2.2).

The final item on the income statement is a statement showing how much of this consolidated profit for the year is attributable to the shareholders in the parent company, and how much is attributable to the non-controlling interest (ie, minority shareholders in one or more of the subsidiaries).

Attributable to equity holders of parent	401.1	364.1
Attributable to non-controlling interest	(0.2)	(0.1)
Profit for the year	**400.9**	**364.0**

You will note that **dividends** are not shown on the income statement. Instead, when directors choose to pay a dividend to shareholders, this is deducted directly from the company's reserves.

3.2.3 Statement of Comprehensive Income: Other Items

The income statement, as described above, includes, primarily, information on income and expenditure from the company's ordinary trading activities. However, there may be other items of income and expenditure, not from trading, which will affect the company's statement of financial position and cash flows. These may include:

- actuarial gains or losses on defined benefit pension schemes;
- profits or losses on revaluation of assets;
- gains or losses on financial instrument hedges.

These are shown separately, under the heading of 'Other Comprehensive Income', to distinguish them from the core income and expenses of the company. In general, most of these items are not realised gains or losses and could be reversed with a change of market conditions. They will usually not be taken into account when calculating any of the company ratios discussed in Sections 5.2–5.3 of this chapter.

3.3 Statement of Cash Flows

Learning Objective

2.4.1   Know the purpose of the statement of cash flows; its format as set out in IAS 7

2.4.2   Understand the difference between profit and cash flow and their impact on the business

3.3.1   Purpose of the Statement of Cash Flows

Cash flow statements show how a company's cash has been generated over the accounting period and how it has been expended. The statement is vital in helping investors, lenders and directors understand whether the company is generating adequate cash to:

- continue to invest in non-current assets, to support the future growth of the company;
- pay its suppliers as they fall due;
- support its pensioners in the longer term; and
- service its capital providers by making interest and redemption payments to lenders, and paying dividends to shareholders.

It also helps directors to anticipate future funding requirements and cash surpluses, and to formulate strategies to deal with these.

3.3.2   Format of the Statement of Cash Flows

The cash flow statement draws on information contained in both in the statement of comprehensive income and the statement of financial position to show where the company generated cash and cash equivalents and where it spent cash and cash equivalents during the financial period.

Under IFRS, the relevant accounting standard is **IAS 7 (Statement of Cash Flows)**, which stipulates the required format for cash flow statements. Under IAS 7, there are three areas of its activities where a company can generate and spend cash. These are:

- **Operating activities** – generally, cash flows arising from generating revenue and meeting the company's costs of managing its operations.
- **Investing activities** – generally, cash flows arising from the management of the company's assets, both in investing in new assets and selling existing ones.
- **Financing activities** – generally, cash generated from raising new loans and issuing new shares; and cash spent on repayments of loans and redemptions of shares.

All of the company's cash flows can be allocated to one of these three areas.

Cash and Profit Compared

Before we look at the format of the cash flow statement in more detail, it might be helpful to clarify why profit and cash are not the same.

- Revenue, as shown in the income statement, is based on sales invoiced, and not on cash received. During the course of the financial year, a company will receive cash from customers in relation to invoices sent out during the previous year; it will also receive cash from customers in payment of most of the invoices sent out during that year; but it will also still have issued invoices before the year-end that have not been paid by the end of the year. Therefore, its cash receipts will not be the same as the amount of sales it makes.
- In the same way, expenses, as shown in the income statement, are based on costs incurred during the year, rather than invoices paid. During the year, the company will pay any unpaid invoices from the previous period, and pay most of the invoices received during the period, but probably still have invoices left unpaid at the year end.
- In addition, some of the company's expenses are not cash expenses. Consider depreciation (you may wish to revisit Section 3.1.8). This does not represent cash spent during the year, but is just a notional allocation of expense to a particular period. Similar examples include amortisation and goodwill impairment. Another example is when a company makes a loss on the sale of an asset; the company has in fact sold the asset for cash, but, because the NBV of the asset was higher than the cash proceeds, it is deemed to make a loss. In this case, the statement of cash flows shows the positive cash receipt, but the income statement shows 'loss on sale of asset' as an expense.

Cash Flows from Operating Activities

The amount of cash flows arising from operating activities is a key indicator of the extent to which the operations of the entity have generated sufficient cash flows to repay loans, maintain the operating capability of the entity, pay dividends and make new investments without recourse to external sources of financing.

Source: IAS 7

Cash Flows from Operating Activities	2015 (£ millions)	2014 (£ millions)
Operating profit	574.8	529.8
Depreciation and amortisation	119.3	123.1
Impairment	2.3	6.4
Loss on disposal of property	6.9	5.5
Other non-cash items	(32.8)	(24.9)
(Increase)/decrease in inventories	(59.3)	9.7
(Increase)/decrease in trade receivables	(29.0)	6.0
(Decrease)/increase in payables	11.7	31.1
Cash generated from operations	593.9	686.7
Corporation tax paid	(141.9)	(115.2)
	452.0	**571.5**

The accounting standard governing the presentation of statements of cash flows is IAS 7. This allows two alternative presentations of cash flow from operations.

The direct method (shown below) shows the cash received from customers and paid to suppliers and employees. Alternatively, the indirect method starts with the operating profit figure from the income statement, and then provides a reconciliation to arrive at the cash generated from operations.

Using the **indirect method**, the cash flow statement is constructed as follows:

- Start with the operating profit figure from the income statement.
- Adjust for any non-cash expenses or profits within operating profit: common adjustments include depreciation, amortisation, goodwill impairment and provisions, all of which are expenses deducted to reach operating profit. To arrive at cash flow, we must add back these non-cash expenses, to work out the cash element of operating profits.
- Adjust for any expenses or revenue that fit more appropriately into 'cash flow from investing' or 'cash flow from financing'; an example of this is any profit or loss on disposal of assets.
- Adjust for changes in working capital over the year, as shown in the statement of financial position. This adjustment is necessary, because of the difference between revenue/expenses and cash, explained earlier. The adjustment to make is:
  - add opening trade receivables, deduct closing trade receivables (or, to put it another way, add any reduction in trade receivables, deduct any increase in trade receivables);
  - add opening inventory, deduct closing inventory (or add any reduction in inventory, deduct any increase in inventory);
  - deduct closing trade payables, add closing payables (or deduct any reduction in trade payables, add any increase in trade payables).
- Deduct corporation tax actually paid during the year. This is usually calculated as opening tax payable (from the previous year's statement of financial position) plus corporation tax for the year (from the income statement) less closing tax payable (from the year-end balance sheet).

Using the **direct method**, the cash flow statement does not show any reconciliation to the income statement but instead shows the gross cash flow received from customers and the gross cash flow paid to suppliers. An example is shown below (note that this example does not relate to ExampleCo plc).

Cash Flows from Operating Activities	2015 (£ millions)	2014 (£ millions)
Cash receipts from customers	1,000	980
Cash paid to suppliers	(320)	(300)
Cash paid to employees	(220)	(210)
Cash paid for other operating expenses	(100)	(90)
	360	380
Interest paid	(55)	(50)
Taxes paid	(100)	(80)
Cash generated from operations	205	250

Format of Cash Flows from Investing Activities

Cash Flows from Investing Activities	2015 (£ millions)	2014 (£ millions)
Proceeds from sale of property	1.9	0.4
Purchase of property, plant and equipment	(120.6)	(98.6)
Payment of deferred consideration	(19.4)	0.0
Interest received	0.9	0.9
Total	**(137.2)**	**(97.3)**

The company's investing activities relate principally to acquisitions or disposals of non-current 'capital' assets such as land, buildings, machinery, and other significant investments. This is referred to as **capital expenditure** as discussed in Section 3.2 of this chapter.

This section of the statement of cash flows also shows amounts spent on acquisitions of businesses, and proceeds from the disposal of these. In the case of ExampleCo, we can see that in 2015 it paid £19.4 million in deferred consideration. This relates to an acquisition in an earlier year, where the consideration was payable some time later. This illustrates the fact that the statement of cash flows records the payment of the consideration as and when it is actually paid, rather than when the transaction is completed.

This section may also include interest received and dividend income. Under IAS 7, interest and dividend income may be included either under 'cash flows from operating activities' or 'cash flows from investing activities', at the discretion of the company and its auditors.

A company's survival and future prosperity are dependent upon its replacing its fixed assets, in order to remain efficient. Ideally, these assets are financed with capital of a similar duration to the economic life and payback pattern of the asset; otherwise the company will have insufficient funds to finance its operating activities.

Format of Cash Flows from Financing Activities

Cash Flows from Financing Activities	2015 (£ millions)	2014 (£ millions)
Repurchase of own shares	(221.6)	(101.8)
Employee share scheme	(68.7)	(5.5)
Proceeds/(repayment) of bank loans	115.0	(75.0)
Repurchase of corporate bonds	(51.3)	(46.6)
Interest paid	(21.6)	(32.1)
Payment of finance lease charges	(0.3)	(0.4)
Dividends paid	(129.6)	(108.5)
Total	(378.1)	(369.9)

This final section of the statement of cash flows shows fund flows arising from the company's capital sources, including income from raising new debt or issuing new shares, and cash outflows for debt redemptions and repayments, or share buybacks. It also includes purchases of shares for the employee share scheme, and the servicing of both debt and equity – in the form of dividend payments and interest payments. Note that, under IAS 7, interest payments may be shown either here, or under 'cash flow from operating activities'.

4. Free Cash Flow

Learning Objective

2.4.3   Understand the concept of free cash flow, including EBITDA and NOPAT, and the difference between enterprise cash flow and equity cash flow

2.4.4   Understand the concept of cash available for debt servicing

The term 'free cash flow' is defined differently by different users. However, for the purposes of corporate finance investment and evaluation, and for this syllabus, it is defined as the cash flow generated by a company's underlying activities, after tax, but excluding any financing deductions or income. Note, however, that you may see different definitions of free cash flow in other contexts.

Free cash flow is not an accounting concept, but a measure that is widely used by analysts.

- It is a measure that identifies what cash the company generates from its underlying operations, after necessary investment for future growth.
- It is also used by credit and investment analysts to understand the ability of a company to service and repay debt.
- Free cash flow forecasts are used to calculate the value of a company on a discounted cash flow (DCF) basis.

There are two alternative measures of cash flow: enterprise cash flow and equity cash flow.

4.1   Enterprise Cash Flow

The enterprise cash flow is the free cash flow of the company before considering payments made to any of the providers of finance to the firm. The providers of finance to the firm are both the lenders and the equity holders. The enterprise cash flow will, therefore, be the free cash flow before deduction of interest payments or debt repayments, and before the payment of dividends to shareholders. It therefore represents the cash flow available to service the needs of both debt and equity providers.

In the UK, enterprise free cash flow is usually calculated as follows:

	£ millions
Operating profit	**1,000**
Add back non-cash items*	300
EBITDA/Operating cash flow	**1,300**
Deduct tax on operating cash flow @ 24%**	(312)
Deduct capital expenditure	(150)
Adjust for changes in working capital***	(100)
Enterprise free cash flow	**738**

*   Non-cash items include depreciation, amortisation, impairments and provisions. EBITDA is earnings before interest, tax, depreciation and amortisation (and, in practice, before impairments and provisions).

**   Note that this is not the actual tax paid, which would be reduced by any tax relief available in respect of interest on debt. This is the tax on the operating cash flow only.

*** Changes in working capital: positive cash flows arise from increases in trade payables and decreases in inventory and receivables. Negative cash flows arise from decreases in trade payables and increases in inventory and receivables.

Note also that the tax is calculated based on the operating cash flow. This is the approach in the UK, where depreciation is not tax-deductible. Instead, companies may deduct certain 'capital allowances'. These are generally more restricted in their application and have not been included in the example above. In non-UK countries, where depreciation is usually tax-deductible, the tax is deducted from EBIT, as follows:

	£ millions
Operating profit	**1,000**
Less tax on operating profit (at 24%)	(240)
Net operating profit after tax (NOPAT)	**760**
Add back non-cash items	300
Deduct capital expenditure	(150)
Adjust for changes in working capital	(100)
Enterprise free cash flow	**810**

4.1.1   Cash Flow Available for Debt Servicing (CFADS)

A variant on the metric of enterprise free cash flow is **cash flow available for debt servicing (CFADS)**. This measure is useful to banks in particular, to establish a potential borrower's debt capacity, and on an ongoing basis to measure whether that borrower's ability to service its debt is improving or deteriorating. The calculation is carried out in the same way as for enterprise free cash flow, but a number of adjustments are made, primarily restricting capital expenditure to maintenance capital expenditure. The resulting cash flow figure can then be compared with existing or expected debt service obligations (interest and repayment) to see how far the company's obligations are covered by its CFADS.

Example

Stable ltd's cash flow information is as follows:

	£000s
EBITDA/Operating cash flow	1,500
Cash taxes payable	(250)
Capital expenditure	(450)
– of which maintenance capex	(250)
Changes in working capital	(100)
Interest payable for the year	(100)
Debt repayment for the year	(300)

CFADS is calculated here as EBITDA less taxes, maintenance capex and changes in working capital: ie, £900,000. Its total debt service obligation for the year is £400,000. Its debt service obligation is therefore covered 2.25x by its CFADS. As a general rule, a company whose CFADS is high relative to its debt service obligations is more stable than a company where this is not the case.

Once again, you should note that CFADS is not an accounting measure and many institutions have their own different approaches to its calculation.

4.2 Equity Cash Flow

In contrast to enterprise cash flow, equity cash flow is the free cash flow available for the shareholders alone. This cash flow is calculated after deduction of the cost of servicing debt providers (net of any associated tax relief) but before any dividend payments to the shareholders.

This is normally calculated as follows:

	£ millions
Operating profit	**1,000**
Add back non-cash items	300
EBITDA/Operating cash flow	**1,300**
Deduct interest payable	(200)
Pre-tax cash flow	**1,100**
Deduct tax on pre-tax cash flow (24%)	(264)
Deduct capital expenditure	(150)
Adjust for changes in working capital	(100)
Equity free cash flow	**586**

4.3   EBITDA and NOPAT

In calculating both enterprise and equity cash flow, we have added back non-cash items to the operating profit from the income statement. In most cases, depreciation, amortisation and impairment comprise the majority of the non-cash items and the figure calculated by adding these back to operating profit is known as EBITDA (earnings before interest, tax, depreciation and amortisation/impairments).

EBITDA is normally stated before exceptional items. It therefore provides a useful indication of the underlying pre-tax cash earnings of the company, before tax, financing costs and capital expenditure. It is widely used in valuing and analysing businesses, as well as establishing debt capacity.

EBITDA is not an IFRS measure, and so UK companies are not required to show EBITDA on the income statement. You will need to refer to both the income statement and the statement of cash flows to calculate it. Under US GAAP, however, EBITDA must be shown on the income statement and is very strictly defined.

Net operating profit after tax (NOPAT) is another measure which helps analysts to focus on underlying earnings. NOPAT represents the profits made by the company before payments made to any of the capital providers, ie, before interest payments and dividends. It takes into account the tax on these pre-interest profits, rather than the actual tax paid by the company, which is reduced by the tax relief available on any interest payments. This figure is useful in helping to establish a company's capacity to raise and service debt capital, as well as providing a clearer picture of underlying operating performance.

NOPAT is calculated as:

$$\text{Operating profit} \times (1 - \text{tax rate})$$

5.   Financial Statements Analysis

Why Analyse Financial Statements?

There are three main groups of analysts of financial statements:

- Suppliers and lenders.
- Investors.
- Management.

Each group analyses many of the same performance ratios but for differing reasons.

Trade suppliers and lenders want answers to the following (and more) questions:

- What is the customer/borrower's ability to pay interest and invoices and repay debt at maturity?
- How reliable are the customer/borrower's cash flows? All obligations must be met with cash; so sometimes cash flows can be more important than profit performance.
- What is the company's capital structure? When a company already has significant debt, can it raise additional short-term financing?

Investors (shareholders) are concerned with another line of questioning:

- How do the company's key performance ratios compare with competitors?
- How much risk is in the company's capital structure?
- Is the company's market valuation perceived as low or high compared with competitors?
- What are the company's expected annual returns?
- Does the company pay dividends; can it sustain them in a future downturn?

Management require answers to more searching questions:

- How well has the firm performed and why?
- How well have management themselves performed?
- Which division is performing the best (in terms of growth, return on capital, cash flows)?
- What are the strengths and weaknesses of the company's financial position?
- What should their strategy be regarding dividends and financing?

Any meaningful analysis must compare the performance of a company:

- Year-on-year – what trends are emerging?
- In comparison to other companies in the same sector – in relative terms, how is the company performing?

This workbook considers the three types of ratios that have a wide application across a number of sectors. These are profitability ratios, gearing (or solvency) ratios, and investor ratios, and these are discussed further in the following sections of this chapter.

For the purposes of this section, we have illustrated the ratios with historic data from the financial statements for ExampleCo plc shown at the start of this chapter, together with estimates for the current year, to provide more helpful trend information.

5.1   Profitability Ratios

Learning Objective

2.5.1   Understand the following key ratios: profitability ratios (gross profit margin; operating profit margin); return on capital employed; return on equity; liquidity (including quick ratio and current ratio)

2.5.2   Be able to calculate the following key ratios: gross profit; operating profit margins; return on capital employed; return on equity; liquidity (including quick ratio and current ratio)

Profitability ratios provide a standardised method of calculating how well the company controls costs relative to turnover, and how well it uses its assets to generate profits. Four common ratios are:

- Gross profit margin.
- Operating profit margin.
- Return on capital employed.
- Return on equity.

Although these ratios each tell a different story, they are closely linked.

5.1.1   Gross Profit Margin

The gross profit margin measures the profit a company generates after deducting the cost of goods sold (ie, in the basic business operation). The margin is most appropriate for retail and manufacturing companies and less useful in service industries. The margin (%) is calculated by dividing gross profits by turnover (revenue).

$$\text{Gross profit margin} = \frac{\text{Gross profit}}{\text{Turnover}} \times 100$$

ExampleCo's gross margin for 2015 was 29.2%, calculated as:

$$\frac{£1,008.7}{£3,453.7} \times 100$$

Gross margins vary widely from sector to sector, so, for valid comparison, only same-sector companies can be compared. To understand whether ExampleCo's gross margin is 'good' or not, the analyst should calculate the gross margin of its competitors, and see how ExampleCo compares with these.

The other feature to consider is the trend. ExampleCo's gross margin trend is:

Year	2016 (estimated)	2015	2014
Gross profit	£1,015.0m	£1,008.7m	£996.9m
Turnover	£3,500.0m	£3,453.7m	£3,406.5m
Gross profit margin	29.0%	29.2%	29.3%

Analysts would have to investigate whether this very slight decline was an industry-wide phenomenon or one specific to ExampleCo. There could be many reasons, such as commodity price movements or competitor pressure, and a full understanding will require more extensive research.

5.1.2   Operating Profit Margin

The operating profit margin measures a company's level of profitability after both cost of production and operating expenses have been deducted from turnover.

$$\text{Operating profit margin} = \frac{\text{Operating profit}}{\text{Turnover}}$$

ExampleCo's operating margin for 2015 is 16.6%, calculated as follows:

$$\frac{574.8}{3,453.7} \times 100 = 16.6\%$$

Reviewing the trend over three years, we can see that ExampleCo's operating profit margin has been improving.

Year	2016 (estimated)	2015	2014
Operating profit	£590.0m	£574.8m	£529.8m
Turnover	£3,500.0m	£3,453.7m	£3,406.5m
Operating profit margin	16.9%	16.6%	15.6%

Operating margins are improving, where gross margins are declining somewhat, indicating that the company is controlling its operating costs effectively to make up for pressure on production costs.

5.1.3   Return on Capital Employed (ROCE)

Return on capital employed calculates the operating profit generated by the company as a percentage of the capital invested in it. Note that this profit is shown before deduction of financing costs, taxation or dividends; this ratio focuses on the performance of the underlying business operations, relative to the total capital invested in these business operations. This focus means that it is easier to compare, on a like-for-like basis, the performance of two businesses with very different financing structures.

This ratio is calculated as follows:

$$ROCE = \frac{\text{Operating profit (EBIT)}}{\text{Total capital employed}}$$

There are a number of different approaches to calculating 'total capital employed'. For the purposes of this syllabus, however, total capital employed equals non-current assets plus net current assets (current assets minus current liabilities). On this basis ExampleCo's total capital employed was £959.4 million in 2015. Its operating profit was £574.8 million.

ExampleCo's return on capital employed for 2015 was therefore 59.9%, calculated as follows:

$$\frac{£574,800,000}{£959,400,000} = 59.9\%$$

Year	2016 (estimated)	2015	2014
Operating profit	£590.0m	£574.8m	£529.8m
Total capital employed	£960.0m	£959.4m	£935.4m
ROCE	61.5%	59.9%	56.6%

5.1.4 Return on Equity (ROE)

Return on equity calculates the profit attributable for shareholders, as a percentage of the equity capital invested. In comparison with ROCE, this calculation focuses on profit after interest and tax, to establish the return that shareholders are generating on their investment.

ROE is calculated as follows:

$$\text{ROE} = \frac{\text{Profit attributable to ordinary shareholders}}{\text{Shareholders' funds}}$$

ExampleCo's profit attributable to ordinary shareholders for 2015 was £401.1 million and shareholders' funds were £232.3 million.

ExampleCo's return on equity for 2015 was 173%, calculated as follows:

$$\frac{£401,100,000}{£232,300,000} = 173\%$$

Year	2016 (estimated)	2015	2014
Profit for ordinary shareholders	£420.0m	£401.1m	£364.1m
Shareholders' equity	£250.0m	£232.3m	£133.6m
ROCE	168%	173%	273%

5.1.5 Liquidity

Liquidity is a measure of how easily a company can meet its short-term obligations as they fall due. There are a number of different measures that can be used, but in this text, we will look at the current ratio and the quick ratio.

The current ratio compares the company's current assets to its current liabilities. If it has fewer current assets than current liabilities, its existing resources are insufficient to meet its short-term obligations. It is calculated as:

$$\text{Current ratio} = \frac{\text{Current assets}}{\text{Current liabilities}}$$

If the ratio is less than 1.00x, the company is unlikely to be able to meet its short-term obligations as they fall due, and could be at risk of insolvency. For ExampleCo, the current ratio is as follows:

Year	2015	2014
Current assets	£1,067.3m	£1,041.2m
Current liabilities	£832.9m	£758.1m
Current ratio	1.28 x	1.37 x

Although the ratio has deteriorated since the previous year, at 1.28x, it still suggests that the company should be able to meet its current liabilities using its existing current assets.

Quick Ratio/Acid Test

An alternative and more stringent liquidity ratio is the quick ratio, which is also referred to as the 'acid test'. Like the current ratio, it measures the company's ability to meet its short-term obligations as they fall due. However, it assumes that not all current assets are equally liquid and that some may not be capable of being turned into cash in time to meet a pressing need.

- Cash and cash equivalents are assumed to be available to be liquid and available to meet short-term obligations.
- Receivables (which are shown net of provisions for bad and doubtful debts) are assumed to be relatively liquid in that they could be sold to a factoring company to raise cash if necessary.
- Inventory is assumed not be liquid; selling raw materials, work in progress or finished goods to raise cash will take time and may result in a loss of value.

The quick ratio only takes into account the 'quick' assets of cash/cash equivalents and trade receivables in calculating liquidity. It is calculated as:

$$\text{Quick ratio} = \frac{\text{Current assets less inventory}}{\text{Current liabilities}}$$

For ExampleCo, the quick ratio is as follows:

Year	2015	2014
Current assets excluding inventory	£699.0m	£732.2m
Current liabilities	£832.9m	£758.1m
Acid test	0.84x	0.97x

This shows a deteriorating ratio of below 1.0x for both years, showing that the company cannot meet its short-term obligations as they fall due. It might want to consider arranging an overdraft or revolving credit facility to provide additional short-term funds when required.

5.2 Gearing Ratios

Learning Objective

2.5.3   Understand the following financial gearing ratios: debt to equity ratio; net debt to equity ratio; net debt to EBITDA; interest cover

2.5.4   Be able to calculate the following financial gearing ratios: debt to equity ratio; net debt to equity ratio; net debt to EBITDA; interest cover

Gearing ratios examine how far a company is exposed to financial risk, by evaluating how much debt it has relative to the amount of its equity, and whether it is able to service this debt without undue stress. They do this either by comparing the company's total debt to its total funding (debt plus equity) or to its total equity.

These measures are important to all three of our analyst types (suppliers and lenders, investors, and management).

Companies with high levels of debt in their structure are said to be 'highly geared'. A company which is highly geared (has a high level of debt in its capital structure) has financial obligations which must be met, irrespective of the level of its profits, before any returns can be provided to shareholders. When profits are volatile or falling, the company's ability to service the demands of its suppliers and its lenders falls into question and the position of the company and its shareholders becomes precarious.

Thus, when a company is highly geared, analysts will pay great attention to its ability to meet interest payments on that debt.

As the gearing ratio increases, it can expose the company to higher risks of financial failure. But, in general, debt is cheaper in the long term than equity, so 'gearing up' by borrowing capital is often a cheap way to expand the firm's capital base. The capital structure decision is a pay-off between access to cheap debt, on the one hand, and the compulsory obligation to make annual interest payments, on the other (see Chapter 3).

In examining the company's exposure to financial risk, we should examine both gearing ratios and interest cover. **Gearing** expresses the amount of debt as either a percentage or a ratio of the company's capital and it is helpful to see whether this percentage is increasing or decreasing. **Interest cover** examines the proportion of interest payment to operating profit and demonstrates whether the company is able to meet its interest obligations, and, if so, with what degree of headroom.

Both measures are used in setting a company's banking covenants; ie, a company will be required under its loan agreements to maintain gearing at below (say) 50%, or maintain interest cover at above (say) 3x. With this in mind, we can also use our gearing ratios to evaluate whether a company is at risk of breaching its banking covenants and so at risk of foreclosure on its loans.

There are a number of different measures of gearing; for this syllabus we use two measures: debt to equity and net debt to equity. However, you may also see analysts calculating debt to debt plus equity, or alternatives.

Note also that the term 'leverage' may also be used in place of 'gearing', especially if there is a US connection.

5.2.1 Debt/Equity Ratio

There are a number of different methods of calculating the debt/equity ratio, all with their advantages. For the purposes of this syllabus we define it as follows:.

$$\text{Debt/equity} = \frac{\text{Total interest-bearing debt (short term + long term)}}{\text{Total shareholders' equity}}$$

ExampleCo's debt to equity ratio for 2015 was 256.6%, calculated as follows:

$$\frac{£10.2 + £115.0 + £471.2}{£232.4} = 256.6\%$$

In itself, this is not a particularly useful figure. A gearing calculation is only helpful when compared with other companies in the sector, or with the previous or subsequent year(s) – as below. Changes in gearing levels may give an indication that a company is becoming more, or less, risky from the point of view of investors and lenders.

The calculation for ExampleCo below shows us that the gearing ratio has decreased since 2014. This indicates a reduction in financial risk, and is a useful calculation, especially when used in conjunction with other calculations such as a net debt/equity ratio or interest cover.

Year	2015	2014
Total debt	£596.4m	£525.6m
Total shareholders' equity	£232.4m	£133.4m
Debt to equity ratio	256.6%	394.0%

5.2.2 Net Debt/Equity Ratio

When a company has significant amounts of cash on its statement of financial position, this is available to pay interest and repay debt, which reduces its exposure to financial risk. If this is the case, it may be more useful to take this cash into account in calculating a net debt/equity ratio. Here the calculation is:

$$\text{Net debt/equity} = \frac{\text{Total debt (short term + long term) less cash}}{\text{Total shareholder equity}}$$

For ExampleCo plc, the net debt/equity figure for 2015 is:

$$\frac{596.4 \text{ (debt)} - 49.3 \text{ (cash)}}{232.4} = 235.4\%$$

Once again, this calculation is most helpful when used to show year-on-year trends, or in conjunction with other financial ratios.

5.2.3 Interest Cover

The interest cover ratio shows a company's ability to meet interest payments out of current profits. The ratio indicates the degree to which the company's pre-interest earnings/profits cover annual interest charges. This is particularly useful when the company's loan agreements specify an interest cover covenant which stipulates that operating profit must be maintained at, say, 4x interest expense, as it provides a very clear and timely warning of any danger of a breach of lending covenants.

Once again there are a number of different versions of interest cover, but for the purposes of this syllabus the definition to apply is as follows:

$$\text{Interest cover} = \frac{\text{Earnings before interest and tax (EBIT)}}{\text{Interest expense}}$$

For ExampleCo in 2015:

$$\text{Interest cover} = \frac{574.8}{24.3} = 23.7x$$

During the three years we are examining, ExampleCo's cover ratios are improving, and this suggests that the company has only limited financial risk, based on this measure. If we wanted to carry out further analysis, we would also compare ExampleCo's ratios with those for other companies in its sector.

Year	2016 (estimated)	2015	2014
EBIT	590.0	574.8	529.8
Interest expense	24.0	24.3	25.3
Interest cover	24.6x	23.7x	20.9x

5.2.4 Net Debt to EBITDA

Comparing a company's net debt to its EBITDA (earnings before interest, tax, depreciation and amortisation/impairment) gives an indication of the company's ability to meet its repayment obligations. If its debt is 1x EBITDA, the company could (broadly, and in theory) repay its debt in full out of one year's pre-tax operating profits. If its debt amounts to 8x EBITDA, it will take it eight years to repay its debt and is clearly more highly geared and more risky.

In conjunction with the other measures discussed above, this is a useful measure of a company's financial stability. Most loan agreements include a net debt to EBITDA covenant, whereby the borrower commits to maintaining at least the required ratio of debt to EBITDA agreed with the lender.

The calculation is:

$$\text{Net debt/EBITDA} = \frac{\text{Total debt (short term + long term) less cash}}{\text{EBITDA}}$$

For ExampleCo plc, the net debt/EBITDA ratio for 2015 is:

$$\frac{596.4 \text{ (debt)} - 49.3 \text{ (cash)}}{574.8 \text{ (EBIT)} + 121.6 \text{ (Depreciation, amortisation, impairments)}} = 0.786$$

5.3 Investor Ratios

Learning Objective

2.5.5 Understand the following investors' ratios: earnings per share; diluted earnings per share; price earnings ratio (both historic and prospective); enterprise value to EBIT; enterprise value to EBITDA; net dividend yield; net dividend cover; price to book

2.5.6 Be able to calculate the following investors' ratios: earnings per share; diluted earnings per share; price earnings ratio (both historic and prospective); enterprise value to EBIT; enterprise value to EBITDA; net dividend yield; net dividend cover; price to book

The following ratios are often classified as investor ratios, since they have a significant influence on company share values.

- Earnings per share.
- Diluted earnings per share.
- Price/earnings ratio.
- Net dividend yield.
- Net dividend cover.
- Enterprise value/EBIT (earnings before interest and tax).
- Enterprise value/EBITDA (earnings before interest, tax, depreciation and amortisation/ impairments).
- Price to book ratio.

5.3.1 Earnings per Share (EPS)

Earnings per share shows the annual profit per share attributable to ordinary shareholders.

The EPS calculation aims to match the earnings generated by the company with the number of shares contributing to the earnings. If profits remain constant but more shares are issued, the EPS figure will fall. If profits remain constant, but shares are cancelled during the year, the EPS ratio will increase. In order to calculate EPS correctly, the denominator must show a weighted average number of shares in issue during the year.

When new shares have been issued as a result of a bonus issue (or an issue where there is a bonus element), this bonus element must be eliminated to make the calculation of EPS comparable with that for previous or subsequent years.

The numerator shows profit attributable to ordinary shareholders; ie, after deduction of interest, tax and preference dividend (if any), but before deduction of the ordinary dividend.

$$\text{Earnings per share} = \frac{\text{Profit attributable to ordinary shareholders}}{\text{Weighted average number of ordinary shares}}$$

ExampleCo's net profit available to ordinary shareholders during 2015 was £401.1 million. The notes to the accounts state that the weighted average number of ordinary shares in issue was 180.7 million in 2015 and 193.1 million in 2014.

Based on this information, ExampleCo's EPS for 2014 was 221.9p.

Year	2016 (estimated)	2015	2014
Profit for ordinary shareholders	£420.0m	£401.1m	£364.1m
Weighted average number of shares	175.0m	180.7m	193.1m
EPS	240.0p (prospective)	221.9p (historic)	188.5p (historic)

Once again, this information is of little significance unless we can see a trend. As shown above, ExampleCo's EPS grew significantly in 2015 and there is further growth expected in 2016. Investors will expect that, as EPS grows, so will the value of their shares.

The EPS result is closely watched by many investors and it is quite common for analysts to forecast earnings per share for the following year, in an attempt to measure growth prospects. This requires, of course, an estimate of expected profit, as well as the expected weighted average number of shares in issue in the following year. This ratio is referred to as a 'prospective' EPS, to differentiate it from the historic ratio, reported in the financial statements.

5.3.2 Diluted Earnings per Share

The measure of EPS shown above is referred to as **basic EPS**, as it is based on the existing share capital, without taking into account any potential future issues of shares.

A second measure of EPS is **diluted EPS**. This takes into account both the ordinary shares currently in issue, and those that it may be obliged to issue in the future. For example, most firms issue stock options to senior employees as part of their compensation packages; these employees may exercise their options to acquire new shares at a predetermined date and price in the future. In addition, many companies issue convertible debt securities, which they may convert into equity shares at some point in the future. In both cases, the company has entered into a conditional commitment to issue more shares in the future.

The accounting standard which applies to the calculation of diluted EPS is **IAS 33**. This requires us to look at the effect of new share issuance on both the numerator and the denominator of the EPS calculation.

When calculating the potential dilution relating to outstanding convertible securities, IAS 33 states that a company would increase the number of shares outstanding by the number of additional shares arising on full conversion. This makes the denominator larger. Net income (in the numerator) is then adjusted by the interest saved due to full conversion (eg, if convertible debt is converted to equity, no further interest is payable on the debt). If the net effect of these two actions is dilutive (ie, reduces EPS), the company must report this. If, however, the net effect is not dilutive, the company makes no change and does not report 'diluted EPS'.

Example

Mayflower plc has profit after tax of £1,500,000. It currently has 2,000,000 shares in issue. Its basic EPS is therefore 75p (£1,500,000/2,000,000).

Mayflower has £700,000 of convertible debt in issue, with a coupon of 3%. This is convertible at a rate of £4/share. The interest is subject to corporation tax at 28%.

If Mayflower converts the debt, the effect will be as follows:

- 175,000 new shares issued (700,000/4) increases the denominator to 2,175,000.
- £15,120 interest is saved (700,000 x 3% x (1–28%)); this increases the numerator to £1,515,120.

Diluted EPS is therefore 69.66p (£1,515,120/2,175,000).

The treatment of stock options and warrants is rather more complicated.

IAS 33 recommends the use of the 'treasury method' in calculating the diluted EPS. This increases the number of shares outstanding by the number of 'free shares' that are effectively issued if the exercise price is less than the current share price. Although this method is described below for completeness, you are not be expected to do this calculation in the exam.

The IASB describes this as follows: *'Assume 100 options are outstanding with an exercise price of 8 and a current share price of 10. On exercise, 100 additional shares will be issued for proceeds of 800, but this can be analysed into 80 shares issued at full market price (which is not regarded as dilutive) plus 20 shares issued for no consideration, which is the dilutive effect.'* That is, 20 shares are added to the denominator in this example.

Example

Mayflower's current share price is 750p, and it has 100,000 options in issue with an exercise price of 700p. On exercise, 100,000 new shares would be issued for proceeds of £700,000. This can be broken down into 93,333 shares at 'full' price (ie, 700,000/750p), and 6,667 shares for no consideration (the balance).

To calculate diluted EPS, the number of shares outstanding is increased by 6,667 (the number of 'free' shares issued) to a total of 2,006,667. The net profit remains at £1,500,000. This brings the diluted EPS to 74.75p.

5.3.3 Price Earnings Ratio

The price earnings ratio (or P/E ratio) is a measure which relates the EPS to the company's current share price. It is sometimes referred to as the multiple of the company's earnings that the market is prepared to pay for its shares. It is calculated as:

$$\text{P/E ratio} = \frac{\text{Share price}}{\text{EPS}}$$

P/E is a helpful way for analysts to compare valuations of company share prices. A company whose P/E ratio is high is generally viewed as an 'expensive' stock, while a company whose P/E ratio is low might be viewed as 'cheap'.

Note that all the other ratios we have seen so far are based on data drawn from published financial statements. The P/E ratio takes into account a market share price – which is a much more volatile figure than published profits.

There are two main types of P/E ratio: **historic** and **prospective**.

A historic P/E ratio is calculated as follows:

$$\text{Historic price earnings ratio} = \frac{\text{Current share price}}{\text{Historic EPS (most recent financial year)}}$$

The P/E ratio differs from other ratios we have seen so far in that the numerator uses the market price of the share rather than any financial statement-generated value. Market prices can be volatile, and so this ratio changes frequently.

In the formula shown above, the share price used relates to a current market share price, but the EPS figure is from published accounts, and relates to a year now ended. For this reason, the multiple is referred to as historic P/E, meaning that it is a 'price-to-historic-earnings ratio'.

However, most investment analysts prefer to base their analysis of a company on its forecast earnings, rather than historic earnings, as this is generally more important to investors. For this reason, they will typically calculate a prospective P/E ratio, which compares the current share price to an estimate of the company's EPS for the current or a future year.

$$\text{Prospective price earnings ratio} = \frac{\text{Current share price}}{\text{Forecast EPS (current or future year)}}$$

ExampleCo's current share price is £22.50.

Year	2016 (estimated)	2015	2014
Share price	£22.50	£22.50	£22.50
EPS	240p	221.9p	188.5p
P/E ratio	9.38x (prospective)	10.14x (historic)	11.94x (historic)

Understanding P/E Ratios

This is one area where a trend does not give the analyst much useful information. Instead, he or she will be more interested in comparing the P/E ratios for ExampleCo with those for other companies in the same sector, to see whether ExampleCo looks cheap or expensive compared with them.

The P/E ratio can be affected by changes in both the nominator (earnings) and the denominator (price), so an analyst needs to look at both these aspects to understand what is driving the ratio. A company may have a relatively high P/E ratio because:

- it has relatively high expectations of growth;
- it has an efficient capital structure;
- it has good-quality management;
- it has a good quality of earnings or assets;
- its price is subject to rumour and speculation (for example, about a takeover bid).

The P/E ratio is not only used to compare the values of companies in the same sector. In Chapter 4 we will see how P/E ratios may also be used to calculate an equity value for a company.

5.3.4 Net Dividend Yield

Just as a P/E ratio will show whether a company is expensive or cheap compared with its peers, a dividend yield will show whether a company is generating a high or a low return to its shareholders in the form of income, compared with its peer group. In this case, the measure calculates the dividend income from a share, as a percentage of the value of that share.

The dividend paid by a company to its shareholders is subject to income tax. The net dividend is the dividend paid by a company to its shareholders excluding the notional tax credit received by UK shareholders.

Dividend yield is calculated as follows:

$$\text{Net dividend yield} = \frac{\text{Net dividend per share}}{\text{Share price}} \times 100$$

ExampleCo paid a net dividend per share of 78p in 2015, and its share price is now £22.50. The net dividend yield (expressed as a percentage) of the company's current share price is 3.47% for 2015, calculated as follows:

$$\text{Dividend yield} = \frac{\text{Net dividend}}{\text{Share price}} = \frac{78p}{2,250p} = 3.47\%$$

Directors will frequently try to maintain a level of dividend yield which makes the return on investment for their company comparable with its sector peers. However, it is helpful to look at dividend yield alongside the dividend cover ratio.

5.3.5   Net Dividend Cover (Dividend Cover Ratio)

The dividend cover ratio measures how far a company's net dividend is covered by its profits for the year.

There are two ways to calculate net dividend cover and each should give the same result.

$$\text{Dividend cover} = \frac{\text{Total profit attributable to shareholders}}{\text{Total dividend paid}}$$

$$\text{Dividend cover} = \frac{\text{Earnings per share}}{\text{Net dividend per share}}$$

ExampleCo plc paid a net dividend per share of 78p in 2015, compared with EPS of 221.9p. This gives a dividend cover ratio of 2.84x.

Falling cover ratios suggest that the company may not be able to sustain dividend payouts at current levels in future years. If a dividend is uncovered (ie, the company is paying a dividend which is greater than its total profits for the year) then it is reducing its retained earnings reserve. Remember that a company may only pay a dividend out of its distributable reserves and not out of its capital reserves.

Note: A US variant is the payout ratio, ie, (1/dividend cover), which would be 35% in this case.

5.3.6   EV to EBIT and EV to EBITDA

There are two further ratios that are extensively used both in investment analysis, and in company valuation (see Chapter 4). Both ratios relate the total market value of a company (debt plus equity) to two operating profit-based figures.

Earlier we saw how calculating a P/E ratio can show whether a company is cheap or expensive compared to its peers. The following ratios are also commonly used in this way:

*   EV/EBIT (enterprise value to earnings before interest and tax); and
*   EV/EBITDA (enterprise value to earnings before interest, tax, depreciation, amortisation and impairment).

These multiples focus on the company's enterprise value as the measure of its value (rather than its equity share price), and use profit before interest and tax to indicate performance (rather than an equity profit figure). They focus more on the underlying business and total capital of the company, rather than on equity returns and pure equity capital.

Enterprise value (EV) is the term for the total value of the company's trading operations, funded by both debt and equity. At its simplest, it is calculated by adding the value of the company's market capitalisation to the value of its net debt – ie, the current value of all of the capital invested in the company. This is discussed in more detail in Chapter 4.

Market capitalisation (MC or market cap) is simply the total value of the company's ordinary shares, calculated by multiplying the company's current share price by the number of shares in issue.

To calculate EV/EBIT or EV/EBITDA multiples, we need to take the following steps:

1. Calculate market capitalisation.
2. Calculate net debt – this is the total short- and long-term interest-bearing debt, less cash and any cash equivalents (eg, marketable securities – see Section 3.1.2).
3. Calculate enterprise value (market capitalisation plus net debt).
4. Divide enterprise value by EBIT or EBITDA (as required) to give an EV/EBIT or EV/EBITDA multiple.

1. ExampleCo's market capitalisation is currently £4,162,500,000, calculated as follows:

$$22.50 \times 185 \text{ million shares in issue} = £4,162,500,000$$

2. ExampleCo's debt has a value (assumed to be market value) of £586.2 million and it has cash of £49.3 million. The enterprise value becomes £4,162,500,000 + £586,200,000 – £49,300,000: ie, £4,699,400,000.

ExampleCo's EBIT in 2015 was £574.8 million. Its historic EV/EBIT ratio for 2015 is therefore 8.18x, calculated as follows:

$$\text{EV/EBIT} = \frac{£4,699,400,000}{£574,800,000} = 8.18\text{x}$$

ExampleCo's EBITDA is calculated as EBIT + depreciation + amortisation + impairments.

Depreciation, amortisation and impairments in 2015 amounted to £121,600,000. This brings EBITDA to £696,400,000. Therefore, ExampleCo's EV/EBITDA ratio for 2015 is 6.75 times, calculated as follows:

$$\text{EV/EBITDA} = \frac{£4,699,400,000}{£696,400,000} = 6.75\text{x}$$

Like P/E ratios, both these ratios are most helpful when comparing them with other companies in the same market sector (see Chapter 4, Section 6). And, like P/E ratios, we can calculate both historic and prospective EV/EBIT and EV/EBITDA multiples.

5.3.7 Price to Book Ratio

The price to book ratio is calculated in a similar manner to a P/E ratio. However, instead of comparing the company's market value to its earnings, we compare its market value to its asset value. This measure is especially widely used in analysing companies whose value is strongly linked to their balance sheet investments, and where assets are regularly revalued to reflect market value – for example, real estate companies, banks or investment managers.

Price to book ratios are used to compare a company with its peers, and see whether it is valued more or less highly. It may also be used to derive a multiple for use in company valuation (see Chapter 4).

The price to book ratio is calculated as follows:

$$\text{Price to book} = \frac{\text{Market capitalisation}}{\text{Net assets (most recent financial statements)}}$$

Or, alternatively:

$$\text{Price to book} = \frac{\text{Share price}}{\text{Net assets per share (most recent financial statements)}}$$

ExampleCo's current market capitalisation is £4,162.5 million.

Year	2016 (estimated)	2015	2014
Market capitalisation	£4,162.5m	£4,162.5m	£4,162.5m
Net asset value	£250.0m	£232.4m	£133.4m
Price to book	16.7	17.9	31.2

End of Chapter Questions

Think of an answer for each question and refer to the appropriate workbook section for confirmation.

1. What are the three main published financial statements and by whom are they used?
    Answer reference: Sections 1.1 and 1.2

2. What are GAAP?
    Answer reference: Section 1.3

3. What is the difference, in accounting terms, between a subsidiary and an associate company?
    Answer reference: Section 2

4. What are the five main sections of the statement of financial position?
    Answer reference: Section 3.1

5. What is the NBV and what are the two methods of calculating depreciation?
    Answer reference: Section 3.1.8

6. What is the difference between capital expenditure and revenue expenditure?
    Answer reference: Section 3.2.2

7. What is the purpose of a statement of cash flows?
    Answer reference: Section 3.3.1

8. Explain the difference between enterprise cash flow and equity cash flow.
    Answer reference: Section 4

9. What is added to operating profit to calculate EBITDA?
    Answer reference: Section 4.3

10. Name the four common profitability ratios.
    Answer reference: Section 5.1

Chapter Three
Capital Structure

This syllabus area will provide approximately 8 of the 50 examination questions

Companies use two principal sources of capital for financing, namely equity and debt. This section discusses the main characteristics of both, and then considers the cost of equity and the cost of debt.

1. Equity

A limited company's share capital can usually be divided broadly into two distinct classes of share: ordinary shares and preference shares. All companies have ordinary share capital but only a minority have preference share capital.

1.1 Ordinary Shares

Learning Objective

3.2.1   Know the typical characteristics of ordinary shares, including: voting rights; rights to dividends; rights to participate in a surplus on winding up

3.2.3   Understand the meaning of the terms 'listed' and 'quoted' in relation to a company's shares

Ordinary shares represent the primary risk capital of a company.

An investor who buys ordinary shares acquires an element of ownership in the company. He or she is referred to as having an **equity interest** in the company. If the company does well, the investor can expect to share (with other shareholders) in that success, but, if the company collapses, the investor risks losing the total value of the investment. He or she is only entitled to receive a share of any value left over once all other claims on the company's resources have been settled.

1.1.1   Equity Returns

Over the longer term, ordinary shareholders have historically been handsomely rewarded for assuming this equity risk. In the short term, however, they have generally experienced a greater volatility in their returns than is experienced in connection with any of the other main asset types.

Equity returns come from two main sources:

- **Distributions** – if the directors of the company consider it appropriate, they may declare a **dividend** to be paid to shareholders out of the **distributable reserves** of the company. Ordinary shareholders do not have any statutory or contractual entitlement to dividends; however, they have the right to approve or reject a final dividend by voting on the subject at the company's annual general meeting (AGM).
- **Capital gains** – shareholders usually have the right to sell their shares and may enjoy capital gains from appreciation in share prices.

In addition it is possible (though unusual) that if the company is wound up there may be a surplus left after all creditors have been paid. This is paid to shareholders, who participate equally. See Section 2.2.1 for further details. In practice, this most frequently happens with investment trusts or other investment vehicles.

1.1.2 Features of Ordinary Shares

When a class of ordinary shares is first created it is assigned a **nominal value** or **par value**. This may be any amount but is commonly £1. The nominal value is fixed, and bears no relationship to the market value of the shares, which may be very volatile. Indeed as the company grows and raises more equity capital, it may sell additional shares at a significant **premium** to the nominal value. However, all new issues of shares must be priced at or above the nominal value; under the Companies Act 2006, they cannot be issued at a **discount** to their nominal value.

Ordinary shares are **irredeemable** as there is no specified provision for their repurchase by the company and shareholders therefore have no right to demand a repayment of their payment for their shares. However, it is possible for a company, with shareholder approval, to buy its own shares in the market (known as a **share buyback**), and subsequently cancel them.

The majority of companies are classified as **limited companies**. Under the Companies Act 2006, shareholders in limited companies have what is known as **limited liability**. This means that they have no personal liability for the payment of the company's debts and their liability extends only to the extent of any outstanding payment on the nominal value of the company's shares held. This compares with the situation of partners in an unlimited liability partnership, who have full and unlimited liability for the debts of the partnership. Limited companies may be either:

- **private limited companies** – designated 'limited' or 'ltd'. Private companies may not offer shares to the public, and are subject to rather fewer regulatory restrictions than public companies; or
- **public limited companies** – designated 'plc'. These are allowed to offer shares to the public, and are subject to greater regulatory restriction.

A plc (unlike a private company) can apply for admission to listing on the LSE or another stock exchange, enabling it to raise capital by selling shares in the equity markets, and provide a trading venue for its investors. However, the majority of plcs do not have a stock market listing, perhaps choosing to avoid the cost and regulatory burden involved. Some of these may raise equity capital through other routes, such as private equity placements.

A company limited by guarantee does not have a share capital or shareholders. Instead, it has guarantors who guarantee the obligations of the company, rather than contributing capital, and their liability extends only to the level of their guarantee. This variant is predominantly used by not-for-profit companies, such as charities.

Companies whose shares are traded on a stock exchange are referred to as **quoted companies** – prices for their shares are quoted. Strictly speaking, only those companies whose shares are admitted to the Official List (ie, traded on the Main Market of the London Stock Exchange) should be described as **listed companies**. A company whose shares are traded on the London Stock Exchange's AIM market is described as 'quoted', 'AIM-listed' or 'AIM-traded' rather than 'listed'.

1.1.3 Shareholder Entitlements

Generally, ordinary shareholders also have the following rights:

- voting rights at AGMs, which allow them to appoint directors, adopt the company's accounts, approve the directors' remuneration report and pass other resolutions;

- voting rights at general meetings which are not AGMs; these meetings are held on an *ad hoc* basis during the year for some special purpose, such as a capital reorganisation or significant transaction;
- information rights, including the right to receive the annual report and accounts and interim financial statements, and to attend and speak at general meetings.

In the majority of cases, shareholders are entitled to one vote per share held.

1.2 Preference Shares

Learning Objective

3.2.2 Know the typical characteristics of preference shares including: redeemable preference shares; cumulative preference shares; convertible preference shares

In addition to ordinary shares, companies can also issue preference shares. Preference shares have priority over ordinary shares when a company declares a dividend, is placed in liquidation or is wound up. That is, preference shareholders must be paid their entitlements before ordinary shareholders are entitled to any distribution. On a winding-up, both preference and ordinary shareholders rank behind all debt holders and other creditors of the company.

1.2.1 Types of Preference Share

The majority of preference shares carry an entitlement to a **fixed dividend**, expressed as a percentage of its face value. For example, a £1 5% preference share will pay a dividend of 5p per annum per share. This dividend must be paid before ordinary shareholders are entitled to receive a dividend. However, the company is not allowed to pay either preference or ordinary dividends unless it has sufficient distributable reserves to do so (see Chapter 2).

Most preference shares in issue are **cumulative**, which means that preference shareholders are entitled to receive all dividend arrears from prior years as soon as the company has sufficient distributable reserves to pay them. Until these arrears have been paid, the company must not pay a dividend to its ordinary shareholders. If the preference shares are not cumulative, holders cannot claim unpaid dividends from earlier years; they are lost.

Preference shares can be **participating**, meaning that they carry a right to a participation in the company's profits (for example, 5% of profit after tax). This might be either instead of, or as well as, the fixed dividend.

Normally, preference shares do not carry **voting rights**. However preference shareholders may have the right to vote in certain circumstances, such as on a change to the rights of the preference shares, or when dividends are in arrears, but only if this is provided for in the company's Articles of Association.

Preference shares can be either **redeemable** or **non-redeemable**. Redeemable shares will be bought back by the company at some future date. They are issued with a predetermined redemption price (usually face value, but sometimes at a premium or discount) and date or series of dates. Redemption may be at the option of the company, or of the preference shareholder, depending on the terms of the shares.

Preference shares can also be **convertible**, which means that they can be converted by the shareholder into new ordinary shares at a pre-specified price or rate, on predetermined dates. In some cases, the conversion is mandatory, while in others, it is optional. If the preference shares are not converted, the shareholder is still entitled to the same fixed rate of dividend until the stated redemption date.

Finally, preference shares may have a combination of these features; for example, a £1 5% convertible redeemable cumulative preference share gives the holder the right to a 5p per annum dividend, 'rolled up' in the event of any arrears, together with the option of either redemption (for £1) or conversion into a pre-agreed number of ordinary shares, in specified circumstances.

2.   Debt

Learning Objective

3.3.1   Know the typical characteristics and differences of the main types of debt instrument including: bank overdrafts and revolving credit facilities; loans; bonds; convertibles; zero coupon bonds; contingent convertible bonds

3.3.3   Know the difference between fixed rate and floating rate interest

3.3.6   Understand the difference between par and premium redemption

3.3.8   Understand the tax treatment of interest for the issuer of debt

3.3.9   Understand that debt can be quoted or unquoted

3.3.10   Understand the key factors in the pricing of debt

Equity is the core finance for companies. The other main form of financing for companies is debt.

Debt generally pays a periodic return to lenders (in the form of interest payments, also referred to as the **coupon**) as well as repayment of the initial sum to the lender by a predetermined date (**maturity**). The payment of interest and repayment of principal are legal obligations of the borrower.

Debt is attractive to companies because most tax regimes permit the issuer to deduct interest payments from their taxable profits, and so reduce their tax charge. This tax reduction (or 'tax shield') has the effect of reducing the effective cost of debt, which helps make it a relatively cheap form of capital.

Illustration

Pelargonium plc and Lily ltd both have operating profits of £2 million. Pelargonium is all-equity-financed; Lily is part-debt-financed and has to pay interest of £500,000.

	Pelargonium	Lily
Operating profit	2,000,000	2,000,000
Interest	0	(500,000)
Profit before tax	2,000,000	1,500,000
Taxation at 28%	(560,000)	(420,000)
Profit after tax	1,440,000	1,080,000

Lily's interest payments are deducted from its profits to calculate its taxable profits, and as a result its tax charge of £420,000 is £140,000 lower than Pelargonium's tax charge of £560,000. Although Lily has £500,000 of interest on the debt, the tax relief of £140,000 reduces the effective cost of debt to £360,000.

2.1 Quoted and Unquoted Debt

2.1.1 Bank Loans

Companies can borrow from banks and other financial institutions; the debt they raise may be referred to as loans or borrowings.

Bank loans may be bilateral agreements (ie, an arrangement directly between a borrower and one bank) or they may be syndicated agreements (ie, a loan provided by a syndicate of banks, organised by a mandated lead arranger). Either way, there is no public trading facility in place for these loans, which may be referred to as **unquoted**, to distinguish them from quoted debt securities (discussed in Section 2.1.2).

The majority of bank loans have **variable rate** interest, which varies with market rates.

It is common for bank loans to have an amortising repayment schedule (when equal instalments are repaid over the life of the loan) although it is also possible to agree a bullet repayment (when all the repayment is made in one instalment on maturity).

Bank loans may be either long or short term, and it is common for borrowers to have a combination of long- and short-term debt to allow them to meet both long-term and short-term funding needs.

Many companies arrange borrowing facilities with their banks ahead of any actual funding need. These could take the form of an overdraft facility. An overdraft allows the company to borrow and repay up to a pre-agreed amount, without further discussion with its bankers, as and when required. It is usually used for short-term funding needs, such as short-term working capital shortfalls. Overdraft interest is typically variable rate, and the sums borrowed are usually repayable on demand.

A company may also arrange a revolving credit facility (sometimes referred to as a RCF or 'revolver'). This is similar to an overdraft in that it allows the borrower to drawdown and repay all or part of the loan as necessary throughout the life of the facility. The facility is available for a pre-agreed period and, providing that the borrower complies with the terms of their agreement, it is not repayable on demand. The company pays a coupon on the drawn-down portion of the facility, and this is usually variable rate; it also pays a commitment fee on any undrawn amount of the facility.

2.1.2   Debt Securities

Larger borrowers can issue debt securities. Bought mainly by institutional investors, these debt securities are traded in the debt capital markets (also referred to as the bond markets, fixed income markets or DCM). The debt capital markets comprise trading through stock exchanges, such as the London Stock Exchange (LSE), as well as over-the-counter, ie, off-exchange.

Debt securities may trade at prices which are at, above or below their book value. As prices for these securities are quoted in the markets, they are referred to as **quoted debt** (unlike bank debt, which is not tradeable and when no prices are quoted). These debt securities may be long-term or short-term obligations, with a variety of characteristics.

Term/Maturity

Long-term debt securities (with a maturity of greater than one year) are commonly issued by larger companies, governments, local governments and financial institutions. These are known as bonds, or loan stock, and account for the largest proportion of the markets for these securities.

Short-term bonds typically have a maturity of between one and three years; medium-term bonds typically have a maturity of between three and ten years; and long-term bonds typically have a maturity of over ten years.

Debt securities with a maturity of less than a year are referred to as a 'notes', 'bills' or commercial paper.

Fixed versus Floating Rate Interest

The interest rate on a loan is frequently referred to as its 'coupon'. The coupon is expressed as a percentage of the nominal value. So, a bond with a nominal value of £100 and a 7% coupon paid semi-annually will pay the holder £3.50 every six months.

The coupon may be fixed rate or floating (variable) rate.

A **fixed rate** is set at the time of issue, and generally remains unchanged for the term of the security. This is usually set in nominal terms. For index-linked bonds, the coupon is expressed in real terms and the bondholder is entitled to this coupon plus an inflation-linked uplift. In a 3% index-linked bond after one year of issue where the RPI inflation rate was 1.5%, the 3% coupon would be increased for the following year by 1.5%, ie, increased to 3.045%.

A **floating rate**, or **variable rate**, is set at the time of issue at a margin over some agreed threshold. In the UK, variable rate debt is usually set at X basis points over the London Interbank Offered Rate (LIBOR).

- A basis point is 0.01% (one per cent of one per cent).
- LIBOR is the rate of interest that major banks charge each other for borrowing, using a range of instruments in the money market, and is set daily for a range of different maturities and a range of currencies. Individual banks submit their own inter-bank rates to ICE Benchmark Administration (which took over the role of administering LIBOR after the 2012 rate-rigging scandal); IBA then publishes the average of these rates.
- The margin of X basis points is referred to as the 'spread' over LIBOR.
- The coupon for a bond is reset by reference to an updated LIBOR figure, typically every three or six months. Since the coupon is reset frequently, interest rates broadly track market rate, and so the price of a floating rate note is less volatile than that of a fixed interest bond.

Example

A bond is issued with a coupon of 150 basis points above three-month LIBOR. When the three-month LIBOR rate is 0.5%, the coupon on the bond is 2% (0.5% plus 1.5%). When the LIBOR rate increases to 0.75%, the coupon increases to 2.25%.

Some bonds may be issued as zero coupon bonds with no interest payable over the life of the bond. This is discussed further in Section 2.5.

Ownership

While title to equities in the UK is usually evidenced in a share register, many debt issuers do not maintain a register of their debt securities. In some cases, issuers maintain an electronic register, while in other cases, the register is maintained by intermediaries. Transfer of ownership typically takes place through a clearing organisation, such as LCH.Clearnet, Euroclear UK and Ireland ltd or the National Securities Clearing Corporation (NSCC), when a trade is settled.

More rarely, a bond is issued in negotiable certificated form (ie, using physical paper certificates). In this case, the legal owner of the bond is the 'bearer' or holder of it and, therefore, the bonds are referred to as 'bearer securities' or 'bearer bonds'.

Transfer

Most bonds are transferable from one owner to another without restriction, either by simple delivery, or by entry in a register.

Bonds may be traded through a stock exchange, like shares, or through an over-the-counter (OTC) dealing facility agreed by the issuer with a bank.

Bearer bonds are certificated instruments. They can be transferred from one holder to another without formality or entry in a register, simply by physically handing over the certificates, as if they were banknotes. This means that bearer bonds qualify as negotiable instruments.

Nominal Value and Market Price

Most UK bonds are issued in units with a nominal or face value of £100, also known as the par value. In contrast to the nominal value of equity shares, a bond's nominal value is of practical significance, as it is the price at which the bond is usually issued and redeemed. Some issues are, however, made and/or redeemed either at a discount or at a premium to par.

Bonds are traded at a price which is linked to their nominal value per unit. For example, a bond with a nominal value of £100 could be priced at £101: in this case, it is trading at a premium to its par value. If its price is £98, it is trading at a discount to its par value.

The market price is affected by a number of factors, including the credit rating of the issuer; the coupon (relative to market interest rates); any covenants or collateral attached to the bond; and the bond's liquidity, which in turn is affected by the size of the issue, and the quality and condition of the markets it trades on.

Illustration

The current benchmark rate for 10-year bonds is 2%.

Premium plc has issued a £500 million 10-year bond with a 3% coupon and a AA credit rating; it is traded on the LSE. Premium plc is therefore liquid, with a good credit rating and a coupon in excess of market rates, and is priced above par – at, say, 105.

Discount plc has issued a £100 million 10-year bond with a 1.5% coupon and a A– credit rating; it is traded over-the-counter. It is less liquid, with a lower credit rating and a coupon below market rates. It is priced at a discount – at, say, 95.

Principal and Redemption

The principal amount of a bond is its nominal value. The bond issuer is obliged to repay the principal to the person who is the holder of the bond at maturity. Most bonds are redeemed at par (ie, for their nominal value) but some may be redeemed at a premium to par value, particularly if they bear low coupons, or no coupon at all, or are index-linked.

The terms of redemption are set out at the time that the bond is issued and include provisions on the timing of redemption. This may provide for the whole of the bond to be redeemed on a specific date or for the bondholders to have the option for redemption at a series of dates.

Structures

A conventional bond has straightforward features, similar to those described above. They can be described as 'straight' or 'vanilla' bonds. Others may have less common features. This includes bonds:

*   with **index-linked** coupon payments and redemption proceeds;
*   without coupon payments; these are known as **zero coupon bonds**;
*   with **conversion rights**; these convertible bonds normally confer a right on the holder to convert them into ordinary shares of the issuer, on pre-specified terms and on predetermined dates;

- with **floating** rather than fixed coupons. These are termed **floating rate notes (FRNs)** or **variable rate notes (VRNs)**;
- with provisions for **early redemption**; a callable bond enables the issuer to enforce early repayment, whereas a bond with a put provision enables the holder to enforce early repayment.

These are discussed in more detail in Section 2.4.

2.2 Security/Collateral

Learning Objective

3.1.1 Understand the elements of capital structure and the ranking of the various different instruments (levels of seniority for equity and debt)

3.3.4 Understand the difference between a fixed and a floating charge

3.3.5 Understand the difference between senior and subordinated debt

The main concern of debt providers is to receive interest and principal payments on time. However, they also wish to retain some degree of protection against the event of default. If possible, a lender will usually aim to take **security** (also called **collateral**, or a **charge**) over some or all of the borrower's assets (or a third party's in the case of a loan guarantee); in the event of the borrower defaulting on the loan, the lender may seize the assets, sell them, and recover their loan from the proceeds. This is similar to the bank or building society's charge over your home to secure an outstanding mortgage – if you don't pay on time, the bank will take your property.

The nature of the security charge may be fixed or floating.

- A **fixed charge** works exactly like the domestic mortgage. Here, the loan agreement clearly identifies specific assets which are pledged as security. They tend to be non-current assets, such as properties and machinery. In the event of default, these specific assets will be seized and sold to repay the company's creditors, with any shortfall forming part of the unsecured liabilities of the company.
- A **floating charge** is a charge over a particular class of assets, such as inventory or trade receivables. It is not possible to identify specific individual assets of this type, as they change day-by-day as the company runs its business. However, at the date of default, the charge attaches to all assets of that class which exist at that date; they will then be seized and sold. Frequently, both a fixed and floating charge will be granted on the same loan.

With a bank loan, the charges are set out in the **loan agreement**. With a bond issue, the security terms are incorporated into a legal **trust deed**, and the borrower's compliance with it is overseen by an independent trustee appointed by the company. If any of these terms are breached, then the trustee has the right to appoint a receiver to realise the asset(s) subject to the charge.

When a company has a number of sources of debt, it is important to clarify which lender is entitled to receive interest and repayments first, and has first claim to the collateral. This is the senior lender. Any other lender is said to be subordinated; it will only receive interest, repayment and access to collateral once the senior lender's claim is met.

- A **senior debt** provider normally takes a fixed and/or floating charge over the assets of the borrower. It will normally have priority in a winding-up and for payment of interest and capital repayments. It will generally impose stricter lending covenants (financial benchmarks and performance requirements), which limit the access of subsequent lenders to the company's cash flows or assets. It is thus in a better position than a subordinated or **junior** lender. In the event of liquidation, senior debt with a fixed charge ranks first in the line of creditors – ahead of subordinated lenders.
- **Junior (subordinated) debt** may have subordinated security, as well as subordination in terms of interest and repayment. It may also be unsecured or even subordinated to unsecured creditors. In the event of a liquidation, subordinated debt holders will not receive any of the liquidation proceeds until senior lenders have been repaid in full. Subordinated lenders typically require higher rates of interest to compensate them, and so junior debt is more expensive than senior debt. Generally, the greater the level of subordination, the higher the cost of the debt.

2.2.1 Ranking in Liquidation

In the event that the company enters into insolvency proceedings, an insolvency practitioner is appointed to oversee the liquidation of its assets, through the sale of the business or of individual assets. The proceeds of this liquidation are distributed in strict order, as follows:

1. Fixed charge holders are paid first (after the costs of realisation up to the value of the proceeds from the sale of the assets, subject to the fixed charge).
2. Preferential creditors: these are primarily employees' arrears of pay and holiday pay, up to specified limits.
3. Floating charge holders (apart from a proportion which may be reserved for unsecured creditors).
4. Unsecured creditors, such as HMRC, unsecured lenders or trade creditors, and any shortfall to secured creditors after realising the proceeds of the assets subject to the charge(s).
5. Subordinated creditors, if any (those who have agreed to be subordinated to unsecured creditors).
6. Preference shareholders, if any.
7. Ordinary shareholders receive any surplus.

If the proceeds are not sufficient to pay the fixed charge holders in full, there will be no payment for preferential creditors. Unsecured creditors will only receive any of the proceeds once all the creditors ranking above them have been paid in full. In a liquidation, it is unusual for unsecured creditors to be paid in full, and it is common for shareholders of an insolvent company to receive no payment at all.

Clearly, the required returns of each class of investor are affected by their position in this table; so that ordinary shareholders require the highest potential returns to compensate them for their risk, while the fixed charge holders are satisfied with the lowest return, given their seniority.

2.3   Returns on Quoted Debt

Learning Objective

3.3.7   Understand the yield to maturity of loan stock

The return on quoted debt is made up of two elements: the coupon and any profit or loss on redemption. This return is usually described as a yield and expressed as a percentage of the market price.

2.3.1   Running Yield and Yield to Maturity

The **running yield** is the percentage return on the investment in the bond which is provided by the coupon alone. For example, a bond which is issued at 90, and pays a coupon of 5%, has a running yield of 5.5% (5% / 0.90). This may also be referred to as a 'flat yield'.

An alternative measure is the **yield to maturity** (also referred to as the 'gross redemption yield'). This is a combination of the running yield and the gain or loss that will occur if the bond is held until it is redeemed. It is calculated over the life of the bond to give an average annual compound return. It is usually stated as a gross yield, with both the coupon and the gain/loss on redemption stated before deduction of tax.

Example

A two-year £100 bond is issued at £105 and pays a coupon of 7%. It will be redeemed at par.

The running yield is 6.67% (7/1.05).

An approximation of the yield to maturity is calculated as follows:

Investment:	(105)
Income year one:	7
Income year two:	7
Loss on redemption:	(5)
Total income:	9
Annualised income (9/2):	4.5
YTM:	4.5/105 = 4.3%

In the example above, the yield to maturity is lower than the running yield because the market price is higher than the bond's par value and the investor will suffer a capital loss if they hold it to maturity. If, however, the market price is below par, a capital gain is made if the investor holds the bond to maturity, and so the yield to maturity is greater than the running yield.

When an issuer is calculating the ideal redemption value for the bond, it will take into account the yield that investors are typically seeking for this kind of investment, based on market data. If the bond's coupon appears low, the premium on redemption (or the discount on issue) will be adjusted until the redemption yield is in line with market levels.

A more precise calculation for yield to maturity takes into account not just the cash flows, but the timing of these cash flows, as clearly a premium received in year ten is of less value to an investor than an equivalent premium received in year two. This approach calculates the yield to redemption for a bond using the internal rate of return (IRR) method shown at Chapter 1, Section 4.3.

2.4   Hybrids (Convertible Securities)

Learning Objective

3.3.1   Know the typical characteristics and differences of the main types of debt instrument including: bank overdrafts and revolving credit facilities; loans; bonds; convertibles; zero coupon bonds; contingent convertible bonds

Hybrid securities contain features of both equity and debt. The most common hybrid is the **convertible bond** (sometimes referred to as a convertible loan stock or debenture).

The convertible bond pays interest in the same way as straight bonds. Additionally it offers the holder an option to 'convert' the bond into a specified number of ordinary shares in the issuing company at a specified future date. The **conversion price** is set at the time of issue and is typically 10–30% above the underlying share price at that time. The price difference is known as the **conversion premium**. The **conversion ratio** refers to the number of shares which can be 'bought' with £100 nominal value convertible bonds.

Example

Transformer plc has issued a £100 bond with the right to convert to 40 shares in 2017. The conversion price is therefore:

$$\frac{100}{40} = £2.50$$

Transformer's share price is currently £2.10. The conversion premium is therefore:

$$\frac{2.50 - 2.10}{2.10} = 0.190, \text{ ie, } 19.0\%$$

The right to convert the bond into shares cannot be separated from the bond itself. Thus, in order to exercise the right to acquire shares, the bondholder must surrender the convertible bond to the trustee of the issue, who will then deliver the agreed number of shares in return.

The coupon on convertibles is generally lower than for straight bonds of the same issuer with similar duration because the conversion option may well turn out to have value that investors are prepared to pay for. The price of the convertible rises as the value of the underlying ordinary shares increases, although not at exactly the same rate.

The attractions of a convertible to an investor are:

- If the company prospers, its share price will rise and, if it rises enough, conversion may lead to capital gains.
- If the company's share price declines, the investor will retain the bond and redeem it at par on the maturity date.

The borrower should consider the following:

- It can offer lower interest than on a similar 'straight' bond, and benefit from tax relief on the interest; this makes it relatively cheap finance, as investors will pay a higher price because of the possibility of a capital gain.
- However, as convertible bondholders exercise their options, existing shareholders will see their interest diluted. This was discussed earlier in Chapter 2, Section 5.3.2.
- A convertible issue may be an attractive option when shares are 'underpriced', and this can make it an inexpensive way to issue shares.

In a convertible bond, the investor has the right to decide whether to convert or redeem the bond. In a **reverse convertible**, the issuer has the right to decide whether the bond is converted or redeemed. In a **mandatory convertible**, the bond *must* be converted in specified circumstances.

Exchangeable bonds share all the characteristics of convertibles except one. Whereas convertible bonds may be converted into shares in the issuing company only, exchangeable bonds are converted into shares in another company. This is either a subsidiary of the issuer, or another company or companies in which the issuer has a substantial equity interest.

Contingent convertible bonds (sometimes called CoCos) are also converted into shares of the issuer. However, the bonds are converted on a contingent basis: that is, if some predetermined event arises, the bonds are mandatorily converted into equity. The commonest example of this is in the banking sector, where banks are required to maintain core tier one capital (equity and retained profits) of at least 7% of their risk-weighted assets. A bank can issue a contingent convertible bond, which is convertible in the event of its tier one capital falling below (say) 5%. When tier capital falls below this threshold, the bond is converted into equity, immediately adding equity to the bank's capital base. These instruments were widely used during the banking crisis.

CoCos can be highly complex and are more risky than conventional convertibles. Due to this, the FCA restricts their distribution to retail investors.

Convertible bonds are, in many ways, very similar to convertible preference shares. Both carry the option of redemption or conversion and a fixed rate of dividend/coupon. The differences are that the dividend on a preference share is not tax-deductible and the preference share ranks lower in a liquidation than the convertible debt.

2.5 Zero Coupon Bonds

Learning Objective

3.3.1 Know the typical characteristics and differences of the main types of debt instrument including: bank overdrafts and revolving credit facilities; loans; bonds; convertibles; zero coupon bonds; contingent convertible bonds

Zero coupon bonds are bonds with a coupon of zero (ie, no interest). Instead these bonds are sold at a deep discount to par value, with the discount reflecting the interest forgone.

The return to bondholders is provided entirely in the form of a capital gain on redemption. The bond price will increase as they approach maturity, but the value will tend to be very much more volatile than interest-bearing bonds. These bonds tend to be relatively long term, compared with other corporate bonds. Zero coupon bonds are most attractive to investors who are not seeking income but looking for long-term capital uplift, eg, for inheritance planning purposes.

For tax purposes, part of the capital gain is treated as interest and so attracts tax relief.

Example

Zilch plc is issuing a five-year zero coupon bond and needs to establish the issue price. Companies with similar credit ratings are currently issuing bonds with a yield of around 5%.

Assuming a required yield of 5%, the issuance price may be set at the present value of the redemption value, discounted at 5% over the five years of the bond's life, as follows:

$$\text{Issue price} = \frac{100}{(1 + 0.05)^5} = 78.35$$

2.6 Alternative Forms of Debt Financing

Learning Objective

3.3.2 Know the typical characteristics of the following alternative ways of debt financing: invoice factoring; asset-based lending; finance leasing; sale and leaseback agreements

Companies may also raise debt finance from non-traditional sources, as well as through issuing debt instruments or borrowing.

2.6.1 Invoice Factoring

Invoice factoring (also called debt factoring) is a common source of short-term financing involving the sale or assignment of a company's sales invoices to a third party (the factor). The factor buys the company's trade receivables (in the form of the company sales invoices) for a sum which is typically 80–90% of the face value of the invoices, depending on the quality, terms and age of the company's receivables book. The factor takes on responsibility for collecting these debts and, once they have been collected, pays over the balance of the invoice amounts – less a fee. This means that the company can raise working capital finance from the factor, rather than waiting for its customers to pay their invoices.

Example

Cashless ltd sells its goods on 60-day terms. It has recently invoiced its customers a total of £25,000 and now needs to buy additional inventory to fill new customer orders. It would be expensive to use its overdraft to borrow the cash it needs, so it decides to pursue factoring.

Cashless approaches a factoring company. The factor offers it £20,000 within 24 hours, in exchange for the right to collect the £25,000 of trade receivables. Cashless is now able to use this £20,000 of cash in its operations. In 60 days' time the factor collects the full £25,000 from the customers, and pays Cashless the balance of £5,000, less its fee.

2.6.2   Asset-Based Lending

Asset-based lending is a term used for debt finance which is secured by assets such as plant and machinery, inventory and trade receivables. It is usually provided by specialist asset-based lenders, frequently alongside invoice factoring or overdraft facilities, and it may be provided to meet short-term working capital needs, or for longer-term purposes. In some cases, lenders will be prepared to take intangible assets, such as brands or patents, as security.

In asset-based lending, the lenders provide a secured term loan of up to (say) 80% of the value of the assets – depending on the type and quality of the asset. The term of the loan will depend on the life, quality and type of the assets used as security for the loan.

Unlike a factoring company, an asset-based lender will not take ownership of the assets unless the borrower defaults on the loan, in which case it may enforce the security.

2.6.3   Finance Leasing

Finance leasing is widely used as a source of long-term financing for companies. Under this arrangement, companies lease, rather than buy, their long-term assets (notably plant and machinery) with the aid of finance from a leasing company, which owns the asset over its working life. Thus, the lessee (the borrower company) enjoys the use of the asset as though it were owned, and makes monthly payments to the lessor (the lender/leasing company). These monthly finance lease payments are made up of a payment for the assets, together with a finance charge.

With finance leasing, economic ownership of the asset – along with the accompanying risks and rewards – lies with the lessee, and the assets are leased for the greater part of their economic life. This means that the lessee is responsible for long-term repairs, maintenance and insurance, even though the legal title to the asset stays with the lessor. If these features are not part of the lease agreement, the lease is instead described as an **operating lease**.

When calculating gearing and other financial ratios, finance lease liabilities must be included as part of the company's debt finance, and the finance charge on the leases must be included in interest payments.

IAS 17 sets out the criteria for classifying a lease as either an operating lease or a finance lease. It also sets out the required accounting treatment for finance leases in the accounts of lessees as follows:

- At the start of the lease term, finance leases should be recorded as an asset (in non-current assets) and a liability (in non-current liabilities). The value is the lower of the fair value of the asset, and the present value of the minimum lease payments.
- Finance lease payments should be split out between the finance charge and the reduction of the outstanding liability.
- The leased assets shown on the statement of financial position should be depreciated in the same way as assets which are owned outright.

Note that in finance leases the assets acquired are shown on the company's statement of financial position. This is an example of on-balance-sheet finance.

2.6.4 Sale and Leaseback

A **sale and leaseback** is another means of financing non-current assets, and property in particular. In this case the company sells one or more of its properties to a bank or specialist financing house, in return for a cash payment at the property's market value. Simultaneously it enters into a lease agreement to rent the property from the bank so that it continues to have the use of the asset in its operations, in exchange for payments. These rental payments may be at market rates, index-linked, or based on the value of the transaction.

The advantage of sale and leaseback for a company is that it is a means of raising cash for operational purposes, debt reduction or investments, releasing the capital tied up in the company's non-current assets. Ratios such as ROCE (see Chapter 2, Section 5.1.3) may be improved, as the company's capital employed is reduced. There may also be tax advantages to sale and leaseback financing.

The disadvantage is that the company may be perceived as having a weaker banking covenant, now that it has disposed of assets which could have been used as collateral, and may be perceived as having 'sold off the family silver'. It may also lose some of its operational flexibility, as it gives up the freedom to use the property as it wishes.

Note that this is an example of **off-balance-sheet financing** as the assets used by the company are no longer visible in its balance sheet.

3. Cost of Capital

Learning Objective

3.4.1   Understand the meaning of the weighted average cost of capital

3.4.2   Be able to calculate the weighted average cost of capital

There are a number of considerations for directors in deciding what form of capital they should select in financing their companies. Relative risk, market conditions, shareholder considerations, collateral, cash flow and lender attitudes are all relevant. However, a major consideration is the relative cost of capital.

It will be clear that debt is always a less expensive source of capital than equity, because it:

* provides a tax shield, reducing the amount of tax a borrower pays (see Section 2);
* is less risky for the investor, as it ranks above equity for distributions and on a winding-up; so that a lender should require a lower return than an equity investor (see Section 2.2.1).

The cost of capital is an important issue for two reasons. First, it makes economic sense to keep the cost of financing down. Second, the company's cost of capital is the discount rate which is used in a cash-flow-based valuation of the company and has a significant impact on the value of the company. This is discussed in more detail in Chapter 4.

In summary, the cost of capital is the rate (in percentage terms) that firms expect to have to return to their providers of capital (eg, shareholders and lenders). It is possible to calculate a cost for each of debt and equity, and from these we can then calculate a single **weighted average cost of capital (WACC)** which can be used as the discount rate for valuation.

3.1   Using WACC in DCF

The **discounted cash flow** method of valuation is one of the fundamental tools of corporate finance. It requires an estimate of future cash flows to be discounted at an appropriate discount rate, to establish a present value of future cash flows. The appropriate discount rate represents the minimum return that its debt and equity investors require as a return on their investment.

When determining the appropriate discount rate, corporate financiers therefore calculate the cost of each form of capital (equity and debt) and then calculate a weighted average of these costs, to produce a single figure that can be used as a discount rate. The WACC is sometimes described as the opportunity cost of capital; (ie, the amount of return that a rational investor could expect to get from another investment of similar risk).

The formula for the WACC of a company with two sources of capital (debt and equity) is set out below:

$$WACC = \frac{(K_d \times MVd) + (K_e \times MVe)}{(MVd + MVe)}$$

where:

K_d = Cost of debt (after tax).
MVd = Total debt (at market value).
K_e = Cost of equity.
MVe = Total equity (at market value).

Example

Cormorant has £500 million market capitalisation, and £200 million of debt (at its market value). Its after-tax cost of debt is 2.5%, and its cost of equity is 6%. Its WACC is:

$$WACC = \frac{(0.025 \times 200{,}000{,}000) + (0.06 \times 500{,}000{,}000)}{(200{,}000{,}000 + 500{,}000{,}000)} = 0.05, \text{ ie } 5\%$$

When calculating WACC, there are a number of key points to remember.

- **Use of market values of debt and equity** – the weightings of debt and equity in the calculation should be based on current market values of debt and equity, not historic accounting book values. WACC is the current expected return on a firm's securities based upon current market price. This is the return a new investor requires now as an inducement to purchase the company's bonds/shares in the market.
- **Use of target or optimal capital structures** – in the example above we have used existing market values of debt and equity. The corporate financier may not have the data available to do this (for example, when valuing a private company) or may be proposing a new capital structure. In such a case, it is more appropriate to substitute the target capital structure of (say) 40% debt:60% equity. As the WACC is used to discount long-term future cash flows, it should be based on the long-term target capital structure.
- **After-tax cost of debt** – since debt interest is an allowable cost in most tax jurisdictions, the effective cost of debt is the after-tax cost of debt. When a company is loss-making, the appropriate effective cost of debt is the pre-tax cost, as there are then no profits to shield.

3.2 Calculating the Cost of Debt (K_d)

The first step in calculating WACC is to calculate the **cost of debt**. The formula for the cost of debt is:

$$K_d = Yield \times (1 - t)$$

where:

K_d = cost of debt.
Yield = coupon (for untraded debt) or yield to maturity (for traded debt).
t = tax rate.

The cost of debt represents the cost to the company of raising debt finance, after allowing for the tax shield on the debt. The current coupon on the company's existing debt may not be representative of this, particularly if the debt was raised in different market conditions or at a different stage of the company's life. Instead, the cost of debt is best represented by the yield on the company's outstanding quoted debt.

When there are a number of different types of debt, we may calculate a **weighted average cost of debt**, using the same approach as we have adopted for WACC above.

Example

KayDee plc has the following debt in issue:

Debt 1: £100m 5% bonds currently trading at 104, with a yield to maturity of 4.5%.

Debt 2: £50m 7% bonds currently trading at 110 with a yield to maturity of 5%.

The corporation tax rate is 20%.

The cost and market value of the bonds is as follows:

	Cost (pre-tax)	Cost (after tax)	Market Value
Debt 1	4.5%	4.5% x (1 – 20%) = 3.6%	£104m
Debt 2	5%	5% x (1 – 20%) = 4.0%	£55m

The weighted average cost of debt is:

$$\frac{(104 \times 0.036) + (55 \times 0.040)}{(104 + 55)} = 3.74\%$$

3.2.1 Nominal Value, Market Value and Yield

Learning Objective

3.4.7 Be able to calculate the present value of a bond (three-year)

It may be helpful here to have a reminder of the relationship between nominal value, market value and yield. The cost of debt is calculated by reference to required yield and market value, not on coupon and nominal value. This is partly because bonds are often issued or redeemed at a discount or premium to nominal value, and partly because investors are, after all, more interested in total yield to maturity than in coupons alone.

The market value of a bond is equal to the present value of the coupon payments, discounted at investors' required rate of return. In Chapter 1, Section 4.1.2, we learned how to calculate the present value of multiple future cash flows, using the following formula:

$$\text{Price} = \sum \frac{CF_n}{(1+r)^n}$$

where:

Σ = sum of cash flows discounted for each year.

CF_n = cash flow received in period n (coupon payments and principal repayment).

r = rate of return (yield-to-maturity).

n = number of compounding periods.

We can adopt exactly the same approach to calculate the market value of a three-year bond.

Example

Bondmaster plc has an 8% bond in issue with three years to maturity. The yield to maturity of similar bonds in the market is 4.5%, and you can assume that is the required return for investors. Assuming redemption at face value (ie, 100) what is the present value of the bond?

$$\text{Market value} = \frac{£8}{(1+0.045)^1} + \frac{£8}{(1+0.045)^2} + \frac{£8}{(1+0.045)^3} + \frac{£100}{(1+0.045)^3}$$

$$\text{Market value} = 7.66 + 7.33 + 7.01 + 87.63$$

$$\text{Market value} = £109.63$$

The market value of the bond is only the same as the nominal value (£100) if the coupon is exactly equal to the required rate of return and if the bond was both issued and redeemed at par.

3.3   Cost of Equity (K_e)

Learning Objective

3.4.3   Know that the cost of equity is equal to the expected rate of total return on shares

3.4.4   Understand what beta measures in relation to equities

3.4.5   Know that the expected rate of total return on shares can be estimated using the Capital Asset Pricing Model (CAPM)

3.4.6   Be able to calculate expected return using the CAPM formula

As we can see above, calculating the cost of debt for companies is fairly straightforward. The calculation of the cost of equity (for either quoted or private companies) is more difficult.

We have already set out the principle that a company's cost of capital is equal to the return required by investors in that company. For equity capital, that return comprises a mixture of dividend and capital gain. As there is no contractual commitment to provide a particular level of dividend and gain, the calculation involves a degree of estimation, either of likely gains and dividends, or of investors' likely expectations.

In practice, a variety of methods can be used to estimate the cost of equity. The most common of these is CAPM.

3.3.1 Capital Asset Pricing Model (CAPM)

The **capital asset pricing model (CAPM)** is often used to estimate the cost of equity capital. The CAPM (pronounced cap-em) model is based on the risk/reward pay off: that is, the relationship between the risk of investing in company shares, and the expected reward required for that level of risk.

CAPM is a **risk premium model** which asserts that the return or opportunity cost of holding an asset should be no less than the return on holding a riskless asset plus a premium for the risk associated with holding the target asset. The **risk premium** required for holding the target asset depends upon the relative riskiness of the target asset when compared with a well-diversified portfolio of similar assets.

In practice, then, to calculate the cost of equity under CAPM we need to establish:

- the minimum return required for investing in a risk-free investment; this is generally taken to be the return on mid- to long-term government bonds;
- the minimum premium required for investing in a diversified portfolio of equities; this is generally derived from data on actual market returns over an extended period; and
- a measure of the relative riskiness of the particular investment in question. This is measured statistically by the share's beta factor (ß).

Putting these elements together, the CAPM formula is as follows:

$$K_e = r_f + (\text{ß} (r_m - r_f))$$

where:

K_e	=	Cost of equity or expected return.
r_f	=	Risk-free rate of return.
ß	=	Beta of the target stock (see below).
r_m	=	Equity market return.

CAPM starts by assuming that no rational investor would accept a return less than that which is available on risk-free investments (r_f). It then goes on to say that to be prepared to invest in risky assets (ie, equities), rational investors require a premium to compensate them for the additional risk involved. This is the market risk premium or equity risk premium, ie, the excess over market risk; and can be summarised as ($r_m - r_f$). Finally, CAPM recognises that not all equities have the same level of risk. Therefore, when considering the required return for a particular stock, the market risk premium is adjusted, by multiplying it by the beta for that particular stock. Beta is a measure of a share's riskiness compared to the stock market as a whole.

The following sections examine each component of CAPM in more detail.

Risk-Free Rate

The risk-free rate is the return on a security that has negligible default risk. Theoretically, any stable government security in the company's home market (eg, gilts for UK companies) can be used. For company valuation, medium- to long-term government bonds are used to determine the risk-free rate. A commonly used rate is the yield-to-maturity on ten- or 15-year gilts.

Market Risk Premium (Equity Risk Premium)

The market risk premium is the difference between the expected return on a market portfolio (broadly the stock market as a whole) and the risk-free rate. Independent research organisations carry out research into the historical gap between returns on government bonds and returns on the equity markets over time, and this research is frequently used to assess the risk premium going forward. The premium over an extended period of time (20–50 years) is more reliable, as the long-term relationship between stock market returns and the risk-free return is relatively stable. Short-term data may show very wide variations and may not be reliable as an indication of investors' needs.

The equity risk premium can be expressed as $r_m - r_f$.

For example, if the FTSE All-Share Index has returned an average of 9% over the last 30 years, and the average long-term UK government bond return for the same period was 4%, the equity risk premium is 5%. This suggests that equity investors expect a return 5% higher than the risk-free rate, to compensate them for the risk of investing in the equity markets.

The assumption surrounding the equity risk premium can have a huge influence on the assumed cost of equity for companies. In the UK, the risk premium may lie in the range of 4–6% above risk-free rates, depending on the data source.

Beta (ß)

The beta coefficient measures the extent to which the returns of a given stock move in line with a market index (such as the FTSE All-Share Index). It is used as a measure of the volatility, and therefore the risk, of a particular stock relative to that index.

Betas are calculated statistically from historic data and can be industry-, sector- or company-specific. A company with a beta of 1.0 is expected to move in line with overall market returns. A beta of 1.5 implies that if the index (overall market) moves by 1%, the target stock will move by 1.5% in the same direction as the market. It is more volatile than the market, and therefore deemed to be more risky; investors should seek a higher return to compensate. A beta of 0.80 implies that if the overall index moves by 1%, the target stock will move only by 0.8%; it is therefore less volatile and (by implication) less risky; investors should be satisfied with a lower return than on a market portfolio.

The beta for most companies falls within the range of 0.6 and 1.5; the weighted average is, of course, 1.0.

CAPM Example

15-year gilt yields are 3.00%. Zephyr's beta is 0.82, reflecting the relatively low volatility of its shares compared to overall market returns. Assuming UK market returns have averaged 8.00% over the last 20 years, Zephyr's cost of equity is calculated as:

$$K_e \quad = \quad r_f + (ß \times (r_m - r_f))$$

$$K_e \quad = \quad 3.00\% + (0.82 \times (8.00\% - 3.00\%))$$

$$\quad = \quad 3.00\% + 4.10\%$$

$$\quad = \quad 7.10\%$$

By contrast, a riskier company, Tornado, has business activities which are much riskier than Zephyr's. This is reflected in the market place by its higher beta of 1.15, so its cost of equity in the same market conditions as Zephyr above is calculated as:

$$K_e \quad = \quad r_f + (ß \times (r_m - r_f))$$

$$K_e \quad = \quad 3.00\% + (1.15 \times (8.00\% - 3.00\%))$$

$$\quad = \quad 3.00\% + 5.75\%$$

$$\quad = \quad 8.75\%$$

Thus, CAPM suggests that holding Zephyr stock is about 20% less risky than holding Tornado stock, and so the appropriate costs of equity are 7.10% for Zephyr but 8.75% for Tornado.

3.4   Using Cost of Debt and Cost of Equity to Calculate WACC

Full WACC Example

Whacky plc has the following features.

Interest rate	6%
Beta	0.90
Debt market value	£5m
Debt book value	£4.5m
Equity market value	£20m
Equity book value	£10m
15-year gilt yield	3.00%
Company tax rate	20%
Equity market returns	8.00%

The WACC is determined as follows:

First, calculate the cost of debt: 6% x (1 − 20%) = 4.80%

Secondly, calculate the cost of equity: 3.00% + (0.90 x (8.00% − 3.00%)) = 7.50%

Thirdly, using market values, calculate total capital outstanding: £5m + £20m = £25m.

Finally, complete the formula to determine the WACC value:

$$WACC = \frac{(Kd \times MVd) + (Ke \times MVe)}{(MVd + MVe)}$$

$$= \frac{(0.048 \times 5) + (0.075 \times 20)}{25}$$

$$= \frac{1.740}{25}$$

$$= 0.0696$$

$$WACC = 6.96\%$$

End of Chapter Questions

Think of an answer for each question and refer to the appropriate workbook section for confirmation.

1. A company's share capital can be divided broadly into two distinct classes of share. What are they?
   Answer reference: Section 1

2. What is nominal value also known as?
   Answer reference: Section 1.1.2

3. When a company declares a dividend, which shares have priority?
   Answer reference: Section 1.2

4. Why are debt issues attractive to companies?
   Answer reference: Section 2

5. Who ranks highest and who ranks lowest for pay-out in a liquidation?
   Answer reference: Section 2.2.1

6. What is the most common form of hybrid security?
   Answer reference: Section 2.4

7. Which is the more expensive source of capital for a company– debt or equity?
   Answer reference: Section 3

8. What is the formula used to calculate WACC?
   Answer reference: Section 3.1

9. What is the formula used to calculate cost of debt?
   Answer reference: Section 3.2

10. What is the formula used under CAPM to calculate cost of equity?
    Answer reference: Section 3.3

Chapter Four

Introduction to Business Valuations

This syllabus area will provide approximately 9 of the 50 examination questions

1. Introduction

The value of a business is a highly subjective matter. The value of a company may be greater to a potential purchaser than it is to the current owner, perhaps hoping to retire; and it may be even greater to a second purchaser who hopes to achieve strategic benefits from its acquisition.

Just as there are numerous definitions of value, there are many valuation methods: discounted cash flow, asset-based, dividend discounting and comparable valuations are the most common. The value that an analyst derives for a business may vary considerably, depending on which method is used.

2. Enterprise Value and Equity Value

Learning Objective

4.1.1   Understand the distinction between equity value and enterprise value

4.1.2   Understand the use, advantages and disadvantages of enterprise value

We also have two main definitions of value: enterprise value and equity value.

Enterprise value refers to the market value of all of the operational assets of a business, irrespective of how these are financed. It can be calculated as the present value of the cash flows these assets are capable of generating, before deduction of any returns to debt providers or shareholders.

An alternative way of looking at enterprise value is as the total market value of both the debt (including any outstanding preference shares) and the equity of the company – which is equivalent to the total market value of the company's operational assets.

The **equity value** of a business is the market value of the ordinary shares of the company. Lenders and preference shareholders have a prior claim on the assets and profits of a company, ahead of ordinary shareholders. The equity value of the business is the residual of the enterprise value after the deduction of these prior claims.

Enterprise value is a measure which is very widely used in valuation for acquisitions and private equity, as it represents both the value of the underlying business enterprise being acquired, and the total finance needed to acquire and/or refinance that business. Equity value is more commonly used in equity markets valuation and investment analysis, where the need is to establish a market capitalisation or price per share.

Enterprise value can be calculated in two ways.

1. By reference to cash flow expectations:
    Present value of the total free cash flows expected to be generated by the enterprise, discounted at the WACC; this is discussed in more detail in Section 7.
2. By reference to invested capital:
    Market capitalisation (share price x number of shares in issue)   plus;
    preference and other shares (if any)   plus;
    non-controlling (minority) interest (if any)   plus;
    total long-term debt plus total short-term debt   less;
    total cash and cash equivalents.

This gives the total capital invested in the business enterprise; ie, the enterprise value.

There are a number of alternative ways of addressing some of these components. For the purpose of this syllabus, you should use the guidelines shown here:

*   When preference and other shares are quoted, they should be included at their market value (when shown) rather than at book value.
*   Finance leases are to be included as a component of debt.
*   When the debt includes bonds or other debt securities, these should be included at their market value (when shown) rather than at their book value.
*   'Cash and cash equivalents' may include money market deposits or other liquid 'near-cash' assets. These should be included at current market value (when shown) rather than at book value.

In practice, you may see additional components of enterprise value, such as pension deficits, options or warrants, operating leases and investment in associates. They are not included for the purposes of this syllabus.

Illustration

Markap plc has 1,000,000 shares in issue, priced at 220p. Its market capitalisation is therefore £2.2 million: this is its equity value.

Markap also has £1 million of long-term bonds, trading at 99p. Their market value is, therefore, £990,000. It also has £500,000 of unquoted preference shares and £200,000 of cash.

Its enterprise value is calculated as market capitalisation plus preference shares plus net debt (debt less cash); ie:

£2,200,000 + £500,000 + £990,000 − £200,000 = £3,490,000.

Note that the difference between equity value and enterprise value is the sum of the non-equity capital invested in the business. Equity value represents the total of all assets owned by the company, after deduction of amounts owing to other stakeholders; ie, the value owned by shareholders. Enterprise value represents the total of all operational assets owned by the business, irrespective of who they are attributable to.

3. Market, Transaction and Break-Up Values

Learning Objective

4.2.1   Understand the distinction between market, transaction and break-up values of a business

4.2.2   Know how to calculate the market value of a quoted company

4.2.3   Understand how to compare the market values of companies in similar sectors by use of multiples such as P/E ratio, EBIT and EBITDA multiples

There are many definitions of value. This section looks at three of them.

3.1   Market Value

The **market value** of a company is its market capitalisation, as discussed in Chapter 2. You will recall that the market capitalisation of a company is the number of shares outstanding multiplied by the share price; it therefore represents the value of the company's equity capital. It is often referred to as 'market cap' by those in the industry.

ExampleCo plc (see Chapter 2) had 185 million shares outstanding in 2015. With a share price of £22.50, its market capitalisation is calculated as follows:

£22.50 x 185 million shares in issue = £4,162,500,000.

This value may, however, be quite volatile, as the share price could change significantly in the course of a single day.

3.2   Transaction Value

The **transaction value** is a common term used in mergers and acquisitions. The transaction value is the value of the entire company being purchased. It is usually expressed on an enterprise basis: ie, the price being paid for the equity plus the value of the debt. It is calculated using the target company's equity value at the bid price plus the book value of the target company's debt. It is therefore the total cost being incurred by the purchaser.

In a takeover of a public company, the price paid for the equity is likely to be significantly higher than the pre-offer market value. This is because it is normal to pay a 'bid premium' to acquire control of the shares of a quoted company. When a company is rumoured to be the target of a takeover, it is common to see its stock market value increase to a level where it reflects the expected transaction value.

3.3   Break-Up Value

The **break-up value** of the company is the value that would be achieved if the company were liquidated and each of its assets sold separately. In a break-up valuation, the analyst calculates the market values of each asset, assuming appropriate discounts for a forced sale, and then deducts the sum of its total liabilities. Any residual value is the break-up value. This represents the lowest possible value for the company.

In years past, some conglomerates (multi-business companies) traded on the stock market at prices lower than their break-up values. This made them attractive to opportunistic bidders, who would purchase the company, then sell individual assets or divisions for prices totalling more than the bid price – a technique known as 'asset-stripping'.

3.4   Comparison of Values

For a quoted company, it is straightforward to calculate its stock market value as shown above. However, a transaction value might be at a significant premium to its stock market value (historical averages in public takeovers have been 25–40% above market price). If we calculated the same company's break-up value, to establish its hypothetical 'worst-case scenario' valuation, we would expect this to be at a significant discount to the stock market value.

4.   Asset-Based Valuations

Learning Objective

4.3.1   Understand the use of asset-based valuations

4.3.2   Know the limitations of asset-based valuations

An asset-based valuation is simple in concept and relatively straightforward to complete in practice. It can be used in the following circumstances:

- Valuations of asset-based companies, such as real estate firms and fund managers, where the function of the business is to enhance the value of the assets held or managed.
- Valuing a loss-making or severely underperforming business, where a valuation based on earnings would not exceed the balance sheet value.
- Establishing a 'floor' or minimum value for a business.
- Establishing a break-up value for a business – as discussed above.

Apart from these examples, asset-based valuations do have their limitations. They do not reflect the future profit or cash flow potential of a business and they do not usually take account of any goodwill or other intangible assets in a business. Moreover, the book value of assets can also be very dependent on the accounting policies used: for example, IFRS permits the revaluation of properties, while US GAAP does not. This means that the statement of financial position of a company would look very different, depending on the reporting standards used.

In many cases an asset-based valuation may give the lowest value for a company, and for a profitable trading business it will usually substantially undervalue it.

4.1 Calculating an Asset-Based Valuation

Using this method, the business is valued at its adjusted net worth; that is, adjusted assets less adjusted liabilities. The adjustments come from determining any difference between the book and the market value of the assets and liabilities.

Starting with the most recent balance sheet, assets as shown on the balance sheet are adjusted as follows:

- Non-current assets such as land and buildings should be revalued if possible, to reflect current market values.
- Plant and equipment must be checked; is the book value close to current market value, and have they been depreciated appropriately?
- Current asset values are calculated as of the date of the valuation. Trade receivables are assessed to check they have been properly provided for (ie, allowance made for non-payment). Inventory may have to be revalued.
- Cash may require adjustment, to reflect any payments of dividends, repayment of debt or generation of cash profits since the balance sheet date.
- Current liabilities are also restated from the date of the most recent balance sheet to reflect the current level of creditors.

The resultant figure represents an enterprise value (total assets less current liabilities, equivalent to the operational assets of the company). To carry on further and work out an equity value, we would then deduct the company's net debt to calculate an adjusted net asset value.

This process generates a value for the business on a 'going concern' basis – ie, assuming that the company is expected to continue to operate for the foreseeable future. If the company is insolvent, or expected to fail, then a break-up basis of valuation should be used.

A variation on an asset-based valuation is the price-to-book method. This is discussed further in Section 6.4, alongside other relative valuation methods.

5.   Dividend-Based Valuations

Learning Objective

4.4.1   Understand the use of dividend-based valuations

4.4.2   Be able to calculate a valuation of a business using the dividend valuation model

4.4.3   Understand the limitations of the dividend-based valuation

The dividend yield valuation model can be used to determine the equity value of a business with steady profitability and a consistent dividend payout ratio. It can also be used to value minority shareholdings.

5.1   Dividend Discount Model

The basis for the calculation is the **dividend discount model**. This assumes that the value of a firm is based on next year's dividend (Div_1), divided by its cost of equity (K_e) less the expected dividend growth rate (g). The formula is as follows:

$$\text{Share price} = \frac{Div_1}{K_e - g}$$

If we adopt the expected dividend per share for Div_1 in the formula above, we can calculate a value per share. If instead we adopt the expected total dividend payout for Div_1, the result will be an equity value for the whole company.

To return to ExampleCo plc, we know that last year's dividend was 78p per share. Let us assume that the dividend is expected to increase by around 8% to 84p next year, and that its cost of equity is 12%. Therefore,

$$\text{Price} = \frac{84p}{0.12 - 0.08}$$

$$\text{Price} = \frac{84p}{0.04}$$

$$\text{Price} = 2,100p$$

In this example, the value based on the dividend growth model comes a little below the market price of ExampleCo plc, which is now around £22.50 a share. The model does not always throw up results that are close to the current trading value as it is highly dependent on the assumptions about the growth and discount rates (see below).

There are potential pitfalls when valuing on a dividend basis. First, it depends on a predictable dividend stream; it would be misleading to use this approach if a company has paid out a special dividend, or if dividend payouts or profitability are uneven. Second, the growth (g) assumption is critical to the final value. To illustrate, examine the difference in value derived for ExampleCo using 5% or 10% dividend growth.

	Example 1	Example 2
Cost of equity	12%	12%
Est. dividend growth rate	5%	10%
Dividend	78p	78p
Discount rate	7%	2%
Share price	1,170p	4,290p

5.2   Dividend Yield Approach

There is an alternative approach to calculating a dividend-based value for a company, based on the dividend paid by the company, discounted using the dividend yields calculated for comparable quoted companies.

Using this approach, we can calculate a share price as:

$$\text{Share price} = \frac{\text{Dividend}}{\text{Dividend yield}}$$

The question is, how do we establish the dividend yield? We will make the assumption that investors in similar companies will require similar levels of dividend yield. If we can calculate the dividend yield for comparable companies, this will give us a good indication of a reasonable dividend yield for the company we are valuing.

As a reminder, a dividend yield is calculated as:

$$\text{Dividend yield} = \frac{\text{Dividend}}{\text{Share price}}$$

Let us assume we are to calculate a share price for a company, Divvy ltd. Divvy has just paid a dividend of 25p per share. The steps to calculating the value for Divvy are as follows:

1. Identify comparable quoted companies (in this example we will just use one).
    - Divvy's closest comparable company is Coco plc.

2. Calculate dividend yields for the comparable company(ies), based on their share prices and dividends, and establish a mean yield.
    - Coco has paid a dividend per share of 10p and has a share price of 333p; its dividend yield is therefore 3% (10/333). We will now assume that this dividend yield is appropriate for Divvy.

3. Divide the target's dividend by the comparable company's yield to derive a share price for the target.
    - Divvy's 25p dividend divided by Coco's yield of 3% = a share price for Divvy of 833p per share.

6. Relative Valuations

Learning Objective

4.2.3   Understand how to compare the market values of companies in similar sectors by use of multiples such as P/E ratio, EBIT and EBITDA multiples

4.5.1   Understand the use of an earnings-based valuation

4.5.2   Be able to calculate the equity value of a business using the P/E ratio

4.5.3   Be able to calculate the enterprise value of a business using EBIT and EBITDA multiples

---

6.1 Earnings-Based Valuation

Analysts often rely on comparable values to determine an appropriate price for a company. The analyst will calculate a number of investment ratios for similar companies in the same industry, including the P/E ratio, EV/EBIT and EV/EBITDA, which were discussed in Chapter 2. This approach assumes, broadly, that all companies in the same sector, with similar characteristics, should share the same or similar investment ratios. Therefore, if we can calculate investment ratios for a range of similar companies in a sector, these ratios can be used to derive a value for any other company in that sector.

This technique is called comparable valuation, relative valuation or earnings-based valuation, and in this context the ratios are referred to as 'earnings multiples'.

Comparable valuations can be used to:

- determine whether a public company share is trading in an appropriate range (ie, is it overvalued or undervalued relative to its peers);
- determine the value of a private company.

In overview, the process is as follows:

- Identify comparable quoted companies (or transactions involving the sale and purchase of similar companies.
- Identify price data (in the form of share price, market capitalisation and/or enterprise value) for each comparable company.
- Identify the relevant earnings data for each comparable company (this is discussed further later in this section).
- Calculate the earnings multiples for each comparable company.
- Evaluate the multiples, taking into account the differences between the comparable companies and the company being valued, and if necessary adjust the multiples to make these more appropriate.
- Apply the multiples to the earnings data of the company being valued, to derive a value range.

All of the four ratios discussed in Sections 6.3 to 6.6 below help in determining the value of a business and can be used for valuing both listed and unlisted companies.

The earnings multiples approach is also often referred to as the 'capitalisation of earnings' approach to valuation.

6.2 Comparable Company Data

The first step of the analyst is to identify data on comparable companies, that is, quoted companies that are similar to the company being valued. The analyst must identify price and earnings data for each company and could assemble this data in a table similar to the one below.

Company	Market Capitalisation (£ millions)	P/E Ratio Historic	P/E Ratio Prosp.	EV/EBIT Multiple Historic	EV/EBIT Multiple Prosp.	EV/EBITDA Multiple Historic	EV/EBITDA Prosp.	Price to Book Multiple
A	728.3	17.7	16.2	9.9	8.6	7.5	5.9	2.0
B	919.7	19.9	15.9	10.3	8.7	6.0	5.3	2.3
C	1,200.6	14.3	12.4	7.9	6.5	6.6	5.7	1.3
D	842.3	15.4	14.6	6.9	5.8	5.6	5.4	1.7
E	808.0	14.7	13.9	7.0	6.6	5.8	5.1	1.7
Average		16.4x	14.6x	8.4x	7.3x	6.3x	5.5x	1.8x

where:

x   =   times.
Prosp =   prospective.

In this case, all five of the comparable companies are from the same industry and the analyst believes that they are similar in terms of product line, extent of operations, gearing and risk, etc. They are all roughly the same size, as measured by market capitalisation, although Company C is larger than the others.

However, determining what is a 'comparable' firm is not always so straightforward and is often open to interpretation. There are a number of key areas of difference between companies, and these can create difficulty in selecting companies as comparables. These include:

- different size and future growth prospects of companies;
- differences in the riskiness of the business;
- differences in the scope of product offerings;
- variance in customer base;
- different geographic reach;
- different gearing levels;
- differences in the asset base, including intangible assets;
- different levels of current and future profitability.

All these factors have an impact on the valuation of the comparable companies, and a valuer must use judgement in drawing conclusions as to the appropriate multiples to be used for the value range.

6.2.1 Information Issues

Learning Objective

4.1.3 Know the differences between public and private companies with respect to the availability and reliability of company information; the typical sources of such information; and the various responsibilities of public and private companies to make information available or respond to information requests

One particular issue to bear in mind is the different levels of information available for public and private companies.

Publicly quoted companies are required by the rules of their stock exchanges to disclose full information to the market on a timely basis.

For example, London Stock Exchange Main Market-listed companies must file statutory IFRS annual reports and accounts within four months of the year-end, and must file half-yearly accounts within two months of their half-year-end. The level of information provided in the accounts is very extensive (and was discussed in more detail in Chapter 2). Companies which are also quoted in certain other jurisdictions (such as the US) must additionally publish quarter-end accounts. They must also disclose publicly any price-sensitive information, such as changes in strategy, financial position or trading conditions, as soon as possible. All such information must be made available freely on the company's website as well as in hard copy from the company itself.

In addition, most of the larger quoted companies are the subject of analytical research by the company's broker and other investment houses. These companies generally provide analysts with further explanation and respond to queries on request, and analysts put a great deal of effort into calculating estimates of prospective earnings – although it is unlikely that these would be verified or confirmed by the company, which tends to restrict itself to broad-brush forward-looking statements. Thus, there is no shortage of detailed information about the financial status and prospects of public companies.

By contrast, UK **private companies** file either IFRS or UK GAAP statutory accounts within nine months of their year-end. These contain much less detailed information than is required for public companies. Smaller private companies are allowed to file only abbreviated financial statements, with no cash flow statement, and the level of explanation is very limited. In the smallest private companies there may be no requirement for their accounts to be audited. Private company accounts are filed and available for public inspection at Companies House, but only on payment of a fee. There is no requirement for interim financial statements, and of course the concept of price-sensitive information is not relevant for private companies so it is unusual to see financial disclosure beyond the bare minimum required by the Companies Act. There is also no coverage of these companies by analysts, until they are proposing to raise equity in an IPO, and they are under no obligation to make information available or to respond to information requests.

This asymmetry of information can make the identification of comparable companies and the application of the ratios difficult.

6.3 Price Earnings Ratio

The best known earnings valuation method is the price earnings ratio (PER or P/E ratio (see Chapter 2, Section 5.3.3). This shows the relationship between the company's share price and its profitability, expressed as a multiple of earnings. The earnings figures used are those earnings attributable to ordinary shareholders after deduction of interest, tax, minority interests and preference share dividends (ie, net profit per equity share, before ordinary dividends). However, exceptional or one-off profits or expenses should not be included in the earnings.

The P/E ratio is calculated as:

$$\frac{\text{Market price per share}}{\text{Earnings per share}}$$

An alternative approach to the method is to take the market capitalisation of the company divided by net profit per equity share. The resulting multiple is identical.

As a simple example, consider Company X with earnings attributable to ordinary shareholders of £5 million. To value this company, its advisers would analyse comparable quoted companies, and calculate their P/E ratios. If the P/E ratios of similar quoted companies fell in the range of 8–12, then this would value Company X at between £40 million (8 x 5) and £60 million (12 x 5). If the company had 10 million shares outstanding, the earnings per share would be 50p; applying the same P/E ratio would result in an estimated share price of 400p to 600p.

6.3.1 Prospective Price Earnings Ratio

In the previous example, we have not specified which year's earnings have been used. It is possible to calculate a P/E ratio based on the previous year's reported EPS (in which case it is called a 'historic' P/E ratio), or an expected EPS for a future year (in which case it is a 'prospective' P/E ratio).

The prospective P/E ratio is the current share price divided by the current year's estimated earnings per share. It is also likely that, in practice, the analyst might calculate P/E ratios for future years. If EPS is growing, the prospective multiple will always be lower than the historic P/E ratio. A prospective P/E is calculated and used to calculate a valuation in the same manner as set out above.

Example _____

We are valuing TarCo ltd, which last year reported profits attributable to shareholders of £5 million. It estimates that profits for the current year will be £5.5 million.

Comparable company Analogue plc has a share price of 500p. Its reported EPS was 30p and analysts forecast EPS of 35p for the current year. This gives it a historic P/E ratio of 16.7 and a prospective P/E ratio of 14.29.

Based on historic data, TarCo's value would be in the region of £83.35 million (£5 million x 16.67). Based on prospective data, TarCo's value would be in the region of £78.56 million (£5.5 million x 14.29). Overall, its value range is £78.56 million to £83.35 million.

Prospective P/E ratios are generally regarded as a more reliable approach to valuation than a historic P/E ratio, which is based on historic earnings. This is because share prices are more closely aligned to investors' expectations of future earnings than to their experiences of the past. In the example above, a final valuation is likely to be at the lower end of the valuation range (based on prospective earnings). See Chapter 2, Section 5.3.3.

6.4 Price to Book Value

The market to book value ratio, also called the price to book ratio, is another useful ratio for use in valuation. It is calculated as:

$$\frac{\text{Market capitalisation}}{\text{Net assets (from the latest accounts)}}$$

Its importance is greatest in some sectors, such as banking, investment management or real estate, where asset valuations are most frequently and reliably measured. It is not a reliable measure in other sectors, such as biotechnology or software, where tangible assets are of limited importance.

Some analysts favour this ratio because the book value of assets is relatively constant, which makes it easier to compare over time or across companies. The price to book value ratio can be calculated even when a company's earnings or EBIT are negative. However, the book value does not reflect the assets' earning power or projected cash flows, and is not therefore useful when a significant part of a company's value to investors lies in its goodwill – ie, its ability to generate earnings or cash growth. Unless the assets in question are regularly and reliably revalued, it reflects the assets' original cost and is affected by accounting decisions on matters such as depreciation, impairment, provisioning and amortisation policies.

6.5 EV/EBIT Multiple

An alternative earnings valuation method is to use a multiple of EBIT rather than profit after tax (see Chapter 2, Section 5.3.6). This is calculated as:

$$\frac{\text{Enterprise value (equity plus net debt)}}{\text{Earnings before interest and tax}}$$

EBIT multiples are widely used when analysing public and private companies, and are particularly useful for valuing a stand-alone business for acquisition or when the business (or division) being valued is highly leveraged. The approach used is the same as for P/E ratios, ie, identification of comparable companies, calculation of EV/EBIT multiples for the comparables, and then applying the multiples to the EBIT of the 'target' company to generate a valuation.

As noted earlier, enterprise value represents the total value attributable to all stakeholders (equity and debt providers). It is calculated as the market capitalisation (number of shares outstanding times share price) plus the market value of outstanding debt, net of any cash. EBIT represents the profit available to service both equity and debt holders, and so enterprise value (representing the value attributable to equity and debt holders) is used as the numerator for EBIT-based valuations.

6.6   EV/EBITDA Multiple

A similar ratio relates a company's enterprise value to its EBITDA – earnings before interest, tax, depreciation and amortisation/impairment. See Chapter 2, Section 5.3.6. It is calculated as:

$$\frac{\text{Enterprise value (equity plus net debt)}}{\text{Earnings before interest, tax, depreciation and amortisation/impairment}}$$

EBITDA is often seen as a proxy for pre-tax operating cash flow and is a useful number to use for valuation, particularly in companies or industries that are growing rapidly and may have not yet achieved profitability. The benefits of the ratio are numerous. It can be computed for firms that have net losses and so it can be more appropriate for industries which require a substantial investment in infrastructure and have long gestation periods. For buyouts or highly leveraged transactions, EBITDA multiples capture the ability of the firm to generate cash flows that may be used to support relatively high debt payments in the short term. Finally, the EBITDA multiple permits easier comparison of firms with different financial leverage or different accounting treatments.

As with P/E ratios, a prospective EV/EBIT or EV/EBITDA multiple (based on forecast EBIT or EBITDA) is more useful than a historic multiple.

Relative Valuation Example

Using the data on comparable companies from the table in Section 6.2, we can calculate the value of the equity of Company X, which also competes in the alphabet industry with Companies A to E.

Company X Summary Income Statement for the Year Ended 201y (in £ millions)	
Revenue	310.9
EBITDA	97.6
EBIT	72.0
Net profit	35.0
Current year estimates	
Net profit	39.2
EBITDA	110.0
EBIT	82.0

Company X's balance sheet shows:

Net debt   £40.0 million
Shareholders' equity   £315.1 million

With this information, we can then insert extra columns in the table with the industry average multiples in the second column.

Comparing Values Based on Multiples

	£ million	Average Multiple	Equity Value (£m)
Revenue 201Y	310.9		
Net profit 201Y/P/E	35.0	16.4x	574
Net profit (prospective)/ prospective P/E	39.2	14.6x	572
Shareholders' equity/price to book ratio	315.1	1.8x	567
			Enterprise Value (£m)
EBITDA 201Y/ EV/EBITDA multiple	97.6	6.3x	615
EBITDA prospective/Prospective EV/EBITDA multiple	110.0	5.5x	605
EBIT 201Y/EV/EBIT multiple	72.0	8.4x	605
EBIT prospective/Prospective EV/ EBIT multiple	82.0	7.3x	599

Note that P/E ratios and price to book ratios have an equity value as the numerator, and so they generate the calculation of an equity value. EV/EBIT and EV/EBITDA multiples have EV as the numerator, and so they generate the calculation of an enterprise value.

The range of equity values (calculated from P/E ratios and price to book) is £567 million to £574 million, with an average of £571 million.

The EV/EBITDA and EV/EBIT multiples suggests an enterprise value of £599 million to £615 million. To convert the enterprise value result to an estimated equity value, subtract Company X's net debt of £40 million. This results in a range of values of £564 million to £575 million – in line with the range of other values suggested.

An analyst might conclude that, based on the comparable ratios above, Company X has an equity value in the range of £560 million to £580 million. Note, though, that relative valuations are never precise – they always result in a 'reasonable range' of values.

7.   Cash Flow-Based Valuations

Learning Objective

4.6.1   Understand the use of cash flow-based valuations

4.6.2   Understand the limitations of internal rate of return (IRR) and discounted cash flow (DCF)

4.6.3   Know how to calculate: free cash flow; NOPAT; EBITDA; EBITA; EBITD

4.6.4   Understand the key stages that need to be followed in a cash flow-based valuation: historical analysis; forecasting; calculating a terminal value; identifying an appropriate discount rate, using weighted average cost of capital

4.6.5   Be able to calculate a simple cash flow-based valuation

The discounted cash flow (DCF) approach to corporate valuation follows the bond valuation approach covered in Chapter 1, in that it estimates the present value of a stream of future cash flows.

DCF is very widely used by company managers and corporate financiers alike.

- Company managers use DCF to evaluate investments; if the present value of the cash flows of the potential investment exceed the investment cost, the project is 'NPV positive' and can be pursued. An example of this was shown in Chapter 1, Section 4.2.
- Alternatively, they may establish a required internal rate of return for all projects; if projects do not have the capacity to generate that IRR, the project should be rejected.
- They may also use DCF to compare mutually exclusive projects; the project whose cash flows generate the highest NPV, or the highest IRR, is that which should be pursued.
- Corporate financiers use DCF to calculate the value of companies or businesses for acquisition, disposal or capital-raising, alongside multiples valuation and asset-based valuation.

However, it is much more difficult to estimate the future cash flows of a company or one of its divisions than to determine the interest payments on a bond. From a theoretical perspective, DCF valuations provide the most reliable indications of corporate value, but their use is often limited in practice by lack of reliable cash flow forecasts or by difficulties in estimating the discount rate (WACC).

The steps in determining the value of an enterprise through a DCF valuation are discussed in this chapter. In outline, they are as follows:

- Estimate and analyse future cash flows for a finite period (frequently derived from earnings projections), ensuring proper adjustment for depreciation and amortisation, capital expenditures and changes in working capital.
- Estimate the value of the estimated cash flows after this finite period (called the **residual** or **terminal value**).
- Determine an appropriate discount rate, taking account of the time value of money and the riskiness of the cash flows (see Chapter 3).
- Calculate the present value of all future cash flows, by applying the discount rate to the estimated cash flows and residual value.

7.1 Free Cash Flows

In most instances, companies prepare forecast income statements and statements of financial position (balance sheets). To value using DCF, the corporate financier needs to use these forecasts to determine the cash flows that will be generated to service the providers of debt and equity.

The majority of discounted cash flow valuations are carried out using free cash flows to firm (enterprise cash flows) (see Chapter 2, Section 4). Free cash flows to firm show the cash generated by the underlying economic enterprise, without any adjustment to show the cost of servicing debt, or financial income. They therefore show a 'clean' picture of the value of the underlying business operations being valued.

The free cash flow figure draws information from both the income statement and the balance sheet forecasts. For example, revenue and operating expenses are shown in the income statement, while capital expenditures are only shown on the balance sheet. Depreciation and amortisation are both recorded as expenses on the income statement, but do not reflect any movement in cash.

If possible, a corporate financier will forecast cash flows for a period of five years. In particularly volatile or uncertain industries the forecast period may be only three years, while in more stable industries (for example, utilities) cash flows may be forecast for ten years or even more in exceptional circumstances. Although it can be difficult, the financial model should attempt to capture one whole business cycle (remember, sales do not always rise).

For simplicity, as described in Chapter 2, Section 4.1, our free cash flow forecast starts with earnings before interest and tax (EBIT) from the forecast income statement and is built up as follows:

EBIT	
Less	Taxes (at highest marginal rate)
Equals	NOPAT (net operating profit after tax)
Plus	Non-cash expenses, particularly, depreciation and amortisation, etc
Less	Capital expenditures Changes in working capital
Equals	Free cash flow

Note that interest expense is not included in the free cash flow forecasts. Free cash flow calculates the cash flow that is available to provide a return to both debt and equity providers, and is therefore calculated before deduction of interest.

Following on from this, the tax charge that is included in the free cash flow forecast is not the actual tax that would be paid by the company, as in real life this tax charge is reduced by tax relief on interest payments. As we have excluded interest from the forecasts, we must also exclude the tax relief derived from that interest. Instead, in most countries the cash tax is calculated as EBIT x marginal tax rate (for most companies, this will be the top rate of corporation tax). This is the approach adopted in the examples in this section.

However, you should note that in the UK and some other countries a different approach operates. Because tax relief is not available in relation to depreciation and amortisation in the UK, the tax charge is calculated by reference to EBITDA. Relief is then given in the form of capital allowances.

The calculation that follows illustrates a simplified five-year forecast of free cash flow, for a business whose EBIT is growing at approximately 8% per annum.

(in £ millions)	Year 1	Year 2	Year 3	Year 4	Year 5
EBIT	200	216	233	252	272
Less tax on EBIT (20%)	−40	−43	−47	−50	−54
NOPAT	160	173	186	202	218
Add back:					
Depreciation	50	56	60	66	74
Less:					
Capital expenditures	−60	−65	−67	−70	−77
Increase (decrease) in working capital	−12	−15	−16	−10	−5
Free cash flow	138	149	163	188	210

7.2 Discounting Free Cash Flows

Next, the corporate financier must discount the cash flows by an appropriate discount rate in order to arrive at a present value. The discount rate is usually the weighted average cost of capital (WACC, as seen in Chapter 3, Section 3). The following example uses the free cash flows from the table in Section 7.1 and a discount rate (WACC) of 10%. The discount factor (row 2 in the table below) is calculated using the following formula for each year:

$$\text{Discount factor} = \frac{1}{(1 + \text{WACC})^n}$$

where:

n = number of years.

The discount factor in row 2 is then multiplied by the free cash flow (row 1) for each year to arrive at the discounted cash flow in row 3.

(in £ millions)		Year 1	Year 2	Year 3	Year 4	Year 5
1	Free cash flow	138	149	163	188	210
2	Times discount factor (10% WACC)	$1/(1+10\%)^1$ ie, 0.909	0.826	0.751	0.683	0.621
3	Discounted cash flow	125.5	123.1	122.8	128.1	130.1
4	Total PV of free cash flows	629.6				

Adding each year's discounted cash flow (in row 3) provides the present value of the enterprise free cash flows over the next five years: ie, £629.6 million (row 4).

7.3 Determining the Terminal (Residual) Value

We have now calculated the present value of the cash flows expected over the next five years. But what about cash flows to be expected beyond our forecast period? To attribute a value to these longer-term cash flows, which it may not be possible to forecast in any detail, we calculate a **terminal value**.

The terminal value represents the total value of all the cash flows expected beyond the forecast period (for the example above, this is from the start of year 6 into infinity). It is usually calculated as a single sum, as shown below.

In computing the terminal value for this business, we are going to look at two possibilities. The first assumes that there is no growth in free cash flows following the final year of the forecast – ie, they will remain at the same level each year into perpetuity. The second assumes that there will be continued cash flow growth.

7.3.1 Terminal Value with No Growth

The first DCF approach assumes that the free cash flow continues at the same level as in the final year in perpetuity. The discount rate (r) continues to be the WACC. The perpetuity formula used to calculate a value for these cash flows is:

$$\text{Terminal value (no growth)} = \frac{CF_n}{WACC}$$

where:

CF_n = Cash flow in final year of forecast 'n'.
WACC = Weighted average cost of capital.

Continuing with the same cash flow example, the final year's cash flow is estimated to be £210 million. Assuming steady cash flows, and a WACC of 10%, the terminal value would be:

$$TV = £210 \text{ million} / 0.10$$
$$TV = £2,100 \text{ million}$$

However, the terminal value of £2,090 million is the estimated value as at the end of year five – we now need to calculate its present value. This is done by multiplying the terminal value (£2,100 million) by the year five present value factor of 0.621 (refer to Year 5, row 2 in the table in Section 7.2). The result is a present value of the terminal value of £1,301.6 million.

7.3.2 Terminal Value with Growth

In some instances, a 'steady state' approach is not appropriate. Some companies might legitimately be assumed to continue to grow after the formal forecast period. If the growth is estimated to be a constant, or if we can assume an average growth level, the terminal value can be estimated by using the formula for a growing perpetuity.

The formula to value a stream of cash flows growing into perpetuity is:

$$\text{Terminal value (with growth)} = \frac{CF_n \times (1 + g)}{(WACC - g)}$$

where:

CF_n	=	Cash flow in final year of forecast 'n'.
WACC	=	Weighted average cost of capital.
g	=	Growth rate.

If the business in our example anticipated its cash flow to grow at an average of 2% per annum in perpetuity, the terminal value would increase to £2,677.5 million.

$$\text{Terminal value} = \frac{(210) \times (1.02)}{(0.10 - 0.02)}$$

$$TV = 214.2 / 0.08$$

$$TV = £2,667.5 \text{ million}$$

Discounting the estimated terminal value to the present using the year five discount factor results in a present value of the terminal value of £1,662.7 million (£2,677.5 x 0.621).

Note that the impact on value of relatively low growth of 2% is significant, even in present value terms. Using a growing perpetuity increases the value of the enterprise by £361.1 million. This is the difference between the enterprise value we calculated with no growth in Section 7.3.1 of £1,301.6 million, and the value calculated here of £1,662.7 million. For established businesses, it is generally recommended that the maximum growth rate used in the calculation should not exceed the long-term sustainable growth rate of the economy. In companies operating in the EU or North American economies, a maximum perpetual growth rate of 2% or perhaps 3% would be reasonable. In declining economies or for a declining company a lower level, no growth, or even negative growth should be used.

7.3.3 Determining the Discount Rate

Chapter 3, Section 3 addressed the weighted average cost of capital (WACC), which is used as the discount rate. In our example, we assumed for simplicity that it is 10%.

7.3.4 Determining the Value of the Business

To recap, the enterprise value of a business (whether a division, business unit, private or publicly quoted company) is calculated as the sum of the following items:

Components of Enterprise Value for a Public Company

> **Market capitalisation**
>
> \+   Total debt
>
> \+   Minority interest
>
> \+   Preferred shares
>
> \–   Total cash
>
> \–   Cash equivalents
>
> \=   Enterprise value

Components of Enterprise Value based on DCF

> **Discounted cash flow (from forecasts)**
>
> \+   Present value of terminal value
>
> \+   Surplus assets at the date of the valuation
>
> \=   Enterprise value

Surplus assets are assets that the business owns but does not use in its ordinary operations. If they have value, the assets should be included in the enterprise value calculation as shown above; but make sure that any cash flows generated by these assets are not included in the DCF calculation, or the value will be included twice. For quoted companies, market capitalisation already includes the value of any surplus assets.

Example

To illustrate the calculation of the value of an unquoted company, using the figures calculated above:

	No Growth (£ millions)	2% Growth (£ millions)
Discounted cash flow	629.6	629.6
+ Present value of terminal value	1,301.6	1,662.7
+ Surplus assets (assumed for illustration)	3.0	3.0
Enterprise value	1,934.2	2,295.3

7.4   Calculation of Equity Value

The value of the equity in the business is simply the enterprise value less the market value of net debt, preference shares or other forms of financing. As noted above, lenders and preference shareholders have a prior claim to the assets of a company, ahead of ordinary shareholders. Therefore, the equity value of the business is the residual of the enterprise value after deduction for prior claims. It is equivalent to the business's market capitalisation: ie, it represents the market value of its equity.

Discounted cash flow

+   Present value of terminal value

+   Surplus assets

=   Enterprise value

−   Market value of preference shares

−   Market value of net debt

−   Minority interest

=   Equity value

Our example company has long-term debt with a face value of £315 million, but the market value is £300 million. (Note that we would only use the book/face value when it is not possible to determine the market value of debt or other securities, for example, when these are not quoted.) Therefore, £300 million is subtracted from the enterprise value to determine the equity value.

There are no preference shares outstanding and no minority interest.

Example

Continuing with the example, from Section 7.3.4, the equity value would be:

- assuming no growth in terminal value: £1,634.2
- assuming 2% growth in terminal value: £1,995.3

as fully set out in the following table.

	No Growth (£ millions)	2% Growth (£ millions)
Discounted cash flow	629.6	629.6
+ Present value of terminal value	1,301.6	1,662.7
+ Surplus assets (assumed for illustration)	3.0	3.0
Enterprise value	1,934.2	2,295.3
− Value of debt	300.0	300.0
Value of equity	1,634.2	1,958.6

7.5 Limitations of Discounted Cash Flow

Discounted cash flow is a widely used, internationally recognised technique for valuing companies and analysing investment opportunities. It has the advantage that it focuses on cash revenue and expenditure, the two elements that are crucial in determining whether a company will survive or fail; and because it is centred on cash, there is no scope for accounting manipulation of the figures.

As a reminder, net present value (NPV) is the present value of the future cash flows of an enterprise. This is a very useful concept for investment appraisal – it tells us how much value is created or destroyed in a particular project, given a known investment sum. In business valuation, it tells us the maximum price that a purchaser should be prepared to invest: if the purchaser pays more, then their investment will obviously become NPV negative, unless there are synergies available that are not reflected in the cash flows.

However, there are a number of potential pitfalls in DCF valuation:

- The core of the valuation is reasonable cash flow forecasts covering several years. In some industries it is not possible to predict revenue and expense even for a year or two with any degree of confidence. In all cases, the forecasts are only as good as the assumptions underlying them, on matters such as inflation, sales growth, raw material and staff costs. It is essential to test these assumptions for reasonableness.
- The terminal value can be a very major part of the total enterprise value, particularly when the explicit cash flow forecasts cover only a short period. As the example at Section 7.4 above shows, this terminal value is highly dependent on what may be very subjective growth assumptions, and an analyst might be tempted to 'flex' the assumptions to reach a particular value. It is helpful to cross-check the terminal value for reasonableness using market multiples such as EV/EBIT or EV/EBITDA.
- The underlying discount rate is also based on a number of assumptions (for example, relating to future capital structure, selection of the equity risk premium, and adjustments to peer group beta factors). Again, these should be tested for reasonableness, and the valuer should carry out a sensitivity analysis of the cash flows to establish a value range.

In Chapter 1, we also discussed the other use of DCF: calculating internal rate of return (IRR). This is of limited use in valuing companies, as it relies on knowing the initial investment/purchase price to calculate the return on that investment. However, it is very useful for private equity firms in calculating potential returns for a wide range of opportunities as the basis for their investment decisions.

There can be some practical difficulties in calculating and interpreting IRR.

- IRR can only be used when the initial and subsequent investment sums are known, and it is only suitable for evaluating projects with a finite term (ie, without a terminal value).
- When the cash flows change sign more than once over the investment period (eg, going from negative to positive and then negative again) there may be more than one IRR calculated.
- When a particular time period is cash-positive, the IRR approach assumes that these positive cash balances are received by the investor at a rate equivalent to the IRR; this may well not be the case.
- A project's IRR must be measured against a benchmark (to ensure that projects with a return below this benchmark are not invested). This benchmark should always be at the project's WACC or higher; but in practice many investors apply a subjective standardised IRR benchmark for investment appraisal. This can make it difficult to use IRR and NPV alongside each other.

However, despite these limitations, when they are used appropriately, both NPV and IRR are essential tools for the corporate financier.

End of Chapter Questions

Think of an answer for each question and refer to the appropriate workbook section for confirmation.

1. What is the difference between the enterprise and equity value of a business?
    Answer reference: Section 2

2. What is the difference between transaction value, market value and break-up value?
    Answer reference: Section 3

3. What are the advantages of an asset basis of valuation?
    Answer reference: Section 4

4. When would a dividends-based valuation be used?
    Answer reference: Section 5

5. What is the most common earnings valuation method?
    Answer reference: Section 6.1

6. What is the formula used to calculate a P/E ratio?
    Answer reference: Section 6.3

7. What does EBITDA stand for?
    Answer reference: Section 6.6

8. What is usually used as the discount rate in DCF, and why?
    Answer reference: Section 7.2

9. How is a terminal value calculated?
    Answer reference: Section 7.3

10. What does the terminal value represent?
    Answer reference: Section 7.3

Chapter Five
Corporate Transactions

This syllabus area will provide approximately 10 of the 50 examination questions

5

1. Mergers and Acquisitions

Learning Objective

5.1.1   Know the key types of acquisition or disposal and the reasons why they happen: listed or private; hostile or recommended; owner/manager exit; existing/continuing/new management participation

5.1.5   Know the key features of a transaction governed by the Takeover Panel

Mergers and acquisitions (M&A) are central to the world of corporate finance and to the wider world of global business. The record year of 2014 saw global dealmaking valued at some $3.5 trillion, according to Thomson Reuters statistics, with significant growth experienced in H1 2015. In this chapter, we look at why, and how, mergers and acquisitions take place.

1.1   Mergers and Acquisitions – Terminology

The field of mergers and acquisitions involves the following main types of transaction:

- **Acquisition** – the purchase of a controlling interest in any company, private or public.
- **Takeover** – the acquisition of a publicly quoted company, rather than a private company. Takeovers may be **recommended** (supported by the target's management) or **hostile** (contested by the target's management).
- **Merger** – a combination of two companies, neither acquiring the other. In practice this term is often used misleadingly to describe any acquisition.
- **Disposal/divestment/divestiture** – the sale of a controlling interest in any company. This may involve a trade sale (to a commercial acquirer) or a financial sale (to a financial buyer such as a private equity firm).
- **Spin-off/demerger** – the disposal of a subsidiary of a public company by way of flotation of the subsidiary on a stock exchange, as a separate quoted entity.
- **Scheme of Arrangement** – a Companies Act 2006 process whereby a company may be reorganised, including in such a way that an acquisition, merger, takeover or demerger is achieved.

The principal parties to an M&A transaction include the following:

- **Acquirer** – the person or company making the acquisition. Also referred to as the bidder or, in a takeover, the offeror.
- **Target** – the company being bought and sold. Also referred to as the offeree in a takeover.
- **Vendor** – the person(s) or company selling the target. Also referred to as the seller or, in a takeover, target shareholders.

1.2 Motivations for Acquisition

A well-managed company will only make an acquisition if the acquisition 'creates or enhances shareholder value'. That is, the merged entity must be worth more than the value of the two stand-alone companies. Value creation is usually the result of **synergies**: either revenue synergies (economies of scope) or cost synergies (economies of scale). A synergy results when two companies co-operate in order to produce a better outcome than each entity could achieve on its own. It is sometimes summarised as the '2 + 2 = 5' effect.

Synergies may be achieved in the following areas.

- **Scale acquisitions** – in general, a larger company can achieve better margins and returns than a smaller one, because of its greater buying power and efficient central services. Acquisition is perceived to be a faster way of achieving growth in core activities than organic expansion.
- **Geographic expansion** – buying a company with activities in a different geographical region can give the acquirer access to a wider customer base for its own products and result in revenue synergies.
- **Product access** – buying a company with a complementary range of products enables the acquirer to produce, market and distribute a wider range or a greater volume of goods and services, and can result in revenue and cost synergies.
- **Technology** – an acquirer may buy a company with unique technology, know-how or intellectual property, to apply this to its own products and processes. This can create revenue and/or cost synergies.
- **Logistics** – buying a company with an effective distribution system could help the acquirer to bring its networks closer to customers or raw material sources. This strategy may include vertical acquisitions; acquisitions of businesses further up the supply chain, such as raw materials producers; or acquisitions further down the supply chain, such as customers.
- **Economics** – an acquirer might seek to diversify its activities, by buying a company in a different business. Conglomerate managers argue that this allows them to use central service facilities such as accounting, taxation, shared operating facilities more effectively, and also helps them to smooth earnings over the business cycle. Such mergers are now most frequently undertaken by financial investors such as private equity firms, but are no longer common among western trade buyers, where the emphasis is on optimising core activities.

1.2.1 Synergies and Value

When setting the acquisition price, the acquirer must be clear as to the contribution of potential synergies to the value. The offer price should not include all the potential synergy value, or the target's shareholders will benefit from all the value that the acquirer has yet to create.

Example _____

Bidco is considering the acquisition of Target. Its managers estimate that the deal will result in annual cost savings (synergy) of £10 million in perpetuity. If the WACC (see Chapter 3, Section 3) of the merged company (Bidco-Target) is 10%, the total synergy value is £100 million (£10 million/10%).

If Target's current value is £350 million, the absolute maximum price that Bidco could offer, before destroying shareholder value, is £450 million (£350 million stand-alone value plus £100 million synergy value). If Bidco did offer £450 million, Target's shareholders would capture all of the synergy value of the merged entity, leaving none of the benefit to Bidco. If the takeover price was £400 million, Bidco would retain £50 million of the synergy benefits, and Target shareholders would receive £50 million of synergy benefits, in addition to the stand-alone value of their shares.

_____

Value is enhanced most often in acquisitions where the bidder already possesses good resident (industry-specific) knowledge, and is able to use that knowledge to turn potential synergies into tangible profits. Value is enhanced least in acquisitions done for tactical or 'personal' reasons (the 'hubris hypothesis').

Most takeover studies conclude that, after the initial share price 'hype' which creates an apparent uplift in value, the market worth of the combined business usually settles back to pre-merger levels. This failure to achieve a sustainable increase in value is thought to be due to:

- over-optimistic claims of synergy gain;
- failure to integrate the businesses in order to achieve the synergies;
- cultural clashes between bidder and target;
- over-paying or lack of due diligence; and
- the cost and effort of acquisition.

1.2.2 Other Motivations

Value enhancement may be the best rationale for acquisition but, in practice, there may be many alternative motives for acquisitions and disposals. These include:

- **Defensive strategies** – protection against competitor movements, or to deflect a hostile bid.
- **Regulatory pressure** – disposals may be required on anti-trust grounds, or acquisitions may be prompted by government pressure (for example, rescue acquisitions during the banking crisis in 2008–10).
- **Financial investment** – acquiring and disposing of businesses is core to the strategy of private equity investors.
- **Opportunism** – in market downturns, assets may be available more cheaply.
- **Personal factors** – a company may be sold due to the retirement of an owner-manager; or an ambitious management team may choose acquisitions to enhance their profile and careers; or a wealthy fan might buy their favourite football team.

1.3 Motivation for Divestiture and Demerger

1.3.1 Disposals by Corporate Sellers

A company might be sold by its shareholders or parent company for a number of reasons.

- **Commercial** – a division or subsidiary no longer fits with the overall group business following major changes in group strategy or market developments.
- **Profit** – the target's trading activities lie in a different sector from the main group and may be valued more highly as an independent undertaking than as part of the group. Alternatively, a loss-making subsidiary might be sold to restore the group's EPS.
- **Financial** – the overall group structure is highly geared, and sale of the target would supply much-needed capital to reduce group debt levels. Alternatively, the target may require significant cash investment, and its sale would release the cash for other activities.

1.3.2 Disposals of Owner-Managed Businesses

Another significant source of disposals comes about when owner-managers of a private company decide to 'exit' the business, for retirement or other reasons. In such cases they may sell out to third-party buyers. Alternatively, a parent company or owner-manager may offer the shares internally to the continuing management. This is referred to as a **management buyout (MBO)** and is discussed in Section 2.2.

1.3.3 Disposals of Portfolio Companies

Private equity firms are major participants in the M&A world. These firms will invest in a portfolio of companies, typically with the aim of improving their financial structure, trading performance and management, with a view to realising a gain on disposal of each company in, say, three to five years' time.

1.4 Public M&A

The majority of M&A by volume involves acquisitions and disposals of private companies. However, many quoted companies will at some time acquire others or become 'targets'; these transactions are relatively high value, attract significant publicity, and can be highly contentious.

In a takeover of a public company, the bidder cannot negotiate with all the target's shareholders directly. Instead, the bidder's board typically negotiates with the target's board in order to agree a price and structure for the offer which the target's board is prepared to recommend to its shareholders. This offer is set out in an **offer document** which is sent to all shareholders. Target shareholders may accept the offer, by completing and submitting an acceptance form, or reject it by taking no action. This type of offer is referred to as a **recommended offer**.

The takeovers that attract the most commentary are those where the target directors are unwilling to sell. These are referred to as **hostile** or unsolicited bids. The resistant target directors have three choices: convince their shareholders not to sell their shares to the bidder, convince the bidder to make a better offer or find an alternative bidder who is more acceptable (the so-called 'white knight').

In a recommended takeover bid, the target directors agree to recommend the takeover to their own shareholders by advising them to support the acquisition and sell their shares to the bidding company. Many hostile bids ultimately end up being recommended, usually after the acquirer has raised the offer price. A recommended offer may also be referred to as a friendly bid, or an agreed bid.

Further details of the processes in public M&A are covered in Section 1.6 below, and in Chapter 6, Section 3.

1.4.1   Regulation of Public M&A

The acquisitions of private companies are relatively lightly regulated; however, public takeovers have the potential to be far more contentious and so are subject to far more extensive regulation. The Panel on Takeovers and Mergers (the 'Takeover Panel') is an independent body with the statutory power to regulate the conduct of takeovers, and the relevant rules are found within the City Code on Takeovers and Mergers (the 'Takeover Code', also known as the 'Blue Book'). The subject of takeover regulation is dealt with in detail in the Regulation paper of this qualification.

1.5   Divestiture and Demerger – Trade Sale or Spin-off

Learning Objective

5.1.4   Know the key features of and differences between a trade sale and a spin-off

5.1.6   Be able to calculate proceeds to holders of ordinary shares in a trade sale or corporate exit

1.5.1   Divestiture Alternatives

Two main types of divestiture are **trade sales** and **spin-offs**.

A **trade sale** involves the sale of a business to a commercial (trade) buyer, as distinct from a financial buyer such as a private equity firm. The most common method involves the preparation of an **information memorandum (IM)** detailing the business activities and related financial results. The IM is circulated to potential purchasers identified in advance by the company's advisers. After an initial round of bids, to ascertain the serious contenders, the number of potential buyers will be narrowed down. The seller then enters into more detailed negotiations with the short-listed bidders. Ultimately, the acquirer offering the best price with the fewest restrictions will be successful.

A **spin-off** involves the flotation, as a separate entity, of all or part of a subsidiary of the parent. The subsidiary is restructured, if necessary, to make it suitable for listing, and shares in the subsidiary are offered for sale to external investors. This generates cash for the parent, from the sale of its shares, and may also raise capital for the subsidiary, through the issue of new shares. The parent company could also retain a stake in its subsidiary. Going forward, the spin-off provides better public information for target shareholders, incentive schemes for management, and more accountability for management, and should lead to better performance and higher value in the longer term. It is an attractive disposal method when market conditions are favourable for IPOs, but only when the subsidiary itself is suitable for listing as a stand-alone company.

A **demerger** is similar to this, but raises no new capital for either parent or target. Instead, the shares in the subsidiary are issued to the parent company's shareholders in the form of a 'dividend *in specie*' (a non-cash dividend). Shares in the subsidiary are then admitted to listing on a stock exchange by way of an introduction. In this way, two listed entities are formed. Shareholders usually retain the same proportionate interest in the two entities as they had in the original parent. Demergers occasionally result in temporary downward pressure on the demerged vehicle's shares, since investors with no interest in the demerged target activity inevitably sell their shareholdings. In the longer term, however, share prices generally recover. Again, this method is only possible when the subsidiary is suitable for a listing as a stand-alone entity, but it does not rely on market conditions for success, since no shares are offered for sale to the public.

1.5.2 Divestiture Proceeds

On a trade sale, it is common for the target to be sold 'debt-free'; that is, without transferring the target's loans and other debt to the purchaser. This means that the target's debt remains outstanding and must now be repaid by the vendor, together with any other sources of finance. The purchase consideration includes payment for both the equity and the debt of the target; effectively, it represents the enterprise value of the target.

If the target were sold with its debt, the acquirer would assume the liability for the repayment of the debt, and the purchase consideration would be correspondingly lower, representing the equity value of the target.

Example _____

Cluster has sold its subsidiary, Solitaire, for £250 million debt-free. Solitaire has debt of £75 million, of which £50 million is a senior secured facility and £25 million is a subordinated unsecured loan. It also has £30 million in preference shares. How much of the consideration is attributable to the ordinary shareholders of Cluster?

On completion, the purchase consideration must be allocated as follows:

	£
Consideration	250,000,000
1. Senior secured loan	50,000,000
2. Subordinated unsecured	25,000,000
3. Preference shares	30,000,000
4. Ordinary shares	145,000,000

The consideration proceeds must be allocated to Cluster's stakeholders in order of their priority on liquidation (this was set out in Chapter 3, Section 2.2.1); however, the disposal of a subsidiary does not typically result in liquidation of that company.

1.6 Financing Acquisitions

Learning Objective

5.1.2 Understand how acquisitions are typically financed and by whom

5.1.3 Understand the basic tax considerations in the UK for acquisitions and disposals

There are four main options when financing acquisitions. The bidder can offer:

- cash in exchange for target shares;
- new bidder shares in a share swap;
- loan notes (effectively, an interest-bearing IOU); or
- a combination of any of these.

Different structures have different tax consequences. Very broadly, a vendor who receives a cash consideration is liable to pay capital gains tax (or corporation tax on the capital gain) in the tax year of the acquisition. However, when the consideration is in the form of paper (loan notes or shares) the CGT payment does not fall due until the shares or loan notes are sold or redeemed. Retail shareholders may benefit from additional reliefs associated with CGT.

Other instruments have been used in the past, such as preference shares or conditional instruments. These can be helpful in structuring private deals. However, in public takeovers, these tend to be less attractive to target shareholders since they have less transparent value and tend to complicate the (usually simple) accept/reject decision that shareholders need to make.

Cash offers tend to find most favour with investors. Cash is certain and easy to quantify, and can be re-invested or spent immediately on receipt. Target shareholders who accept cash do not become investors in the bidder company and are not exposed to post-acquisition risk. Thus, the downside for sellers is the potential earlier payment of capital gains tax and lack of any upside potential.

A bidder with surplus cash will generally seek to use this to fund its acquisitions, particularly when interest rates are low. Otherwise it will have to raise the cash through borrowings (which will have an impact on its gearing ratios) or through an issue of shares (which could dilute the interests of its shareholders).

Share swaps (also known as paper or share-for-share offers) involve the issue of new shares by the bidder. They are a realistic option only for publicly quoted companies whose shares are liquid and transparently priced. They have the advantage of being relatively quick and easy to fund, especially when cash is scarce. However, they dilute bidder shareholdings, and larger issues may require the publication of a prospectus, which is time-consuming and expensive. During the credit crisis, cash offers were difficult to finance, and so share-for-share offers became common.

Target shareholders must forgo certain cash now, in exchange for potential future profits from their bidder shares. If they accept the offer they will be exposed to the bidder's post-acquisition risk, but if they believe that the bidder is likely to create value from the acquisition, this option may be attractive to them. If not, they may sell their shares quickly, which can of course cause a dip in the bidder's share price. Generally, the value of a share offer must be a little higher than in a pure cash offer, to compensate for additional risk as well as dealing and other costs of selling the shares.

Capital gains deferral is available as long as the target's investors keep the consideration shares.

If the target's management will continue to be employed at the target, they are usually required to take bidder shares in exchange for their shareholdings, to ensure their continuing commitment.

Loan notes (also called loan stock or promissory notes) are usually structured as short-term interest-bearing redeemable or convertible debt instruments, which can be issued to target shareholders as consideration; they are similar to a bond or IOU. Although they are normally transferable, they are not usually quoted on a stock exchange. From the seller's point of view, they are less liquid and certain than cash, but less risky than bidder shares. From a bidder's point of view, they have the effect of deferring the payment of cash consideration; ie, target shareholders will receive cash for their shares, but only once the loan notes are redeemed. Also, as they are debt instruments they are taken into account in calculating the bidder's financial ratios, and the interest is tax-deductible.

As with a share offer, capital gains deferral is available until the loan notes are redeemed.

Cash/share/loan note combinations can be structured in a way to optimise the bidder's funding options; for example, an offer might be structured as follows: for every 2 target shares, 1 bidder share plus 85p in cash or 1 bidder share plus 85p loan note. These enjoy a mixed reception with investors. It becomes slightly more complicated to assess the total value, as the market value of the bidder's shares can be volatile.

When the target is a private company, the bidder is able to negotiate with individual shareholders separately and can agree different consideration structures to meet the tax and liquidity needs of these shareholders. If the target is a public company, and the deal is governed by the rules of the Takeover Code, the bidder cannot negotiate individual agreements; all shareholders must receive equivalent treatment and the same structure or options must be made available to all shareholders. If a bidder wants to provide some flexibility of choice to target shareholders, it could offer a **mix and match** option. This gives each shareholder a range of structure options to choose from, for example: the basic offer: 100p cash plus 1.4 new bidder shares. Under the mix and match facility, holders can vary the proportion of cash or shares they take, up to a maximum of [say] 4.5 shares or 150p cash.

2. Private Equity Transactions

Learning Objective

5.2.1   Know the definition of private equity

5.2.2   Know the key features of and differences between: a management buy-out (MBO); a management buy-in (MBI); a leveraged buy-out (LBO); a leveraged buy-in (LBI); a buy-in management buy-out (BIMBO); an institutional buy-out (IBO); a public to private (PTP)

2.1   What is Private Equity?

The private equity industry is one of the main drivers of activity in the M&A market. It can be briefly defined as direct equity investment in private companies, made by professional and/or third party investors, for the short- to medium-term. This investment is usually intended to finance a change in the company invested in; this could be an acquisition, a turnaround, an expansion or a start-up, and the intention is usually to achieve an exit by way of sale or flotation within, on average, three to five years. If possible, the equity investment is usually structured alongside leverage in order to maximise potential gains.

2.1.1   Participants in Private Equity

The main participants in private equity investment are as follows:

Private equity firms raise finance from investors, and establish funds which are then invested in private company shares, to provide returns for investors. These funds are typically structured as closed-end limited partnerships, with a ten-year life. This means that the private equity firm must, over the ten-year period, identify suitable investments; invest in the form of equity and/or other capital; make changes at the company which will enhance the overall value; and then exit their investment, to generate an adequate return to their partners. The private equity firm will take the role of **general partner (GP)** in the fund, and is usually also the **manager** of the fund.

Limited partners (LPs) are the investors in the funds. They may be pension funds, banks, insurance companies, corporate, government institutions, high net worth individuals or other investment entities. Their investment in private equity typically comprises only a small part of their overall investment portfolio, as private equity investment is classed as risk capital.

Portfolio companies are the companies that the fund invests in. These may be early-stage or start-up companies (in which case the investment is usually referred to as **venture capital**), more established companies seeking expansion, development or recovery capital, or businesses being acquired by management or by a third party company. A major part of the industry focuses on buy-out transactions; these are discussed further in Section 2.2.

Management in the portfolio companies are usually required to commit finance alongside the private equity investor, in the form of subscription for equity. It is normal for management to have a different class of equity from that of the private equity investor, and to accept considerable restrictions as the price of the PE firm's investment.

Banks will frequently lend to portfolio companies alongside private equity investors, in order to create the possibility of enhanced, leveraged returns.

2.2 Buy-Out Types

A buy-out is a private equity investment in the acquisition of a company as opposed to investing development capital in a company. Buy-outs take a number of forms, each with their own associated jargon, but, in each case, the private equity firm provides a significant amount of the acquisition finance.

A **management buy-out (MBO)** arises when a team of managers purchases the target from its existing owners. With an MBO, the continuing management team usually comes entirely from within the target.

A **management buy-in (MBI)** occurs when an external management team approaches the existing owners independently with a view to acquiring the company and managing it. The old management is then usually replaced.

A **buy-in, management buy-out (BIMBO)** refers to the combination of buy-out and buy-in, when a mixture of both incoming and existing management collaborate to buy the target, and run it together over the investment period.

An **institutional buy-out (IBO)** is usually instigated and led by private equity funds (institutions) wishing to acquire the target. Existing management may be retained, enhanced or replaced following completion of the buy-out process.

If debt capacity permits, all buy-out transactions typically involve borrowing a large proportion of the purchase price, to minimise the equity finance required and enhance equity returns to the fund and to management. This is referred to as a **leveraged buy-out (LBO)**. When leverage is provided to fund a management buy-in, this is referred to as a **leveraged buy-in (LBI)**.

A **public to private (PTP) transaction** is one in which a private equity firm launches a takeover bid for a company that is quoted on a stock exchange. This is generally a recommended offer, in collaboration with the target's management, and results in the public company becoming privately held.

In all cases, the private equity firm plans to exit its investment in the short- to medium-term, ideally through a trade sale or IPO. A common theme for all buy-outs is that the target's cash flow must be adequate to service the debt used for the buy-out and the future development of the target. Over time, the business should generate sufficient profits and cash flow to repay the debt, so that, on exit, a larger proportion of the value achieved is available for shareholder returns.

Buy-Out Example from Investment to Exit

Target ltd has total assets of £100 million and total liabilities of £80 million (assumed to remain constant over the life of the investment). Shareholder equity, therefore, amounts to £20 million.

Its management agrees to acquire Target for £20 million in an MBO. The purchase is financed by bank borrowings of £15 million secured on company assets, together with £2.5 million of equity provided by management and £2.5 million provided by a private equity firm.

Immediately after the buy-out transaction, Target has total liabilities of £95 million (£80 million + £15 million new debt) and a balance sheet asset surplus of £5 million, represented by the new equity.

Target grows successfully, and at the end of year three the PE firm decides to exit, through a trade sale.

By now, retained profits of £20 million have been generated and Target has assets of £120 million and liabilities of £95 million. Assuming that the company is sold for an enterprise value of £120 million, the proceeds are used first to repay the debt, and the equity balance is then shared between the PE fund and management, as equity investors. (Note that this example assumes no dividends or debt repayments before exit.)

Period	Pre Buy-out	Post Buy-out	End Year 3	Exit Value
Assets	100	100	120	120
Liabilities	−80	−95	−95	−95
Net assets	20	5	25	25

Equity Returns

Year	0	1	2	3
Equity investment	(5)	0	0	25
IRR				71%

2.3 Structuring and Funding the Buy-Out

Learning Objective

5.2.4 Understand the types of investment and the funding components of a typical: trade sale; MBO/MBI; PTP

5.2.5 Understand the principles applied in determining the levels/ratio of equity and debt that might be available in such transactions

The essential prerequisites for successful buy-out transactions are a strong and able management team, predictable and reliable cash flows in the target vehicle, an ability to acquire the company at affordable price levels, and the ability to secure and service debt finance.

In the example in the last section, we saw a relatively simple structure. The financial structure of real-world buy-outs is usually much more complex than this.

- First, the management must ascertain that the sellers are willing to sell the company, and they must calculate their total funding needs, including acquisition price, debt refinancing, professional fees, working capital and capital expenditure.
- They must then determine how much bank/debt finance is available. This may include secured senior debt, working capital finance, and mezzanine debt if available.
- They must also determine how much capital the management team can contribute in the form of equity.
- Assuming that additional funding is needed, the balance is likely to be raised from private equity providers.
- Both the banks and the private equity firm will need to be satisfied that the deal can meet their expectations of returns. This means, first, that the company must be able to generate sufficient cash to service the debt and, if possible, pay dividends, and, secondly, that the business must be capable of being sold or floated for a higher value in the future, to provide a capital return on exit.

The deal can only go ahead when a workable combination of financing sources is found.

The diagram below (known as the funding triangle) represents the typical funding structure required for management buy-outs.

Banks (Secured Lending)

When deciding how to fund the buy-out, it is usual to start at the bottom layer of the funding triangle: senior bank debt. The team could approach a single bank, or a consortium, though often with large transactions the debt may be syndicated to a number of banks.

The senior lender will usually only lend on a secured basis taking a fixed and/or floating charge over the target's assets. When the lending is secured, the interest will be relatively low. Although the cost will vary with market conditions and the quality of security offered, this senior debt will be the cheapest form of funding for the transaction. Because of this, the buy-out team will raise as much senior debt as possible.

The proportion of bank funding typically ranges from 35% to 50% of total transaction value in normal market conditions. The exact level of bank financing depends on the quality and amount of security available, the interest cover and gearing ratios required by the bank, market conditions, management quality and the company's cash flow forecasts.

Mezzanine Debt

Mezzanine debt is subordinated debt with subordinated or no security, and thus it ranks between senior bank debt and equity in a capital structure. Mezzanine investors require higher returns than senior lenders because they are exposed to higher risk. Typically their required rate of return is between 15% and 20%. This return is made up of relatively high interest (say, 10–12%), together with some form of equity participation such as war-rants to subscribe for equity in the borrower. These warrants are usually exercisable on the repayment of the loan or the exit of the investment – whichever comes first. If the investment performs as expected, the equity element of the loan should add another 5–10% of return to the mezzanine provider.

Mezzanine finance may be supplied by specialist financing groups or by banks. It is not always needed for private equity transactions, but, when required, mezzanine finance typically accounts for up to 20% of the overall transaction value. In larger deals, it is also commonly used as a form of bridging finance, to be refinanced in the high yield bond markets when conditions permit.

Companies that are too small to access the bond markets will often regard mezzanine finance as a natural alternative. Its attraction is the ability to tailor debt structures that closely match the borrower's needs. Bond issues, on the other hand, are much less flexible.

Private Equity Funds

The amount of equity invested by institutional investors – private equity funds and venture capitalists – varies from transaction to transaction according to the perceived risk levels. In good economic conditions, institutional equity may account for 25% to 40% of the total transaction value. The amount of private equity investment available depends mainly, however, on the ability of the transaction to generate an adequate IRR.

Private equity firms establish funds typically for a period of ten years, and these usually aim to achieve an IRR (internal rate of return) of 30–35% over that time. In the early years of the fund the PE firm identifies and invests in a portfolio of investments in companies; over the following three to five years, the individual investments are managed so as to generate significant capital growth and/or income; and in the final years of the fund, the PE firm exits each investment in order to crystallise gains. It then remits the proceeds to its LP investors. Some individual investments generate much more than a 30–35% IRR, and some significantly less. However, no PE firm with a 30-35% IRR target will invest in a company that does not have the potential to deliver a 30–35% IRR, and any actual investment it makes will be capped at a level where this IRR can be achieved.

The private equity firm's investment will often be split between ordinary shares (giving potentially the highest returns) and preference shares or loan stock (ranking ahead of ordinary shares for dividends and on liquidation). Preference shares can also be used to help structure a ratchet (see Section 2.4 below) to protect their returns.

Management Equity

Finally, the top portion of the funding triangle represents the management team's capital contribution, which is used to subscribe for management's own equity shares in the target. The investment (for them) constitutes pure risk capital and rarely exceeds more than 10% of the total funding. Management is generally expected to invest as much as they can possibly afford in order to align their interests closely to the long-term success of the MBO and the interests of their investors. This funding may come from personal loans, mortgages or personal savings.

The investment structure shown here gives a very broad example of how a transaction could be structured and each deal will, of course, be different. For example, financing for an asset-intensive business or an infrastructure project, with strong collateral or guarantees, will attract a much higher amount of senior debt, while a technology investment may be almost entirely funded by equity and loan stock.

2.4   Private Equity Terms – Glossary

Learning Objective

5.2.3   Understand the key terms and phrases typically used in private equity and debt transactions: debt/equity ratio; gearing/leverage ratios; capital structure, ie, types of shares and their rights (eg, dividend, liquidation preference, redemption conversion, anti-dilution, pre-emption, voting); ratchets; investment hurdles; 'drag and tag' provisions; good leaver/bad leaver; 'pay to play'; bridge finance; burn rate; capitalise; carried interest; co-investment; mezzanine debt; down/follow-on round; founder shares

Private equity business uses a large number of technical terms. The more common ones are discussed below:

- **Bridge finance** – a form of short-term finance provided (primarily) by banks to purchasers to meet temporary finance needs in the period between agreeing a deal and permanent finance becoming available. It could take the form of a bond issue or, more usually, a term loan or facility. Bridge loans typically carry high interest rates to protect the lender if the borrower fails to secure long-term finance. The arrangement is usually secured on the acquirer's assets.
- **Burn rate** – the monthly quantity of cash consumed by companies to meet current expenditure levels. The term is most commonly used by venture capitalists to describe the quantity of funds consumed or 'burned' during a start-up period when companies develop new products, prior to selling them.
- **Capitalise** – an alternative to paying interest on a loan is to capitalise the interest. This means that the interest is added to the total loan as an additional obligation, rather than paid in cash. The next year's interest is then calculated by reference to the new, higher total of the loan. Loan agreements which allow capitalising interest are referred to as 'Pay-in-Kind' or 'PIK' loans.
- **Co-investment** – a co-investment occurs when one or more private equity or venture capital funds invite others to avail themselves of an investment opportunity. Co-investors are typically the venture capital managers or investors known to the fund (often limited partners of the fund). Thus, co-investors enjoy greater investment opportunity – initially through the main fund making the investment and then also through direct holdings.

- **Down rounds/follow-on rounds** – a follow-on round is a second or third tranche of finance required by companies. Follow-on rounds are common in venture capital arrangements when small firms require additional capital for survival, before becoming self-sufficient. A 'down round' is a follow-on round of finance set at lower prices per share than prior rounds. Investors dislike down rounds, as they reduce investment-carrying values on the balance sheet.

- **Drag and tag provisions** – drag-along rights allow the PE investor to compel management to agree to the sale or flotation of the company. Thus, if the institution receives an offer for the company, management can be forced to sell their holding. Tag-along rights allow the management or other minority investor to 'tag along' with any offer from a third party to buy the PE firm's shares. These provisions are part of the protections provided for institutional investors and management in the investor agreement.

- **Founder shares** – originating stock owned by company founders. Some founder shares confer additional rights. Common devices are 'clawback' provisions when affected shares may be retained or 'clawed back' should the founder depart. The clawback amount varies in proportion to the time the departing founder spent at the company.

- **Gearing/leverage ratios** – gearing (also known as leverage) ratios are measures which quantify the proportion of a company's capital provided by debt finance. Common gearing ratios include the debt:equity ratio; net debt to EBITDA; and net debt:equity. Changes to a company's gearing ratios provide valuable information as to whether the company is becoming more, or less, risky. See Chapter 2, Section 5.2.

- **Good leaver/bad leaver** – reference to treatment meted out to departing members of the management team. Terms are defined in shareholder agreements between the PE firm and management, and vary widely; usually, though, good leavers are those who depart through no fault of their own (eg, redundancy, illness); bad leavers go voluntarily (resignation) or are dismissed for cause. Good leavers may be entitled to receive value for their investment at 'good' prices; bad leavers receive reduced amounts or may forfeit their investment.

- **Investment hurdle** – the minimum required return rate for investors; often referred to as a **hurdle rate** (see Chapter 1, Section 4.4). Carried interest computations are affected by hurdle rates (see 'carried interest' below). Typically all fund profits are paid to the limited partners, until they have achieved a cumulative return equal to the hurdle rate (say, 8% of invested funds). Only then will the general partner start to share in any of the fund's returns.

- **Carried interest** – a share of profit that general partners (GPs) in venture capital, private equity and hedge funds receive in addition to annual management fees charged. In a typical fund, profits made are allocated as follows. Up to a predetermined hurdle rate (say 8%) all profits are paid to the limited partners (LPs); once the LPs returns have met the hurdle rate, future returns are then allocated to the GP until it, too, has achieved its hurdle rate of 8%. After this, further returns are allocated between the GPs and LPs so that the GP is paid a 'carried interest' of, usually, 20%, and the LP receives the balance of 80%.

- **Pay to play** – a clause in a financing agreement whereby any investor that does not participate in a future round agrees to suffer significant dilution compared to other investors. One mechanism provides that investors' preference shares are automatically converted to ordinary shares, which in essence ends any preferential rights of an investor, such as the right to influence key management decisions or take priority in distributions and on winding up.

- **Mezzanine debt** – this is subordinated debt accompanied by an equity 'kicker' in the form of equity warrants. The debt may be unsecured or have subordinated security, and it also ranks behind the senior debt in insolvency. It is typically bullet-repayment (ie, repaid in one instalment on maturity) and cannot be repaid until the senior debt is repaid. These terms represent high risk to the lender, who requires a high return in compensation – typically, 15-20%. This is usually made up of a combination of relatively high interest, and warrants to subscribe for shares in the borrower, exercisable either on maturity of the loan or on a change of control, constituting an exit from the investment. It is called 'mezzanine' because it ranks between senior debt and equity.
- **Ratchets** – this is a structure that determines the eventual equity allocation between groups of shareholders. A ratchet enables a management team to increase its share of equity if its company is performing well. This could be achieved by allocating part of the equity investment to convertible redeemable preference shares; if management perform well, then all or part of their preference shares are converted into equity. The final equity allocation in a company therefore varies, depending on the performance of the company and the rate of return that the private equity firm achieves.

3. Quoted Equity Transactions

3.1 Institutions, Individuals, and Intermediaries

Learning Objective

5.3.1 Know the main types of investor and their ability to invest in either or both of quoted and unquoted shares: pension funds; insurance companies; collective investment schemes (including open-ended funds and closed-ended funds); venture capital investors (including venture capital trusts in the UK); directors/employees; private individuals; family offices

There are three main groups of participants in the secondary equity markets: intermediaries, institutions and individuals. Institutions and individuals buy and sell company shares and other financial assets, while the intermediaries facilitate the sale and trading of shares (including new issues) for companies.

- **Individuals** – these may be connected with the company (eg, directors, managers and employees of companies who own shares in their employer). Since the 1980s, large institutional investors have pushed to 'align the interests of management and shareholders'. One way of doing this is to remunerate employees with company shares. The belief is that, if the company performs well due to the manager's actions, the stock price will increase and the manager's wealth will increase (this is the doctrine of 'agency theory'). Additionally, individual investors may be third parties unconnected with the company, investing either directly or through a stockbroker. These are generally referred to as 'retail investors'.
- **Intermediaries** – typically these are investment banks and brokers. They are active in both the primary market (initial public offerings of company shares to investors) and the secondary market (facilitating the selling and trading of shares that have already been issued).

- **Institutions** – these are professional investors, generally managing funds on behalf of other investors. During the past 50 years, institutional investors have grown enormously and now own more than 80% of shares outstanding on the London Stock Exchange and AIM. There are five main types of institutional investor:

    - pension funds;
    - insurance companies;
    - mutual funds (unit trusts, investment trusts, OEICs and hedge funds);
    - private equity firms;
    - venture capital firms (including venture capital trusts).

Pension funds, mutual funds and insurance companies invest primarily in **quoted shares**. It is rare for one of these funds to have more than 10% of its assets invested in unquoted equity. On the other hand, private equity and venture capital firms specialise in **unquoted equities** – their goal is to achieve higher returns than available in the stock market by investing in fewer, often riskier shares, outside the restricted and regulated world of the public equity markets. Individuals are generally limited to investments in quoted entities. Company managers/directors might invest in either, depending on whether their company is quoted or not.

3.1.1 Pension Funds

Pension funds are the largest source of investment capital in the UK, with over £1,700 billion of funds under management in 2015 (source: OECD). Employers and employees make contributions to the fund, to provide income for employees on their retirement. Not all of the funds are invested in shares; pension funds are required to maintain diversified portfolios, and invest in a number of different asset classes. The challenge for pension funds, as for all investors, is to balance their investments in low risk assets, such as gilts, with investments in high return assets, such as equities, at the same time as ensuring they have sources of short-term income as well as long-term growth. These include equities as well as corporate and government bonds, property and private equity funds but, in recent years, many funds have been looking for new sources of income, leading to more diverse investing. The proportion of these funds held in equities has varied over the years, from 68% in 2003 to under 40% in 2015. However, most pension funds are not allowed to invest directly in unquoted companies; instead, they usually invest through private equity funds or in stock market quoted companies that invest in unquoted companies, such as certain investment trusts.

As major investors, pension funds are very active in corporate governance and corporate performance. Their umbrella organisation is the National Association of Pension Funds (NAPF) (see www.napf.co.uk).

3.1.2 Insurance Companies

The two types of insurance company are life assurance and general insurance companies. Both are major investors in equities, but the two types of firm have a different investment focus, based on the length (duration) of policies written.

Life insurance policies typically have a term of five to 30 years, or the life of the policyholder. This gives them a long-term investment focus and such companies tend to hold high proportions of long-term instruments such as ordinary shares and long-term or perpetual bonds in their portfolios.

General insurance companies cover motors, building and contents, etc. They have a shorter-term investment horizon, reflected accordingly in their lower shareholdings in equities; their portfolios have a stronger weighting to short- or medium-term bonds.

The insurance industry has a similar interest in corporate governance to the pensions industry and is represented by the Association of British Insurers (ABI) (see www.abi.org.uk).

3.1.3 Mutual Funds

Mutual funds are collective investment vehicles that maintain diversified share portfolios and hold other assets on behalf of investors (mainly individuals). They charge annual fees to manage the portfolio. Mutual funds are the best way for investors with limited funds to gain cost effective entry to markets. A mutual fund accommodates investors with as little as (say) £1,000, by allowing access to well-diversified portfolios at much lower brokerage rates than they could achieve privately. A fund manager may operate a number of funds, each with a different investment focus and with a different portfolio mix.

The industry has seen strong growth in the last 20 years, with OEICs and unit trusts increasing in value eight-fold between 2003 and 2013. As the scale of business has increased and internationalised, some managers have moved away from executing large trades through stock exchanges and are instead using so-called 'dark pools' – inter-firm, off-exchange trading centres where large blocks of shares can be bought or sold with minimal transparency.

Unit trusts, OEICs and investment trusts are common kinds of mutual fund in the UK.

Despite their name, **investment trusts** are investment companies that trade on a stock exchange like any other company. Pricing of investment trusts is continuous (their shares trade all day) and is based upon both share supply/demand characteristics as well as fund net asset values. Investment trust shares can and usually do trade at prices representing a premium or discount to the underlying net asset value per share. An investment trust must trade only on a regulated market, and must spread its investment risk, although it can invest in shares, land and other assets (from 2012). It can retain a maximum of 15% of its income in any accounting period and must distribute the remainder as a dividend. It is not subject to tax on gains made on disposal of its investments.

Unit trusts are not companies. They are formed under a 'trust' structure, and investors buy units in the trust. They are not traded on an exchange, but units usually trade once per day at a price approximating to the net asset value per unit. As with investment trusts, unit trusts are not subject to tax on any capital gains made within the fund. Unit trusts are examples of **open-ended funds** in that they do not have a fixed capital base; instead, they can issue or redeem units at any time with no limit.

In recent years many unit trusts converted into **open-ended investment companies** (OEICs; also referred to as investment companies with variable capital or ICVCs). These are similar to unit trusts, but are structured as companies, whose shares can be traded on stock markets. As open-end funds, they can issue and redeem shares at any time. Both unit trusts and OEICs are required to maintain a diversified portfolio.

Hedge funds are a specialised variant of mutual funds usually sold to large sophisticated investors, such as institutions, including pension funds and insurance company funds. Hedge funds enjoy lower levels of regulation than unit trusts, OEICs or investment trusts, which are widely marketed to retail investors. They manage highly strategically focused portfolios, often 'short selling' shares, and invest in many assets not available to other more regulated mutual funds such as private companies. Some hedge funds take an 'activist' approach, taking strategic stakes in companies in order to influence the company's strategy and direction.

A further variant is the **family office**. These are private firms that manage the funds of wealthy families (or individuals). They provide similar services to private banks. Some are single-family offices which focus their attention on a single family with investable wealth typically of at least $100 million. Others are multi-family offices with a number of clients with wealth of $5 million or more. The family offices can provide savings for their clients through pooling investments to reduce transaction costs, as well as providing financial and investment advisory and transaction services.

3.1.4 Private Equity

The investors described above are all investors in public capital markets. However, many investors also diversify their portfolios by investing in alternative investments. Private equity (described in Section 2) is an alternative investment class that has gained increased popularity among institutional investors, notably because of its low correlation to broad equity market movements and the higher-than-average returns it has historically delivered. Most private equity firms raise funds for investment by launching closed-ended funds (ie, funds with a predetermined limit to the amount of capital they will raise), structured as partnerships, to attract investment from institutional investors. The fund is then invested in a portfolio of private companies.

Additionally, while private equity is a key source of funding for many companies, the exit route for many private equity investments is in the form of a stock market flotation, so that there is a strong linkage between the fortunes of the public and private equity markets. Private equity and venture capital firms may also be stock market investors; once a portfolio company has become listed, the original private equity investor may retain an equity stake, so that it can still participate in its future growth.

3.1.5 Venture Capital

Venture capital is a sub-category of private equity. Here, start-up finance and early-stage capital is provided to small, but potentially fast-growing, unquoted companies, with investors reaping their reward from realising the (often significant) equity stake they take in the business, either through a trade sale or a flotation on the stock market. The majority of venture capital investment takes the form of relatively small equity investments, often provided in stages, by specialist institutions. It is usually seen as the high-risk end of private equity, and investors therefore seek proportionately higher returns.

However, **venture capital trusts (VCTs)** were introduced in 1995 in order to allow individual investors to participate, indirectly, in early-stage venture capital investments. VCTs are companies with shares listed on a regulated market, and are essentially a class of investment trust. VCTs are restricted to investing in equity, loans and preference shares in unquoted trading companies with no more than £15 million gross assets (pre-investment) and fewer than 250 employees. In this context, an unquoted company excludes any main market-listed company, but includes companies quoted on AIM or ISDX Growth Market (previously PLUS). VCTs are not allowed to invest more than 15% of their portfolio in any one company, invest more than £12 million in any one qualifying company (£20 million for 'knowledge-intensive companies') or invest in property or finance companies.

A unique feature of VCTs is that they offer significant tax advantages. A VCT is exempt from corporation tax on any gains arising on the disposal of its investments. Investors in VCTs may also be entitled to various income tax and capital gains tax reliefs, providing that their VCT shares are held for five years. These reliefs include:

- Exemption from higher-rate income tax on dividends from ordinary shares in VCTs.
- Income tax relief at 30% of the amount subscribed for new shares, up to a maximum of £200,000 per tax year, providing that the VCT shares are held for at least five years.
- Any gain made on disposal of VCT shares is free of capital gains tax.

The restrictions and reliefs shown are those for the 2015–16 tax year, and are not comprehensive.

The relief for dividend income and gains applies whether the VCT shares were acquired at issue or subsequently via a stock exchange trade. The income tax relief is only available for initial subscriptions for ordinary shares in VCTs.

The **Enterprise Investment Scheme (EIS)** is another government initiative designed to help smaller higher-risk companies to raise finance by offering a range of tax reliefs to investors who purchase new shares in those companies. The difference between investing in an EIS and a VCT is that, under EIS investments, the investor invests directly in the small company, while with a VCT the investor buys shares in the VCT which then invests in a portfolio of small company investments.

3.2 Initial Public Offerings (IPOs)

Learning Objective

5.3.2 Understand the roles of the professional advisers in an IPO: reporting accountants; sponsor; nominated adviser (Nomad); underwriters; lawyers; PR consultants; independent expert

5.3.8 Understand how the book-building and pricing process works

5.3.9 Understand secondary market liquidity and its importance

IPOs are one of the central activities of the corporate finance department. In 2014, the strongest year since 2007, 376 IPOs raised €49.5 billion for European companies and a further 258 listings raised €39 billion in the first three quarters of 2015 (Source: PwC IPO Watch).

3.2.1 Rationale for an IPO

A flotation is the name given to the initial sale of company shares to the public and the listing thereafter of the shares on a stock exchange. Flotation is also referred to as an **initial public offering (IPO)** or may also be referred to as a primary offering. The process of flotation is complex and involves much time and activity from company management and advisers (including investment bankers, brokers, lawyers, and accountants).

Companies may float for a number of reasons:

- to raise cash for expansion;
- to give them access to capital in the future;
- to realise an exit for existing investors;
- to gain status and credibility;
- to create currency for further share-based acquisitions;
- to incentivise management through access to transparent share schemes.

However, a significant issue for companies 'going public' is the reduction in control that will follow. Most market rules have provisions in relation to liquidity, requiring sufficient shares to be in public hands so that a liquid market is created (where the shares may be readily traded). This usually requires the issue of additional shares to third parties, such as the institutional investors described in the previous section. In most markets, management cannot restrict the transfer of shares from one party to another. As a consequence, management must accept the fact that external investors have a right to attend, speak and vote at general meetings, and that they will scrutinise and challenge the board's strategies and performance.

Note that a company which is going through an IPO, or which is listed on an exchange, is referred to as an 'issuer' in the UKLA rules, or as an 'applicant' or 'AIM company' in the AIM rules.

3.2.2 IPO Alternatives

A company seeking to list its shares on a market has a number of options open to it.

- **Introduction** – no shares are issued or sold; existing shares gain a trading facility on the market. There must be adequate shares in issue to create a liquid secondary market.
- **Retail offering** – offer of shares to retail shareholders. Only realistic when the issuer is a well-known company. Requires a high degree of public relations input and can create a wide shareholder base.
- **Institutional offering** – offer of shares to institutional investors. Quicker process and creates a narrower shareholder base.

In most cases, a company seeking to list in the UK must retain the services of an adviser. This adviser is known as a sponsor if a company is seeking a premium listing on the Main Market of the London Stock Exchange, and is a nominated adviser (Nomad) if it seeks admission to AIM. The adviser assists with the overall IPO process including the preparation of documentation; the latter is discussed in Chapter 6.

Any listing of shares on the Main Market of the LSE must be approved by the Financial Conduct Authority (FCA). Any admission to the AIM market must be approved by the LSE.

3.2.3 Sponsors

The **Main Market** of the LSE provides two types of listing: premium, with enhanced regulatory requirements; and standard, with lesser requirements.

In a UK premium listing, the issuer appoints a financial adviser, typically an investment bank, to act as sponsor. No sponsor is required for a standard listing.

The role of the sponsor in an IPO is:

- to confirm to the FCA, via its UK Listing Authority (UKLA), that the company is suitable for listing;
- to advise the company and its directors on their obligations under the rules;
- to confirm the accuracy and completeness of the information provided in the company's prospectus (through commissioning due diligence);
- to liaise with the UKLA.

Only firms approved by the FCA may act as sponsor.

In addition, the issuer appoints at least one **broking firm** to advise it on pricing and marketing of the issue. The broker also handles communications with investors prior to the issue and arranges underwriting (see below). Often, an integrated investment bank will perform both the sponsor and broking roles. For a standard listing, a financial adviser will prepare a prospectus and liaise with the UKLA; this **financial adviser** is typically also a firm which is approved to act as sponsor, even though it is not required to act as a sponsor on this transaction.

3.2.4 Nominated Advisers (Nomads)

When a company seeks admission to AIM, it must appoint a nominated adviser (Nomad) to advise it on the issue, and confirm to the LSE that the applicant is suitable for admission to AIM. Unlike a sponsor, the Nomad (or a replacement Nomad) remains as adviser to the AIM company for as long as it is quoted on AIM.

The Nomad must be a firm approved by the Exchange to act as a Nomad. Its role is to:

- determine whether the applicant is suitable for admission to AIM, including carrying out due diligence; in this context it owes a duty of care to the Exchange;
- manage the flotation process, liaising with the Exchange and other advisers;
- satisfy itself that the applicant has adequate systems and controls in place for compliance with AIM rules;
- co-ordinate the preparation and publication of the AIM Admission Document (see Chapter 6);
- continue to advise the AIM company on a continuing basis after the flotation.

The AIM company must also appoint a **broker** to advise on pricing, provide research on the flotation and to support trading in the company's shares on an ongoing basis.

3.2.5 Other Advisers

The sponsor or Nomad must liaise with a wide range of other advisers on an IPO, as follows. Note that in this section we use the term 'issuer' for both AIM and main market companies.

Legal Advisers

The issuer's lawyers assist in the production of the issue documentation. They also assist in the process of verifying the issue documentation and other legal documents, they advise on the directors' legal and other responsibilities and they carry out legal due diligence. Typically at least two firms will be involved, one acting for the company and another for the sponsor or Nomad.

Accountants

The issuer's accountants also play a major role in the IPO. Firstly, they carry out financial due diligence, involving a detailed investigation into the company's financial affairs. Their conclusions are presented in a 'long-form report'. A key element of this includes confirming that the company has adequate working capital for at least the next 12 months.

They may also act as reporting accountants on the issue. In this capacity, they must confirm that the financial information provided in the prospectus is either directly reproduced from its audited accounts, or, if the accounts have been restated, confirm that they are 'true and fair'. When the issuer includes forecasts or a pro-forma statement in the prospectus, the accountants must confirm that these have been prepared appropriately.

Public and Investor Relations

It is common to appoint public relations and investor relations consultants. These advisers must co-ordinate any proposed advertising, relations with the media, and press conferences. The larger the deal, the more important it is to ensure that the issuer is well known in the investment community. Where the offering is intended to include a high proportion of retail investors, the PR exercise becomes very important.

Following flotation, the PR firm adviser assists the issuer's investor relations team with the preparation of its annual and half-yearly report and accounts, and announcements regarding the issuer's results and any other significant events. The investor relations team are expected to monitor the issuer's investor base, ensure that the board communicate effectively with investors, and organise and manage regular presentations to investors and research analysts.

Independent Experts

In certain cases, the sponsor will retain an independent expert to advise on specific aspects of the issuer's affairs. This could be, for example, a real estate adviser, a surveyor, or a mining expert. Their role is to provide a report to be included in the prospectus. See Chapter 6, Section 5.4.

Book-Runners

In a large offering, the investment bank may form a syndicate with other banks to assist in the sale and underwriting of the shares. Syndicate members are usually selected on the basis of their ability to distribute shares to investors and to provide company research following the offering, and their role is to promote and market the shares to their client base and contacts. The size of the syndicate will depend on the size and structure of the offering, and on any existing banking relationships that the issuer may have.

The lead bank is referred to as the book-runner, or global co-ordinator if shares are being offered in multiple jurisdictions. However, these terms are not used consistently with the same meaning by all parties in all countries.

3.2.6 Pricing and Marketing the Issue

When the IPO takes the form of a placing to institutional investors, it is usually marketed through a 'book-building' process. The function of book-building is to build up interest in the shares, as well as to establish a share price which reflects the interest level of potential investors, thus minimising the risk of shares being left unsold or being sold too cheaply. The marketing of the issue is dealt with by the lead investment bank, which will decide which investors to target.

The first stage is the completion of due diligence. Next, the issuer's advisers start work on drafting the prospectus, for approval by the UK Listing Authority (UKLA, part of the FCA). Initially, this is prepared to near-final form – omitting only pricing details, which will be inserted once the marketing process is nearly complete.

Using this draft prospectus and other marketing information, the issuer's management and advisers make presentations to institutional investors, known as roadshows. The roadshows include a combination of one-on-one meetings with the most important institutions and breakfast-, lunch- and dinner-time presentations to selected groups of fund managers and analysts. During these meetings, management and the advisers try to build up interest in the IPO, as well as gauging the appetite of investors, which will guide their final views on pricing of the shares.

Based on feedback from the roadshows, the issuer's management, advisers and any underwriters decide on a price range for the shares. The investment bank's book-running team now contacts institutional investors to discuss the range; and investors indicate their demand for shares at different price levels, so that the bank can build up an order book. Subsequently, the book-runner, in discussion with the issuer, may then vary the size of the issue, or its price, or both, in an attempt to satisfy the level of indicated demand. The book-runner then sets the price of the issue at a level high enough to maximise proceeds for the issuer, but low enough to encourage demand in the secondary market.

In pricing the issue, it is important to try to ensure that the price is at a level where the offer is oversubscribed so that applicants receive fewer shares than they applied for. This creates a degree of unsatisfied demand, so that investors will purchase shares in the market following the offering. This, in turn, means that trading in the shares in stimulated, creating liquidity in the secondary market for the shares. Secondary market liquidity is vital to a modern and efficient capital market, as it creates the means of meeting investors' needs for transparent pricing and liquidity, as well as an environment for companies to access funds readily.

In many flotations there is uncertainty as to the extent of demand for the shares. If this is the case, the issuer may choose to have the offering underwritten. Its investment bank will usually perform this role for a fee, entering into a commitment to buy any shares which remain unsold after the IPO. In larger deals, this obligation may be syndicated to sub-underwriters.

The final stage of the new issue marketing process is the allocation of shares to investors, once the price has been set and all orders placed. While the decision on price is fundamental to the success of the issue, the allocation policy has an important role, not only in the after-market, but also in the maintenance of a strong and stable shareholder base.

The allocation of shares from a new issue is made by means of an allotment letter (or placing letter if the new shares are issued through a placing) which entitles the recipient to a specified number of shares, subject to payment. If the offering is oversubscribed, the sponsor and brokers must determine how to allocate the shares which will mean that there is a scaling down of allotments. If the offer is undersubscribed, the underwriters must take up any unsold shares.

In larger issues, the offer may include a 'greenshoe' or 'over-allotment' option. This is a provision in the prospectus which allows the underwriters and issuer to sell up to 15% more shares than originally planned, if the demand for the shares is higher than expected.

3.3   Raising Further Equity Capital – Secondary Offerings

Learning Objective

5.3.3   Understand why a company may choose to raise additional capital via: a rights issue; a placing; a placing and open offer

5.3.4   Understand the basic mechanics including the options available to a shareholder and role of any underwriters of: a rights issue; a placing; a placing and open offer

5.3.5   Understand pricing of secondary issues as mandated by UK relevant rules and guidelines: Institutional Voting Information Service (IVIS); National Association of Pension Funds (NAPF); Pre-emption Group of the Financial Reporting Council; UK Listing Authority (UKLA)

5.3.7   Understand the effect of clawback by qualifying shareholders under a placing and an open offer

5.3.10   Understand the consequences of equity issuance on corporate control

Companies often experience the need for additional capital after their initial offering. This may be for expansion finance, to fund acquisitions, to refinance debt or to raise working capital. In the UK, the main methods for secondary offerings are rights issues, placings and open offers.

Rights issues and open offers are offers of new shares to the company's existing shareholders. A placing is an offer of new shares to shareholders, who can be new or existing investors. These are described in more detail later in this section.

First, though, we must consider the effects of any secondary issue on corporate control and shareholder interests.

3.3.1 The Consequences of Equity Issuance on Corporate Control

A key consideration for shareholders is the degree of control they have over the actions of management and the use of the company's assets. For example, in the UK, a 75% shareholding carries the power to pass a special resolution, including a resolution to amend the company's Articles of Association, or to de-list the company. A shareholding in excess of 25% is sometimes referred to as 'negative control' or 'blocking control' as it carries the power to block the passing of a special resolution. A shareholding in excess of 50% carries 'legal control'; it gives the right to pass (or prevent the passing of) an ordinary resolution, such as those to elect directors or to approve significant transactions.

The issuance of new equity, through a secondary offering, may have significant consequences for shareholders who are concerned to maintain their existing shareholding. When new shares are issued to incoming shareholders, the holdings of existing shareholders may be diluted to a level where their existing control is reduced below an acceptable level. When this new issue is very significant, there is a risk that incoming shareholders may implement changes which are contrary to the wishes, strategy and financial interests of existing shareholders.

Example

Dilute ltd has 100 shares in issue and four shareholders, each owning a 25% interest in the company's shares. At present, each of them has an equal holding, and therefore at least three of the shareholders must collaborate to pass either an ordinary or a special resolution.

Dilute's directors now decide to issue a further 35 shares to a new shareholder. The revised shareholdings are now as follows:

- Original shareholders each own 25 / 135 = 18.5% each.
- New shareholder owns 35 / 135 = 25.9%.

The new shareholder now has 'blocking control', and his agreement would be required to pass a special resolution. All of the original shareholders would now have to collaborate in order to pass an ordinary resolution.

The consideration of corporate control is central to the regulatory framework that applies to secondary offerings in the UK, and in particular the concept of pre-emption rights.

3.3.2 Pre-Emption Rights

Investors in UK quoted companies are protected from forcible dilution of their ownership stake by pre-emption rights. These provide, under the Companies Act 2006, that, when a firm wishes to issue new shares in exchange for cash, it must first offer those shares to its existing shareholders in proportion to their existing shareholdings. Thus if a shareholder owns 25% of the existing shares, he or she has the right to acquire 25% of the new shares – maintaining the holding at 25%. This protection from dilution of holdings is enshrined in both company law and in the UKLA Listing Rules. Assuming the shareholder 'takes up' the right to subscribe to the new issue, his or her proportionate share in the overall equity of the company will be preserved.

If a company wishes to offer shares to new shareholders, or selectively to certain shareholders, it must seek shareholder approval for the disapplication of these pre-emption rights, through passing a special resolution at a general meeting. This approval will cover both the number of shares to be issued and the price at which they are issued, to ensure that incoming shareholders pay a fair price. It is normal for a listed company to seek a general disapplication of pre-emption rights at its AGM, to allow flexibility for small *ad hoc* share issues over the course of the coming year (but see further details below).

Companies making rights issues must follow the rules laid out in the Companies Act, the UKLA rules and those of any exchange on which its shares are listed.

UK Guidelines on Pre-Emption Rights

The Companies Act 2006 provides that pre-emption rights can be disapplied by a shareholder vote at an AGM. However, public companies do face some non-statutory restrictions on this disapplication.

As mentioned earlier, the major institutional investors (pension funds, insurance companies and other investment firms) are members of their individual representative organisations, such as the Investment Association (IA) and the National Association of Pension Funds (NAPF). Where these bodies have interests in common, for example in relation to corporate governance matters, these interests are, in turn, represented by specialist groups, including Institutional Voting Information Service (IVIS), the Financial Reporting Council (FRC) and the Pre-Emption Group, who provide guidelines for issuers and investors.

- The IVIS is part of the Investment Association. It is a leading provider of corporate governance research, analysing annual reports, meetings and corporate governance of UK-listed companies and highlighting areas of concern for shareholders. Through the IA, it contributes to the work of the Pre-emption Group (see below).
- The FRC is, of course, familiar as the organisation responsible for accounting and auditing standards in the UK. It also has a key role in UK corporate governance, as the sponsor of the UK Corporate Governance Code (for companies) and the Stewardship Code (for investors). Both of these Codes are covered in the Regulation section of this qualification. It supports the Pre-Emption Group.
- The Pre-Emption Group was originally founded in 2005 to produce a Statement of Principles for investors to take into account when considering whether to approve a disapplication of pre-emption rights. Its current Statement of Principles was published in March 2015 and its members include representatives from the corporate sector, IA, NAPF, ABI and others. The FRC acts as its secretariat.

Pre-Emption Guidelines

The Guidelines apply to all UK and non-UK premium issuers, and to all issues of equity securities undertaken to raise cash for the issuer or its subsidiaries, regardless of the legal form of the transaction. They set out what the Group considers to be 'routine' and, therefore, of limited concern to investors. In summary, this would be:

- a general disapplication of pre-emption rights at an AGM for issues of up to 5% of a company's issued equity securities, provided that the total shares issued under a general disapplication does not exceed 7.5% over a rolling three-year period;
- an additional annual disapplication level of 5% of the issued equity securities, provided that this is earmarked for a specific acquisition or capital investment which is recent or imminent;

- a general AGM disapplication of pre-emption rights to apply for no more than 15 months, or until the date of the next AGM;
- a maximum discount to the existing share price of 5%, other than in exceptional circumstances.

The Guidelines also give a non-exhaustive list of considerations for investors when voting on a specific disapplication of pre-emption rights.

If any offering falls outside the 'routine' guidelines for size and pricing of issues, the Pre-emption Group requires the company to present 'a strong business case' before investors should vote in favour of the issue.

3.3.3 Rights Issues

In the UK, the majority of major secondary offerings are currently rights issues, ie, offers to existing shareholders in accordance with their pre-emption rights.

In a rights issue, the company offers new shares to all existing shareholders in proportion to their existing holding: for example one new share for every five shares owned (a 'one-for-five' or '1:5' rights issue), at a discount to the current market price. The offer is made by sending each shareholder a **provisional allotment letter** (known as a PAL), which sets out his or her entitlement to shares. This PAL may be transferred to a third party.

The shareholder has the right, but not the obligation, to participate in the offering by purchasing new shares in proportion to their existing holding. Alternatively he or she may decline the offer and do nothing, or may sell on the rights in the market to a third-party investor, by transferring the PAL to them. Rights which are transferable in this way are said to be 'renounceable'.

A company may choose a rights issue to raise additional capital:

- if it considers that its existing shareholder base is supportive of management's strategies and likely to invest further;
- if it is in financial difficulty, needs to raise equity finance, and thinks it is unlikely that new external shareholders would be prepared to invest in the circumstances. In this case, the issue is known as a 'rescue rights issue' and the price will be heavily discounted relative to the existing share price.

3.3.4 Open Offers

An open offer is similar to a rights issue in that existing shareholders are offered new shares in proportion to their existing holdings. Like a rights issue, it is a pre-emptive offer. However, in an open offer, a shareholder who does not wish to take up their shares does not have the option of selling the rights on the open market. The shareholders have an entitlement to purchase new shares, but this right is not renounceable. They have only two options: taking up the offer, or not doing so.

Accordingly, open offers tend to be less popular than rights issues. Because of this, it is common for an open offer to be carried out alongside a **placing**, whereby the shares are placed with institutional investors on a conditional basis, before being re-offered to existing shareholders. Any shares required to meet shareholder demand are 'clawed back' from the institutions.

A company may use a **placing and open offer** when it wishes to offer all shareholders the chance to participate in the equity offering, but doubts the likelihood of all the required funds being received, and prefers to introduce new shareholders rather than underwrite the offer.

3.3.5 Placings

A placing is the sale of a company's shares to a limited number of institutional investors, who are either not existing shareholders, or represent only a proportion of them. It is a non-pre-emptive issue (ie, does not comply with pre-emption rights).

A company may only carry out a secondary placing with the approval of its shareholders, and therefore is only likely to use this approach when it does not consider that its existing shareholders are likely to invest in a rights issue, or when it wishes to broaden the shareholder base. This might be the case if the placing is particularly large, or if the company has recently undertaken a rights issue and shareholders are unlikely to invest in a second one.

A company is restricted in carrying out placings by the Pre-Emption Guidelines.

3.3.6 Setting the Price

Rights Issues

One of the most important aspects of a rights issue is setting the terms and the price of the new shares. Typically the new shares are offered at a discount to the prevailing trading price on the stock exchange, to make them attractive to shareholders. In most instances, the discount is set between, say, 15% and 20%, although when a company is in financial difficulty a deep discount of up to 50% may be applied.

Secondary offerings must, in most cases, remain open for ten business days. In that time it is possible for share prices to fall below the issue price. Should this occur, no rational investor would be prepared to purchase new shares when existing shares could be bought in the market at the lower price; for this reason, for safety, the issuer usually has the offer **underwritten**. This means that, if the share price falls below the purchase price or the shareholders do not subscribe to the issue, the underwriter will buy any unsold shares so that the company is guaranteed to receive the issue proceeds. Underwriting can be expensive, particularly for small issues, so where there is uncertainty about the take-up of an offer, the issuer must decide between reducing the offer price, amending the number of shares to offer and taking on the cost of underwriting. Rights issues, especially underwritten ones, are uncommon on AIM.

The only regulatory restriction on the pricing of a rights issue is the Companies Act provision that shares cannot be issued at a discount to their nominal (par) value.

Placings and Open Offers

In both a placing and in an open offer by a main market issuer, the Listing Rules restrict the pricing, by setting a maximum discount of 10% below the pre-issue share price. Any discount in excess of 10% would require specific approval by shareholders in a general meeting. There is no such restriction for a rights issue.

A further restriction is imposed in the Statement of Principles of the Pre-emption Group. The guidelines seek to restrict the discount in a placing to 5% below the middle of the best bid and offer prices immediately before announcement.

Placings are less restricted on AIM, where the Listing Rules do not apply and, as a result, are the most common form of equity fundraising.

3.3.7 Calculating the Theoretical Ex-Rights Price

Learning Objective

5.3.6   Be able to calculate the theoretical ex-rights price

An important consideration for shareholders in a rights issue is the effect of the new issue on the share price. It is possible to calculate the theoretical ex-rights price (ie, the expected price after the rights issue).

Example

Bridge plc has 125 million shares in issue, currently trading at 240p per share. The company needs to raise £50 million in order to complete several projects; its advisers recommend a rights issue.

They suggest an offering of 25 million shares at 200p per share (a discount of around 17% on the current price). The ratio of new shares to old is 25:125. Thus for every five existing shares an investor owns, he is entitled to purchase one new share at 200p. This is a 1 for 5 rights issue (the ratio of 25:125 simplified).

On issue, the share price is likely to fall from its current 240p, reflecting both the new monies raised and the new shares issued. The price to which the shares are likely to settle is referred to as the theoretical ex-rights price and is calculated as follows:

Five existing shares at current price of 240p	1,200
One new share for cash of 200p	200
Value of six shares	1,400
Theoretical ex-rights price of one share (1,400/6)	233p

The theoretical ex-rights price of one share is (1,400/6) = 233p

When the shareholder sells the rights on, by selling the PAL, the value attached to the right will be the **ex-rights price less the rights price**. In the example above, this would be 233 – 200, or 33p per share. In this case, the buyer of the rights would receive a signed PAL from the seller and would be prepared to pay the seller up to 33p to acquire the right, plus 200p (the rights price) to acquire shares estimated to trade at around 233p if the issue is fully taken up.

$$\frac{\text{Theoretical market value of share ex-rights} - \text{subscription price}}{\text{Number of sold shares required to purchase one new share}}$$

End of Chapter Questions

Think of an answer for each question and refer to the appropriate workbook section for confirmation.

1. When might a scheme of arrangement be used?
    Answer reference: Section 1.1

2. Name two types of synergy.
    Answer reference: Section 1.2

3. How is divestiture achieved?
    Answer reference: Section 1.5

4. Name two types of divestiture.
    Answer reference: Section 1.5

5. What are the main options available for financing acquisitions?
    Answer reference: Section 1.6

6. What does the 'funding triangle' represent?
    Answer reference: Section 2.3

7. What percentage of the overall transaction value does mezzanine finance typically account for?
    Answer reference: Section 2.3

8. Who are the three main participants in secondary equity markets?
    Answer reference: Section 3.1

9. Who are the main providers of investment capital in the UK?
    Answer reference: Section 3.1.1

10. What are the options available to a shareholder in a rights issue?
    Answer reference: Section 3.3.3

Chapter Six

Corporate Finance Documentation

This syllabus area will provide approximately 7 of the 50 examination questions

1. Introduction

The corporate finance environment in the UK is governed by a number of regulations. The main ones are described briefly below.

The prime governing legislation is the **Companies Act 2006**, fully implemented in 2009, which covers (among many other matters) mergers and acquisitions, new issues of shares and security on loans. In each of these three situations, the company(ies) involved must file a notice with Companies House of the corporate action that has taken place.

With effect from 1 April 2013, the **Financial Conduct Authority (FCA)** replaced the Financial Services Authority (FSA) as the 'competent authority' that governs the financial services industry in the UK. The FCA regulates most financial services markets, exchanges and firms, by setting standards and enforcing them.

The **UK Listing Authority (UKLA)**, a function of the FCA, is concerned primarily with the behaviour of, and market disclosures made by, listed companies. The FCA publishes the Prospectus Rules, the Listing Rules and the Disclosure and Transparency Rules, which are jointly referred to as the UKLA Rules and which govern the preparation of prospectuses, shareholder approval for certain transactions, and the need to provide full disclosure of relevant matters.

The **Panel on Takeovers and Mergers (Takeover Panel)** is an independent body formed in 1968 to administer the City Code on Takeovers and Mergers and ensure compliance with it. Its statutory functions are set out in Part 28 of the Companies Act 2006 and merger law in the UK is also regulated by the law of the European Union. The main objective of the Takeover Panel is to ensure that all shareholders are treated fairly in takeover bids.

This chapter looks at the various documents that a financier may be involved in drafting or reviewing during the course of their career in corporate finance.

2.   General Corporate Finance Documentation

2.1   Confidentiality Letter

Learning Objective

6.1.1   Understand the purpose and scope of a confidentiality letter

Most corporate finance transactions involve common sets of documentation or include common terms and conditions. The document that is probably most frequently encountered in corporate finance transactions is the **confidentiality letter** or **non-disclosure agreement (NDA)**. The NDA outlines the fact that the vendor (of shares or the entire company/division) is providing non-public information to potential investors or purchasers. The potential purchasers agree that they are receiving confidential information; that they will keep the information confidential; that they will use it only for the purposes of evaluating a potential investment; and that they agree to return or destroy the confidential information (and any copies of this) after they have used it.

By signing the confidentiality letter, the potential investor or purchaser is able to receive non-public information that will allow them to make a full and complete evaluation of the investment opportunity. The vendor gains some comfort in that inside information will not be spread to all its competitors and customers.

The normal rules on insider dealing and disclosure of inside information still apply when an NDA is in place. These are covered in detail in the Corporate Finance Regulation workbook.

2.2   Engagement Letter

Learning Objective

6.1.2   Understand the purpose and scope of an engagement letter

In many transactions the first document to be drafted is the engagement letter – the letter used to engage an adviser for a particular assignment in the first place. Companies undertaking transactions may sign separate engagement letters with corporate financiers, accountants, legal counsel, capital markets specialists and independent industry specialists, among others.

The engagement letter is intended to establish a clear understanding on both sides as regards the adviser's and the company's responsibilities during the planning and execution of the transaction. By setting this out in a formal letter, the potential for misunderstanding (and potential lawsuits) at a later date is greatly reduced.

The typical engagement letter will cover the following items:

- The nature of the proposed transaction.
- Specific services to be provided in relation to the transaction.
- The term of the engagement, if relevant.
- Fees for services, when they are payable and how they are calculated. For example, there could be a retainer payable; a success fee determined as a percentage of the final transaction value; a fee based on time spent; or a combination of these.
- Reimbursement of expenses.
- The responsibilities of both parties.
- Indemnities and limitation of liability for the advisers; this limits the adviser's liability for any liability incurred as a result of the engagement, other than due to its own negligence or misconduct. This may include a 'hold harmless' provision (see Section 3.5).

It may also include certain representations, warranties and indemnification on the part of the client.

2.3 Representations, Warranties and Indemnities

Learning Objective

6.1.3 Understand the meaning, purpose and scope of representations, warranties and indemnities

6.1.5 Understand the use of vendor protection clauses

During the sale process, the vendor and their advisers provide significant amounts of confidential information to the purchaser. The purchaser relies on the accuracy of this information in carrying out their valuation or analysis, and deciding to invest. Therefore, they are concerned to ensure that the information provided is true and complete, and to gain some protection or redress if this is not the case. The vendor is said to **represent** (confirm) that certain information is true and/or complete, and further provides a **warranty** (a promise or assurance) that this is so. The warranties are set out in full in the **sale and purchase agreement** (see Section 3.6), and relate to a number of subjects, such as property, tax, accounting information and pensions. If the representation proves to be incorrect, the purchaser may sue the vendor for breach of warranty and claim damages from them.

In addition, the vendor provides **indemnities** in relation to certain specific matters where there is a known uncertainty; such as the current year's tax liability, or ongoing litigation. Here, the vendor confirms that if a certain event materialises (eg, the tax bill is greater than expected, or the company loses its lawsuit) they will make good the purchaser's expenses or losses. The warranties are underpinned by disclosures (see below).

By providing the warranties and indemnities the purchaser is protected, but the vendor now has a risk of claims. The sale and purchase agreement therefore also includes **vendor protections** including warranty caps. These are limits on the amount that can be claimed for breach of warranty (for example, no more than the total consideration paid) and time limits for warranty claims (for example, 12 months for financial warranties, or six years for tax warranties). This limits the risk to the vendor.

2.4   Disclosures

The scope of the warranties is also limited by the use of **disclosures** against warranties. It would be unreasonable for a purchaser to make claims in relation to matters already known to them before completing the acquisition; but it is important to clarify exactly what information the purchaser has had access to. The vendor therefore seeks the purchaser's confirmation that they have had sight of an extensive amount of information. The information the purchaser confirms they have seen is listed, item by item, in the **disclosure letter**. This is then attached to the sale and purchase agreement and serves as a list of exceptions to the warranties.

2.5   Shareholders' Agreement

A company's Articles of Association govern the relationships between the company, its directors and its various classes of shareholder; they are a public document, and must comply with company law. Alongside the Articles, some companies may also have a shareholders' agreement in place, governing the relationship between all, or specific, shareholders; this is a private, unpublished document and is not governed by company law.

When a company is founded, the founding shareholders may set up a shareholder agreement to cover matters not covered by the Articles; if new shareholders are introduced (for example, when a venture capital or private equity firm acquires an equity stake), a new shareholder agreement would have to be drafted, and this sets out the ground rules for the equity investment. Typically, these agreements are to the benefit of institutional investors but, in any event, they provide clarity as to the obligations and entitlements of each shareholder or class of shareholder.

A typical shareholders' agreement will include the following:

- Who owns the shares (ie, who is party to the agreement).
- Who are the officers and directors.
- Any restrictions on future new issues, eg, anti-dilution clauses, pre-emption rights and tag-along provisions (see Chapter 5).
- Provisions for the death of a shareholder, or their sale of shares.
- How shares are to be valued in the case of a sale.
- Voting, distribution and information rights.
- Any vesting or dis-enfranchisement provisions.
- Management agreements and remuneration.
- Whether shareholders are allowed to pledge their shares as security for a loan.

3. Mergers and Acquisitions Documentation

This section discusses a number of documents which will be encountered in the course of a private company acquisition or disposal. To put this in context, we have set out below the main stages of a company disposal, highlighting when key documents would be used.

For most friendly M&A transactions, the process is usually linear:

- The decision is made to sell the company.
- The vendor hires an investment bank or other financial adviser to manage the sale. The adviser's **engagement letter** will include a **hold harmless clause** (see Section 3.5).
- The vendor and its advisers prepare an **information memorandum** (see Section 3.1) that describes the key features of the business being sold.
- The adviser researches potential bidders, including trade purchasers and private equity firms. In conjunction with the client, the adviser produces a list of potential purchasers to contact.
- A brief letter is sent inviting potential bidders to express interest and request an information memorandum.
- Any interested buyer signs a confidentiality undertaking (**non-disclosure agreement**) and receives the information memorandum.
- The process may differ at this stage.
    - For smaller transactions, purchasers may be asked to submit their best offer. The purchaser who sends the highest bid with the fewest conditions then negotiates exclusively with the vendor. An **exclusivity agreement** (see Section 3.3) is signed at this time.
    - In a larger transaction, two or three bidders may be selected and placed on a shortlist. They will receive more time and information to help them to finalise their bid.
- After a period of due diligence, bidders on the shortlist are requested to make bids. The bidder whose offer is 'best' negotiates exclusively with the vendor.
- The remaining bidder and vendor may sign a **letter of intent** (see Section 3.2) which, while not binding, signifies a serious intention on both sides to complete a transaction. This may include an exclusivity agreement (see Section 3.3).
- The advisers to the transaction may deliver **comfort letters** (see Section 3.4) to the bidder certifying the information that they compiled/reviewed is current.
- The bidder and vendor negotiate a **sale and purchase agreement** (see Section 3.6).
- The bidder and vendor sign the sale and purchase agreement and work towards the closing of the transaction.
- The transaction completes.

3.1 Information Memorandum (IM)

The information memorandum (IM) is a comprehensive description of the business that is for sale, prepared by the vendor and their advisers, and/or the target company's management. It is meant to provide sufficient information for potential bidders to allow them to make a preliminary bid, subject to due diligence. Due diligence will be described in greater detail in the section on equity issue documentation (Section 5).

The IM normally includes the following information:

- nature of the business and brief history; locations; ownership;
- description of the business – products, sales, customers, suppliers, production process and future prospects;
- risks of the business;
- description of the property and other assets owned by the business;
- description of the competitive landscape;
- material legal issues (eg, litigation, patents, etc);
- key managers – brief profiles of those most vital to the success of the business;
- previous two to three years' financial statements, including audit report;
- budgets and forecasts, including cash flow forecasts;
- other relevant information.

3.2 Letter of Intent and Heads of Agreement

A letter of intent and a heads of agreement are similar documents that outline an agreement between two parties (eg, purchaser and vendor) prior to entering into a legally binding commitment. The letter is meant to clarify agreement reached on key points arising in the negotiation of a transaction, and act as a clear statement of the agreement reached for the purpose of drafting the sale and purchase agreement (see Section 3.6). It will often provide safeguards in case a deal collapses during negotiation, such as agreement to exclusivity (see Section 3.3).

Most of these documents contain both binding and non-binding sections. Typical binding sections would include non-disclosure agreements, a covenant to bargain in good faith, and a **stand-still** (which grants the purchaser exclusive negotiating rights for a certain period of time). Non-binding sections would include the proposed transaction value and structure.

3.3   Exclusivity Agreement

Learning Objective

6.2.3   Understand the purpose of an exclusivity agreement

An exclusivity agreement can either be a stand-alone document or part of a letter of intent, as noted above. In order to protect a bidder from doing a lot of work, only to find that the vendor withdraws from negotiations to pursue a better offer, the bidder often seeks to require the target to negotiate with it exclusively. The agreement may provide that the vendor is not allowed to initiate talks with a rival bidder or solicit rival bids ('no shop') or prohibit the vendor from even responding to unsolicited approaches from rival bidders ('no talk').

Exclusivity agreements typically have a time limit written into them, so that each party is motivated to close the deal as soon as possible.

It is normal for an exclusivity agreement to include a **break fee**. A common example provides that if the vendor either starts or continues discussions with an alternative purchaser, he or she must pay all the reasonable costs of the original purchaser from the date of the letter of intent, up to the date of the termination of exclusive discussions. This would include the purchaser's due diligence, legal and advisory fees. In some jurisdictions, break fees might be based on a percentage of the proposed transaction value or a flat 'penalty' payment.

3.4   Comfort Letters and Side Letters

Learning Objective

6.2.4   Understand the purpose of comfort letters and side letters

In new equity issues, the issuer's accountants may be required to provide a **comfort letter** to the underwriters to the issue, confirming that there has been no material change in the issuer's financial condition since the date of the last published financial information. In the context of an acquisition, the advisers may be required to confirm to a bidder that there has been no material change in the target's circumstances.

Side letters are found in a wide range of transactions. They are agreements between some (but not always all) parties to the transaction, which vary some of the terms of the agreement without redrafting the whole agreement.

3.5 Hold Harmless Letters

Learning Objective

6.2.5   Understand the purpose of a hold harmless letter

Hold harmless letters or clauses are the means by which one party agrees in advance to indemnify another in relation to a particular loss. A hold harmless letter or clause may be found in a wide range of agreements, including engagement letters, underwriting agreements, indemnities and insurance contracts.

Specifically, it may provide that one party to a contract undertakes that it will not hold the second party responsible for certain claims and liabilities that the first party may incur in the course of its actions, so that the first party confirms it will not sue the second party for recovery of losses suffered by it.

3.6   Sale and Purchase Agreement

Learning Objective

6.2.6   Understand the purpose and scope of a sale and purchase agreement

The sale and purchase agreement (also known as the SPA) is the culmination of the negotiations of an M&A transaction. It is a legal contract that creates a binding obligation for the seller to sell and the buyer to buy the business, for the price specified and on the terms and conditions outlined in the agreement. These agreements are very lengthy and will typically include:

- a description of precisely what entities and assets are being bought and sold;
- details of the amount, form and timing of the consideration being paid;
- the completion date and terms of completion;
- the treatment of working capital;
- a description of material contracts and mechanism for transfer to new ownership;
- intellectual property issues (eg, transfer of trademarks or patents);
- representations, warranties and indemnities;
- conditions precedent (that must be met before the transaction can complete);
- post-completion matters;
- other details relevant to the particular transaction.

3.7 Takeovers

Learning Objective

5.1.5   Know the key features of a transaction governed by the Takeover Panel

6.4.8   Understand the purpose and scope of a public takeover offer document

Earlier in this section we discussed the processes and documentation required in a **private company** M&A transaction. This is centred on the sale and purchase agreement, which constitutes the contract entered into between purchaser and vendor for the acquisition and sale of the target.

When a transaction involves the acquisition of a UK **public company**, the transaction is generally governed by the rules of the Takeover Code, published and administered by the Takeover Panel. As a result, there are a number of very significant differences between the procedures followed in public offers, as compared with private transactions. (Note that the detailed rules contained within the Takeover Code are covered in detail in the Corporate Finance Regulation workbook.)

The procedure most commonly followed in a recommended public offer is broadly as follows:

1. The potential bidder company (known as the offeror) or its advisers makes an initial approach to the board of the target company (offeree) or its advisers with a view to commencing negotiations.
2. The potential offeror and offeree enter into confidential discussions around the price and structure of a possible offer. The offeree board may provide the offeror with management information or access to due diligence at this stage. The aim is to agree a price and structure which the offeree board is prepared to recommend their shareholders to accept.
3. If there is rumour or speculation about a possible bid, the offeree may be required to make a public disclosure of the approach and talks, disclosing the identity of the potential offeror.
4. Once the identity of the potential offeror is disclosed, it has 28 calendar days to 'put up or shut up' – ie, either announce a firm intention to make a formal offer for the offeree, or declare that it has no intention to make an offer, and be bound by that statement for six months.
5. Once the offeror has announced a firm intention to make an offer for the offeree, it must comply with the strict timetable set out in the Takeover Code. First, it must post a formal offer document (discussed below) to all the shareholders of the offeree company, setting out the price, structure and terms of the offer, which must be made on equal terms to all shareholders. In particular the document sets out the conditions attached to the offer, which include the required acceptance percentage threshold, any regulatory approvals required, and any other conditions included.
6. If the offeree board is prepared to recommend that offeree shareholders accept the offer, it will collaborate with the offeror in the preparation of the offer document, and include within the document a letter to the offeree recommending that they accept the offer to acquire their shares. Otherwise, the board's reasons for not recommending the offer are set out in a separate defence document, also sent to all offeree shareholders.
7. Shareholders who wish to accept the offer must complete an acceptance form and send this to the offeror's advisers. Those who do not wish to accept the offer need take no action.

8. The offeror now has 60 days (from the posting of the offer document) to persuade the majority of offeree shareholders to accept their offer, as the offer is not allowed to complete unless the offeror has control of a majority of the voting rights. Once the offeror has received acceptance forms in respect of shares which (when taken together with shares already controlled by them) give the offeror control of more than 50% of the votes (or a higher percentage, if desired), the offer is said to be 'unconditional with regard to acceptances'.

9. Once all the conditions attached to the offer have been met (or, if permitted, waived), the offer is said to be 'unconditional in all respects'. At this stage the offeror must pay the consideration to the offeree shareholders, and execute share transfers, in line with the Takeover Code timetable.

3.7.1 Takeover Offer Documents

In a takeover of a public company there may be many thousands of target shareholders, so it would clearly not be feasible to try to agree a sale and purchase agreement. Instead, the main documentation takes the form of an offer document. The required contents of the offer document are set out in Rule 24 of the Takeover Code.

The offer document is prepared by the offeror and its advisers, and is sent to all shareholders of the offeree company, as well as to other persons with information rights, such as offeree employees or their representatives. This must be posted to them, or made available electronically, within 28 calendar days of the firm announcement of the offer.

When the takeover is a recommended offer, the document also includes a letter from the offeree chairman to the offeree shareholders, setting out the board's recommendation that shareholders accept the offer, and the justification for this. If the takeover is a hostile bid, this is not included. Instead, the offeree board sends a defence document to its shareholders, explaining the directors' position and urging offeree shareholders to reject the hostile bid.

The offer document is intended to provide all offeree shareholders with sufficient information to enable them to reach a properly informed decision on whether to accept or reject the offer for their shares. This includes, *inter alia*:

- full details of the offer, including the terms of the offer;
- details of the conditions attached to the offer, including the acceptance threshold and any regulatory approvals required;
- proposals for management and employees, or the offeree's places of business;
- full financial information on the offeree (or references to where this is available);
- full financial information on the offeror (or references to where this is available);
- background to and reasons for the offer;
- financial effects of accepting the offer;
- details of the offeror's holdings and dealings in the offeree shares, including those of offeror directors and any other parties connected to the offeror;
- any material contracts entered into;
- the recommendation by the offeree board (if applicable).

The offer document has a contractual element to it. The document contains the formal offer by the offeror to offeree shareholders for the acquisition of their shares. If this offer is accepted (and all associated conditions are met) then the offeror becomes contractually obliged to acquire the shares of any shareholders who have accepted the offer.

4. Loan and Security Documentation

Although the substance of a loan may be fairly straightforward, a typical loan agreement contains a range of complex terms, conditions and provisions.

4.1 Term Sheets

Learning Objective

6.3.2   Understand the purpose and scope of a term sheet

A term sheet is a document which sets out, usually in bullet-point format, the key terms of a proposed lending or investment agreement. A lender's term sheet in relation to a new loan will set out the following:

- amount of the loan (principal);
- interest rate to be paid (coupon);
- payment schedule (whether monthly, quarterly, semi-annually, etc);
- repayment date(s) (maturity).

A term sheet may also be provided in the context of venture capital or private equity investment, when it sets out the terms of the proposed investment, including:

- the amount and form of the investment (eg, ordinary shares, convertible redeemable preference shares or loan notes);
- the investment required from management, and the form of that investment;
- the rights attaching to shares, and the headline terms of a proposed shareholder agreement;
- restrictions on management and/or other investors.

In both cases the term sheet is intended to provide a template for the parties' solicitors to use in drafting the final legal investment or loan agreement, and to act as a framework for negotiation of final terms. It is not in itself a legally binding agreement.

4.2 Loan Agreements

Learning Objective

6.3.1 Understand the concept of taking security in the context of a corporate finance transaction

6.3.3 Understand the purpose and scope of a loan agreement

6.3.4 Understand what guarantees, indemnities and covenants are in the context of a debt transaction

6.3.5 Understand the purpose, scope and limitations of loan representations and warranties

6.3.6 Understand the purpose of an intercreditor agreement

Once the borrower and lender have agreed on the headline loan terms in the term sheet, they move to the negotiation of the **loan agreement**, which is a legal contract.

There are two main types of long-term bank loan:

- **Term loans** – cash advanced at the start of the loan, with the principal repaid at agreed intervals during, or at the end of, the 'term' (life) of the loan.
- **Revolving credit facilities** – when the bank commits to making funds available up to a certain amount, and the borrower may borrow up to that amount and make full or partial repayments, according to their needs, during the term of the loan. This is in essence like a committed bank overdraft.

The main components of a loan agreement include:

- **Preamble and definitions** – setting out the borrower and lender details, and defining various terms that occur later in the agreement.
- **Conditions precedent** – these are conditions that must be complied with by the borrower before the lender will release the funds. The conditions may be legal, financial or structural; for example, the lender might require adequate insurance in place before lending.
- **Terms and conditions** – setting out the amount of the loan, the interest rate (and basis for its calculation), repayment schedule, early payment provisions, fees and penalties for late payment, among others. This section will also state whether the loan is secured or unsecured (see Section 4.2.1).
- **Representations and warranties** – the representations and warranties section of the loan agreement covers statements made by the borrower about its financial and legal status. For example, the borrower must warrant (confirm) that it has the legal authority to borrow funds and that the financial information provided to the bank is accurate and complete. Any misrepresentation usually gives the bank the right to call in the loan and/or sue for damages.
- **Covenants and undertakings** – these are the borrower's commitments to the bank during the life of the loan. Financial covenants are commitments to maintain required levels of interest cover, gearing and net debt to EBITDA, etc. Affirmative covenants relate to the 'wellbeing' of the company: for example, maintaining appropriate insurance cover, and compliance with health and safety requirements. Restrictive covenants include such commitments as not to change management, issue more debt without approval, or issue debt more 'senior' to the existing loan.

- **Events of default** – sets out the conditions on which the bank is allowed to 'call' the loan (ie, demand instant repayment). These usually involve breaches of covenant, missing an interest payment, or missing a principal repayment. They may also include a 'material adverse change' clause, when the loan is callable in the event of any material adverse change.
- **Cross default** – if the company defaults on any of its other loans (from the same or other lenders), this is automatically treated as a default on this loan. This prevents a company from using the proceeds from one loan to pay another loan or favouring one lender over another.
- **Applicable law and jurisdiction** – borrower and lender(s) agree on the jurisdiction that will apply if legal proceedings are necessary. It is usually the home jurisdiction of the bank.
- **Facility agent** – for syndicated loans there is a section that covers the functions, fees and responsibilities of the agent appointed by the syndicate to act on its behalf.
- **Guarantees and indemnities** – if the borrower is part of a group, the bank may seek guarantees and/or indemnities from the parent company. This may also apply when the borrower is a private company; here, major shareholders and/or directors might be asked for guarantees.

4.2.1 Security/Collateral

Loans can be secured or unsecured. A loan is secured when a borrower pledges security (also called collateral): ie, it promises to give the lender a specified asset, if it fails to maintain payments or meet other conditions.

Security may be in the form of a **fixed charge**. In this case, the security is in the form of a specific 'charge' on a particular asset such as a property or piece of equipment. An example of this is a mortgage. The borrower is not allowed to sell the assets without the lender's permission, and must commit to maintaining the value of the assets. In the event of default, the lender can seize that specific asset and sell it to recover its loan.

Alternatively, security may be in the form of a **floating charge**, whereby all of a particular class of assets (such as inventory or trade receivables) are pledged as security for the loan. Over the life of the loan and over the company's trading cycle, these individual items change and their value changes; the company simply commits to maintaining the particular asset class at least at a pre-agreed level. In the event of a default, the lender has the right to seize all assets of that particular class in existence at the time of default.

4.2.2 Intercreditor Agreement

When a company has more than one lender, it is usual for these lenders to enter into an **intercreditor agreement**. This is an agreement agreeing in advance how their competing interests in the borrower will be dealt with. It sets out each lender's entitlement in respect of interest payments, principal repayments, and collateral, both over the life of the loans and in the event of the company's insolvency. The borrower is not a party to this agreement.

The agreement specifies any interest that a lender has in particular assets of the company; for example, a bank providing trade finance may have a lien over specific inventory or a particular receivable, and wants to ensure that a floating charge holder would not be able to seize these assets. The agreement also specifies the priority of each lender with respect to security and payments.

The agreement may also set out how the parties have agreed to act in the event of a default. One common clause is a 'standstill agreement' whereby a junior lender agrees not to enforce security for a specified period, usually until the senior lender has been paid.

In a management buy-out, the private equity investor may structure part of their investment as a loan; in this case, they would also be a party to an intercreditor agreement.

5. Documentation for Equity Issues

5.1 The Prospectus, Long-Form and Accountants' Reports

Learning Objective

6.4.4 Understand the purpose and scope of a prospectus or admission document

6.4.5 Understand the purpose and scope of long-form and accountants' reports

A prospectus is a document prepared to provide potential investors with full information about a company which is proposing to issue new securities, or to list on an equity market. In essence, it contains:

* full information on the offering (price, number of shares on offer, subscription procedure);
* full information on the business of the company (history, industry, management, and operations); and
* audited financial statements, restated as necessary.

5.1.1 Requirement for a Prospectus

A prospectus must be prepared by the issuer, and approved by the FCA, whenever a company:

* seeks admission to listing for its securities on a regulated market; or
* offers shares to the public, unless the total consideration is less than €5 million, or the offer is made to fewer than 150 non-professional investors in any one EEA state.

A regulated market includes the Main Market of the London Stock Exchange, but does not include AIM, which is classified as an exchange-regulated market. When a company seeks admission to AIM, it is only required to prepare a prospectus if it is offering shares to more than 150 non-professional investors in any one EEA state. Otherwise, it must prepare an **admission document**, which has somewhat lighter content requirements and need not be approved by either the FCA or the London Stock Exchange. (Note that this subject is covered in more detail in the Corporate Finance Regulation paper.)

When either a prospectus or admission document is prepared, it must be made publicly available.

5.1.2 Contents of the Prospectus

Within the European Union, the contents of a prospectus are prescribed by the European **Prospectus Directive (PD)**, which provides minimum common standards for all prospectuses issued in relation to the marketing of securities within the EU. Within the UK, these requirements are set out within the Prospectus Rules, published and enforced by the FCA's UKLA function.

In the UK, the prospectus must contain all information needed *'to enable investors to make an informed assessment of the assets and liabilities, financial position, profits and losses, and prospects of the issuer of the transferable securities and of any guarantor; and the rights attaching to the transferable securities'.*
Source: Prospectus Rules 2.1.1

The three elements of a prospectus are:

- **Summary** – this must *'convey concisely, in non-technical language and in an appropriate structure, the key information relevant to the securities which are the subject of the prospectus and, when read with the rest of the prospectus, must be an aid to investors considering whether to invest in the securities'.* The summary must follow a strictly prescribed format under standard headings, and comprise no more than 7% of the prospectus or 15 pages, whichever is shorter. A summary is not required for issues of non-equity securities.
- **Registration document** – this contains information about the issuer and its business, management history, financial information
- **Securities note** – this contains information about the issue and securities to be issued.

The prospectus can be produced as a tripartite document (ie, in three sections, each section being approved separately by the FCA) or, much more commonly, as a single document containing all the requirements for each part, approved as a single document by the FCA.

5.1.3 Non-Financial Information in the Prospectus

The prospectus must contain the following specific information in addition to the financial information outlined in Section 5.1.4:

- **The persons responsible for listing particulars, the auditors and other advisers (banks, brokers and solicitors)** – this section includes the following declaration: *'The directors of [the issuer], whose names appear on page [ ], accept responsibility for the information contained in this document. To the best of the knowledge and belief of the directors (who have taken all reasonable care to ensure that such is the case) the information contained in this document is in accordance with the facts and does not omit anything likely to affect the import of such information.'*
- **The shares for which application is being made** – including a description of the characteristics of the shares (eg, voting rights), the number being offered, and the names of stock exchanges where listing is being sought.
- **The issuer and its capital** – name, registered office and head office of issuer; description of share capital and any changes in the prior three years; controlling shareholders and any other person holding 3% or more of the ordinary share capital.

- **The group's activities** – description of the business of the company, including breakdown of divisional turnover; number of employees; research and development; main investments, etc. This portion of the prospectus is usually the longest. In this section the company gets an opportunity to tell its story, so the prospectus is both a marketing document and a legal document. The section also includes an **operating and financial review (OFR)**.
- **The issuer's assets and liabilities, financial position and profits and losses** – three years of financial results in a comparable table (statement of financial position, statement of comprehensive income and statement of cash flows together with the notes to the accounts). (See Section 5.1.3.)
- **Working capital statement** – a statement by the directors that the issuer's working capital is sufficient to meet its needs for the next 12 months.
- **Management** – directors of the issuer with details of previous work; aggregate remuneration paid to directors.
- **Recent developments and prospects of the group** – general information on the trend of the group's business since the end of the financial year to which the last published annual accounts relate; this may include a profit forecast or estimate and the supporting grounds for the forecast or estimate (including sponsor's statement).

5.1.4 Financial Information in the Prospectus

The prospectus must also contain detailed financial information.

Long-Form Reports

The financial information in a company's prospectus is substantially based on the findings of due diligence, discussed further below. In particular it will rely heavily on the contents of the **long-form report**.

The long-form report is a document prepared by the company's accountants in its due diligence process. This report contains all relevant financial information about the issuer, including its past performance, current financial status and future prospects, and highlights any aspects of the company's structure and operations which could make it unsuitable for listing, or which should be addressed by management. The accountants provide this to the company's sponsor or Nomad in confidence, to provide them with comfort that the company is suitable for listing.

It is also used by the company, its bankers, lawyers and accountants to provide accurate, verified information as the basis of the prospectus.

Accountants' Reports

When possible, the financial information contained in a prospectus is extracted without adjustment from the issuer's published audited financial statements for the last three years, together with any half-yearly or quarterly financial statements published since the last year-end.

However, in some circumstances this is not possible, or would give a misleading impression of the issuer's track record.

This could be the case:

- when the issuer has made significant acquisitions, disposals or other investments during the last three years;

- when the issuer has not filed audited accounts in its current form for three years (in the demerger of a division of a listed company, or the listing of a newly privatised business, for example);
- when the issuer's financial position will be materially changed by the capital to be raised on the IPO, so that its latest balance sheet would give a misleading impression of its financial position going forward;
- when the issue has historically prepared accounts (say) in UK GAAP, but the Listing Rules require these to be included in the prospectus under IFRS.

In these circumstances the accounts would require material adjustment or re-statement to enable them to provide investors with a clear understanding of the company's underlying track record and financial position. The issuer must therefore appoint a firm of reporting accountants to report on the adjustments made and include their report in the prospectus.

Where the report relates to the restatement of historical financial statements – for example, from one GAAP to another, or to consolidate the results of two companies – the report will state that the re-stated figures present a 'true and fair view'.

Very rarely, a company may choose to include financial forecasts in a prospectus. Once again, these would have to be supported by an accountant's report, although in this case, the report will not state that the forecast is 'true and fair'; instead it will say that the forecast has been *properly compiled on the basis of the assumptions made by the directors and the basis of accounting used is consistent with the accounting policies of the company'*.

5.1.4 Proportionate Disclosure for Small Companies and Rights Issues

With effect from 1 July 2012, the requirements for a prospectus for a rights issue are lighter than those for an IPO or secondary placing. This is because it is assumed that those shareholders to whom the offer is made already have, or have available to them, a significant amount of information about the issuer.

A rights issue prospectus needs only to include:

- details of the terms and conditions of the offer;
- information on all material changes to the company's affairs since the date of the last audited financial statements, together with a significant change statement;
- one year's financial information, as well as any interim or quarterly results published since the last year-end;
- information on risk factors relating to the issuer and the transaction;
- information on any material litigation in which the issuer is involved;
- a working capital statement;
- a capitalisation and indebtedness statement.

Furthermore, a reduced level of disclosure is also permitted for small and medium enterprises, or those with an average market capitalisation below €100 million for the last three years. These companies need only include two years' financial information and reduced information on the business and capital, and need not include an OFR or interim financial information.

5.2 Due Diligence and Verification

Learning Objective

6.4.3 Understand the purpose of verification notes

6.4.6 Understand the purpose and scope of a due diligence report

---

Under securities legislation in most countries, the issuer and its directors assume absolute responsibility for the contents of a prospectus. This means that they are liable to civil and/or criminal charges if there is a material inaccuracy or omission in the document. In addition, the sponsor or Nomad to the offering has a separate responsibility to make a reasonable investigation to ensure the accuracy of the offering documents used in a securities offering.

To meet these responsibilities, the advisers commission due diligence before preparation of the prospectus, and carry out a verification process once it has been prepared.

Although this section focuses on due diligence being carried out for the purpose of a flotation, you should note that due diligence is also carried out by the purchaser in the majority of M&A transactions, to increase its knowledge of the target company and reduce its risk.

5.2.1 Due Diligence

The completion of a thorough due diligence examination brings two benefits to the sponsor or Nomad. First, it gives them a deeper appreciation and understanding of the business of their client company, helping them to market it effectively and accurately, and ensuring that they have comfort that the company is in fact suitable for listing. Secondly, the conduct of due diligence protects the managers of the offering from lawsuits from disgruntled shareholders if the price drops dramatically in the market after the launch of the offering. When the due diligence is being carried out by an acquirer in an acquisition, the due diligence report will also form part of the disclosure against warranties.

Due diligence can be divided into three main areas:

- commercial;
- financial;
- legal.

In addition, separate due diligence reports may also be commissioned into specific areas such as tax, pensions, IT, regulatory compliance, operations or environmental damage.

Commercial Due Diligence

Commercial and strategic due diligence helps the sponsor or Nomad more fully understand the business of the issuer and therefore helps them to promote it and to anticipate and manage risks. For 'younger' companies going public, the due diligence process may be the first time since the firm's inception that the senior management has considered its strategy and it can be useful for management to gain this third party insight on the company's strategy, performance, risks and opportunities.

The due diligence review may be carried out by specialists, who will look at the company's products, operations, markets and competitive environment, including:

- key market dynamics – size, trends, value drivers;
- forces driving competition in the firm's markets;
- intellectual property;
- external influences on past and future results;
- sources of competitive advantage/disadvantage;
- quality of implementation;
- sources of risk (industry and company specific);
- key suppliers and customers;
- key success factors.

This review of the company's strategy and industry is accompanied by a review of its operations. The due diligence team interviews key operating personnel as well as visiting the issuer's main operating sites and reviewing its production and administrative procedures, systems and controls.

Financial Due Diligence

The financial due diligence team examines the company's historic and forecast performance, detailing their findings in the accountants' long-form report.

Areas investigated include:

- historic financial statements;
- the condition, ownership and value of assets;
- indebtedness;
- the level and impact of contingent liabilities and provisions;
- historic accounting policies;
- systems and controls, and quality of financial controls;
- working capital position;
- cash flows;
- budgets and forecasts;
- current year management accounts;
- liabilities.

Legal Due Diligence

The painstaking review of all the company's legal documentation is a vital part of the due diligence process. Lawyers examine minutely the company records, contracts, and other documentation.

Some of the most important documents that will be inspected are:

- accountants' letters;
- incorporation documents and shareholder agreements;
- board and shareholder meeting minutes;
- debt instruments, indentures and loan documents;
- documentation regarding issues and repurchases of shares;
- employee benefit plans, including share option schemes;
- employment and consulting agreements;
- joint venture and partnership agreements;

- lease agreements;
- patents, copyrights, trademarks and other documentation evidencing intangible property;
- pending or threatened litigation;
- insurance policies;
- title to real property.

5.2.2 Verification

Verification and due diligence have some similarities in that they both contribute to the accuracy and completeness of a prospectus (or other documents). However, they differ in the level of detail applied to statements in the prospectus.

Due diligence is, by and large, an investigation of the company's historic and current operations. On the basis of the information confirmed in due diligence, the prospectus is drafted.

Verification is a specific, line-by-line examination of the statements made in the prospectus, information memorandum or other document. Each individual statement in the prospectus is verified as a fact and confirmed by a member of senior management, and the source of the information is identified and placed on file in the form of verification notes.

5.3 Underwriting and Subscription Agreements

Learning Objective

6.4.1 Understand the purpose and scope of subscription/placing agreements

6.4.2 Understand the purpose and scope of underwriting agreements

In a share offering, the banks managing the offering and the issuer of the shares enter into either an **underwriting agreement** or **subscription (placing) agreement**. These agreements are similar in that they both set out the obligations of the company and the banks involved in the offering.

5.3.1 Underwriting Agreements

In an underwritten offering of shares, the underwriters agree to buy any unsold shares at the offering price, less an underwriting discount (the amount that the underwriters are paid for their service in selling and underwriting the securities).

For example, a company proposes to issue ten million shares at 180p each. Its bank agrees to underwrite the sale at 140p per share (a discount of just under 7%, referred to as the gross spread). This means that the bank guarantees to the issuer that it will receive £14 million, whether the bank sells all ten million shares or not.

The purpose of an underwriting agreement is to clarify all the terms and conditions associated with the sale of the shares in question. The two parties enter into this formal contract so that there is no chance of a misunderstanding at a later date.

The key elements of an underwriting agreement are:

- **Identification of the parties to the agreement** (there may be more than one underwriter or selling shareholder).
- **Definition of terms**.
- **Duties of the issuer** – for example, to achieve regulatory approval for a listing of the new shares;
- **Representations and warranties** – for example, the issuer warrants it has authority to issue new shares and enter into the underwriting agreement, that there are no encumbrances on the shares being sold, and that the ordinary shares rank *pari passu* with others of their class.
- **Duties of the underwriter(s)** – including the commitment to purchase the shares at the specified price.
- **Price of the offering** – this sets the price that investors will pay for the shares.
- **Underwriters' compensation** – what is the underwriting discount, and how will other expenses be dealt with.
- **Closing date of the offering** – when investors will receive the new shares (known as the 'settlement date').
- **Applicable law and jurisdiction** (the applicable law is typically that of the jurisdiction of the main listing of the shares).

5.3.2 Subscription/Placing Agreement

When a bank is appointed to market an IPO, it enters into a subscription/placing agreement with its client. This sets out its obligations as placing agents with regard to identifying investors and marketing the shares. In the placing agreement, the bankers agree to use their reasonable endeavours or best efforts to place the shares, or to use a book-building process (see Chapter 5, Section 3.2) before setting the price of the offering. Thus, the company may enter into an agreement that says that it will issue up to 'x' shares at a price to be mutually agreed between the company and its bankers.

5.4 Competent Person's Report

Learning Objective

6.4.7   Understand the purpose and scope of a competent person's or independent expert's report

In recent years, AIM has become an extremely attractive source of funding for mining and oil and gas exploration firms. In order to protect investors and potential investors in these technically complex companies, any fundraising for a resources company must contain a summary of a **competent person's report**. The full report itself must be made available to the public. Similar rules apply on the Main Market, and a competent person's report must be included in any prospectus of mining, oil and gas companies.

The report is prepared by industry experts (eg, properly qualified mining engineers) and addressed to the underwriters to the issue, the senior management of the issuer and the directors of the issuer. It contains independent estimates of the quantity and quality of reserves of natural resources that the issuer is attempting to exploit and which comprise the majority of the issuer's assets.

The competent person must belong to a professional organisation with an enforceable code of ethics; the aim of this is to ensure objectivity (as the issuer pays for the report). The competent person must accept full responsibility for the report and as such must also approve those parts of the prospectus where the report is summarised. In addition, the competent person must consent to the disclosure of his or her name and qualifications to the relevant regulator and within the listing documentation.

End of Chapter Questions

Think of an answer for each question and refer to the appropriate workbook section for confirmation.

1.	Which body is concerned primarily with the behaviour of, and disclosure made to, investors by quoted companies?
	Answer reference: Section 1

2.	Define an engagement letter and the items it covers.
	Answer reference: Section 2.2

3.	What is the difference between a warranty and an indemnity?
	Answer reference: Section 2.3

4.	Name the final stage of a private company sale.
	Answer reference: Section 3

5.	Name the two main types of long-term loan available.
	Answer reference: Section 4.2

6.	What are the two main forms of security in a loan?
	Answer reference: Section 4.2.1

7.	When would a prospectus be required?
	Answer reference: Section 5.1.1

8.	What are the three main areas usually covered in due diligence?
	Answer reference: Section 5.2

9.	How do verification and due diligence differ?
	Answer reference: Section 5.2.2

10.	What is the purpose of underwriting?
	Answer reference: Section 5.3

Glossary

Acid Test

Also known as the quick ratio, this is a measure of the ability of a company to meet its short-term obligations. Calculated as current assets minus stocks divided by current liabilities.

AIM

The London Stock Exchange's (LSE) market for smaller UK companies. Formerly known as the Alternative Investment Market, AIM has less demanding admission requirements and places less onerous continuing obligation requirements upon those companies admitted to the market than on those applying for a full list on the LSE Main Market.

Amortisation

Reduction in value of an intangible asset over time; recognised as an annual expense in a company's accounts.

Amortisation Schedule

Loan repayment schedule structured so that the payments made will completely pay off the interest and principal over the agreed period.

Annual general meeting (AGM)

UK-quoted companies must hold an AGM within six months of their accounting reference date. There is no requirement for a private, untraded company to hold an AGM.

Arithmetic Mean

Also known as the simple average. Calculated as the sum of the observations divided by the number of observations.

Asset Class

An investment category. An asset class is a group of investments that tend to perform similarly, for example equities (or domestic equities and international equities). The main asset classes are equities, fixed income, real estate and cash.

Association of British Insurers (ABI)

The trade body that represents the interests of the UK insurance industry.

Auditor's Report/Audit Report

The auditor's report is prepared by a company's independent auditor and confirms whether the accounts present a 'true and fair view' of the company's situation and performance.

Authorised Share Capital

The maximum number of shares that a company may issue. For UK-incorporated companies, this concept was abolished in the Companies Act 2006, but it still applies in many other jurisdictions.

Balance Sheet

Also called the Statement of Financial Position, this is the statement of a company's assets and liabilities at a particular date.

Balloon Maturity

When a loan or bond has low or no repayments in early years, but high repayments in later years.

Beta

A measure of market risk. Beta measures the degree to which the historical returns on an asset (security) change with changes in the market portfolio return. Beta is referred to as an index of the systematic risk due to general market conditions that cannot be diversified away.

Blue Book

Colloquial name for the Takeover Code. This is the set of rules governing takeovers of public and some other companies in the UK.

Bond

A debt security which may be traded in the secondary market, where the borrower (issuer) promises to repay the lender (investor) the principal amount plus any periodic interest charges over a specified period of time.

Bond Indenture

The contract between an issuer and investor that sets out in detail the obligations of the issuer and the rights of the investors.

Bonus Issue

The issue of new, free ordinary shares to a company's ordinary shareholders in proportion to their existing shareholdings through the conversion, or capitalisation, of the company's reserves. A bonus issue makes the shares more marketable by proportionately reducing the market value of each existing share. Also known as a **capitalisation issue** or **scrip issue**.

Book Value

In equity: the total shareholders' equity, as shown on the statement of financial position (balance sheet). In assets: the value as shown in the statement of financial position, as distinct from the market value.

Bookbuilding

The process by which investment banks gather non-binding expressions of interest from investors for a new issue (of shares or bonds).

Break-up Value

Valuation of a company in a liquidation scenario, assuming all assets realised at a discount, represents lowest valuation for the company.

Bridge Loan

Short-term loan to provide temporary funds while more permanent funding is arranged.

Bullet Repayment

When a loan is repaid in one single instalment on maturity.

Burn Rate

In venture capital investment, this is the rate at which the investee company 'burns up' cash invested.

Buy-in Management Buy-Out (BIMBO)

Acquisition of a company from a parent company by its own management, in collaboration with incoming management, backed by private equity funding.

Capital Asset Pricing Model (CAPM)

A theory that describes the relationship between risk and return of a security (ordinary share) and the market overall. The CAPM states that the expected return on a share is equal to the risk-free rate of return plus a risk premium (calculated as the company's beta times the equity market premium). Used to calculate the cost of equity.

Capital Reserves

In a company's balance sheet, reserves created from additions or changes to the company's capital base (eg, from share issues). These are not distributable.

Carried Interest

In private equity, venture capital and hedge funds, the general partner's share of proceeds from investments in excess of the hurdle rate.

Cash Flow Available for Debt Servicing

Calculation of free cash flow which focuses on cash available to service interest and debt repayments. Calculated as EBITDA less cash taxes, maintenance capex and changes in working capital.

Clawback

In an open offer with placing, shares are first placed provisionally with institutions and then offered to the issuer's existing shareholders. Any shares taken up by existing shareholders are then 'clawed back' from the institutions and issued instead to the shareholders.

Co-Investment

In private equity, this is investment by an individual limited partner alongside the private equity fund; alternatively, two funds investment jointly.

Comfort Letter

Letter provided by advisers confirming that there has been no material change since the date of specified information.

Commercial Paper (CP)

Unsecured bearer securities issued by companies with high credit ratings. Commercial paper is a money market instrument with a maturity of up to 270 days. It does not pay coupons but provides a return to investors by being issued at a discount, and redeemed at par.

Common Stock

US term for ordinary shares.

Confidentiality Undertaking

Confirmation that non-public information to be provided to facilitate a transaction will be held confidential and used only for specified purposes. Also called a non-disclosure agreement.

Contingent Convertible Bond

A bond which is converted mandatorily into equity of the issuer in specified circumstances, such as the breach of a lending covenant. Also referred to as a 'Coco'.

Conversion Ratio

The number of ordinary shares that the security-holders will receive on the conversion of a convertible bond.

Convertible Bond/Convertible Loan Stock

A bond that can be converted into a specified number of ordinary shares at the option of the bondholder.

Convertible Preference Shares

A preference share that can be converted into a specified number of ordinary shares at the option of the preference share holder. If not converted, the share may be redeemed.

Corporate Bond

A debt obligation issued by a corporation.

Correlation

The degree of co-movement between two variables, determined through regression analysis and quantified by the correlation coefficient. Correlation does not prove that a cause-and-effect or even a steady relationship exists between two variables, as correlations can arise from pure chance.

Coupon

The amount of interest payable to investors periodically over the life of a bond. Can be expressed in either percentage or currency amounts. Can be fixed or variable: ie, adjusted periodically by reference to a spread over a set benchmark.

Covariance

The correlation coefficient between two variables multiplied by their individual standard deviations.

Current Assets

Assets that are expected to be sold or consumed during the company's trading cycle. Includes inventory, trade receivables and cash.

Current Ratio

The ratio found by dividing current assets by current liabilities.

Debt to Equity Ratio

Measure of a company's financial risk. Calculated by dividing total debt by total equity (shareholders' funds). Also referred to as a gearing ratio.

Default Risk

Also called credit risk. The risk that a borrower or bond issuer will be unable to meet future interest or principal payment obligations.

Defence Document

In a hostile takeover bid, a document sent by the board of the offeree (target) to its shareholders, setting out their reasons for recommending that target shareholders do not accept the offer terms.

Depreciation

Reduction in the value of a tangible asset over time, due to wear and tear, obsolescence or depletion. Allocated over the life of the asset and recognised as an annual expense in a company's accounts.

Disclosure Letter

In an acquisition agreement, the disclosure letter contains a list of information agreed to have been provided to the purchaser by the vendor of a company. Provides exceptions to the general warranties in the agreement.

Discount Rate

The measure used in discounting cash flows, to establish the present value of a sum of money receivable in the future. Usually derived from an interest rate or cost of capital, such as WACC.

Discounted Cash Flow (DCF)

Valuation and investment appraisal methodology; calculates the present value of a series of cash flows receivable in the future, taking into account risk and time value of money.

Diversification

The reduction of investment risk by investing in a wide variety of assets or asset classes.

Divestiture (also referred to as disposal or divestment)

Sale to a third party of all, or the majority of, an asset or trading entity.

Dividend Discount Model (DDM)

A model for valuing the equity of a company, based on the present value of forecast dividends. Can also be used for calculating the cost of equity for a company.

Dividend Yield

Dividend per share divided by share price, expressed as a percentage. May be calculated either gross or net of taxation.

Drag and Tag

Provisions in a private equity investor agreement whereby the private equity firm ensures that management will co-operate in any exit for the investment.

Due Diligence

A detailed investigation into the history, current status and future prospects of a company in connection with a fund raising or acquisition.

Earnings per Share (EPS)

Net profit after tax and before ordinary dividends, divided by the weighted average number of shares outstanding during the period.

EBIT

Earnings before interest and tax. Also known as the operating profit.

EBITD

Earnings before interest, tax and depreciation.

EBIT and EBITDA Multiples

Valuation measures based on enterprise value. Calculated as EV/EBIT and EV/EBITDA.

EBITDA

Earnings before interest, tax, depreciation and amortisation.

Engagement Letter

Letter from an adviser setting out the terms on which they will act for a client in, say, an IPO or an M&A transaction.

Enterprise Value

Value of all the operational assets of a company; equivalent to the total of its equity value plus its net debt, plus any other capital sources, such as preference share capital or minority interests.

Equity Value

Total value of the equity of a company. Equivalent to its shareholders' funds. In a public company this is equal to its market capitalisation.

EV/EBIT and EV/EBITDA

Enterprise value divided by earnings before interest and tax (or earnings before interest, tax, depreciation and amortisation); widely used valuation and analysis metrics.

Ex-Dividend (xd)

The period during which the purchase of a company's shares does not entitle the new shareholder to receive the next dividend paid by the issuer. Shares are usually traded ex-div for a few days before the payment of a dividend.

Ex-Rights (xr)

The period during which the purchase of a company's shares does not entitle the new shareholder to participate in a rights issue announced by the issuing company. Shares are usually traded ex-rights (xr) on or within a few days of the company making the rights issue announcement.

Exclusivity Agreement

Agreement between prospective purchaser and vendor confirming that the vendor will not seek other potential purchasers for an agreed period.

Expected Return

The return on an investment that is anticipated, usually based on historical returns on assets of that kind, and taking risk and duration into account.

Family Office

The investment operation of a high-net-worth family.

Finance Leasing

Finance available for a company. The company leases specific assets from a leasing company, taking responsibility for maintenance and insurance. Assets and liability both appear on the balance sheet.

Financial Conduct Authority (FCA)

A regulator of the financial services industry in the UK.

Financial Gearing

The ratio of debt to equity within a company's capital structure.

Fixed Charge

In a bank loan, security over a specified non-current asset (such as a building or machine).

Floating Charge

In a bank loan, security over a specified class of current assets (such as trade receivables or inventory).

Floating Rate

Interest rate which varies over time; structured as a spread of X basis points over a benchmark rate, such as LIBOR.

Founder Shares

A class of shares held by the founder of a company and usually carry preferential rights compared with other classes of shares.

Free Cash Flow

Cash flow generated by the underlying business operations of a company. Generally shown before interest but after tax, capital expenditure and working capital investment.

Full Listing

Those companies admitted to the UK Listing Authority's (UKLA) official list and traded on the London Stock Exchange's (LSE) Main Market. Companies seeking a full listing must satisfy the UKLA's stringent listing requirements and continuing obligations once listed.

Fully Diluted Earnings per Share

Earnings per share that includes in the denominator both shares in issue, and those that may be issued through exercise or conversion of outstanding options, convertible bonds or other dilutive securities.

Gearing

The ratio of debt to equity of a company. A useful indicator of financial stress, relative to other periods or companies.

General Partner (GP)

The sponsor of a private equity limited partnership; as general partner, has unlimited liability. Usually has responsibility for managing the fund.

Generally Accepted Accounting Principles (GAAP)

The collective body of rules, professional standards, laws, and regulations that the accounting industry is required to follow in the discharge of its audit responsibilities.

Gilts

Bonds issued by the UK government.

Good Leaver/Bad Leaver

In an investment agreement, provisions that tie management into their roles by providing that a 'bad leaver' who quits the company forfeits all or part of their investment.

Goodwill

In acquisition consideration, the premium paid in excess of the net asset value of the target company.

Gross profit

Turnover less cost of goods sold. Represents profit before administration, selling and operating expenses.

Gross Profit Margin

Ratio calculated by dividing gross profit by net turnover. Also called gross margin.

Gross Redemption Yield (GRY)

The annual compound return from holding a bond to maturity, taking into account both interest payments and any capital gain or loss at maturity. Also known as the **yield to maturity (YTM)**.

Heads of Agreement

A non-contractual document outlining terms of the agreement reached, subject to due diligence and contract. Also called heads of terms, letter of intent or memorandum of understanding.

Non-Disclosure Agreement (NDA)

Confirmation that non-public information to be provided to facilitate a transaction will be held confidential and used only for specified purposes. Also called a confidentiality undertaking, agreement or letter.

Hostile Bid

Takeover offer where the management of the offeree company is not prepared to recommend that their shareholders accept the offer.

Hurdle Rate

In private equity, venture capital and hedge funds: the minimum required return of limited partners; all proceeds from investments are paid until these partners have received their minimum required return; after this, proceeds are split between general partner and limited partners.

Hybrid Security

A security with features of both debt and equity, such as a convertible bond or convertible preference shares.

Income Statement

In a company's financial statements, this is the statement of income and expenditure over a period. Part of the Statement of Comprehensive Income. Also called profit and loss account.

Indemnity

In an engagement letter or sale and purchase agreement, a confirmation that one party will not hold the other party liable for any costs arising out of a particular set of possible circumstances.

Indenture

In bonds: formal legal agreement establishing the terms and conditions of a bond issue.

Information Memorandum (IM)

Document setting out a wide range of relevant information in relation to a company which is being marketed for sale.

Initial Public Offering (IPO)

First offering of a company's shares in the market. Also known as flotation.

Institutional Buy-Out

A private equity purchase of a company where the transaction is initiated by the private equity firm rather than by management or another trade purchaser.

Institutional Investors

A financial institution investing on a professional basis. Often manages collective funds; eg, pension funds, insurance companies or unit trusts.

Institutional Voting Information Service (IVIS)

Organisation representing the interests of investors that carries out research into company accounts and activities.

Interest Cover

Measure of a company's financial risk. Calculated by dividing interest paid by either EBIT or EBITDA. Frequently used as a financial covenant in bank loans.

Internal Rate of Return (IRR)

A metric used in investment analysis to establish the average annual return on an investment over the life of that investment. A 'required' IRR is often used as a yardstick to evaluate investments. Calculated by establishing the discount rate at which NPV of a stream of cash flows is equal to zero.

International Financial Reporting Standards (IFRS)

Accounting standards with application in a wide number of countries.

Investment Association (IA)

The trade organisation for UK investment managers. Formed by the 2014 merger of the Investment Management Association and the Investment Affairs Division of the ABI.

Invoice Factoring

Financing available to a company from a factoring company. The company 'sells' an invoice, or invoices, to the factoring company for an up-front payment. The factoring company receives payment of the invoices.

Kd (Cost of Debt)

The after-tax cost of debt of a company; calculated as interest x (1-tax rate).

Ke (Cost of Equity)

The cost of equity of a company, calculated using the CAPM formula or the dividend discount model.

Leverage

Proportion of debt to equity in a company's balance sheet. Also referred to as gearing in the UK.

Leveraged Buy-In (LBI)

A transaction in which a company is acquired by its incoming management using substantial amounts of debt to finance the purchase.

London Inter-bank Offer Rate (LIBOR)

The rate charged between banks for lending to each other and the benchmark rate for lending in the UK.

Leveraged Buy-Out (LBO)

A transaction in which a company is acquired, using substantial amounts of debt to finance the purchase. The company may have been publicly traded.

Limited Partner

Private equity funds are usually structured as limited partnerships. A limited partner (LP) is an investor in a private equity fund; the fund is managed by the general partner (GP).

Liquidity

a. A company's ability to meet its debts as they fall due, out of existing assets; two key measures are the quick ratio and the current ratio.
b. The number of shares available to buy and sell in a market.

Listed (Company)

Admitted to trading on the Main Market of the London Stock Exchange; whereby it is admitted to the Official List maintained by the FCA.

Loan Stock

Short- or medium-term debt securities issued by a company. May be interest-bearing, redeemable or convertible, and may be traded or unquoted.

London Interbank Offered Rate (LIBOR)

The interest rate at which major banks lend to each other in London. A common benchmark for floating rate debt.

London Stock Exchange (LSE)

UK market for listing and trading domestic and international securities. Operates the main market and AIM, among others.

Management Buy-In (MBI)

Acquisition of a company by an incoming management team, backed by private equity funding.

Management Buy-Out (MBO)

Acquisition of a company from a parent company by its own management, backed by private equity funding.

Margin

In bond pricing, this is the level above a benchmark rate implied by the coupon of a bond. If the coupon is 5%, and the benchmark rate (eg, LIBOR) is 3%, the margin is 2% (200 basis points). Also called the **spread**.

Market Capitalisation/Market Value

The total market value of a company's equity. Calculated by multiplying the ordinary share price by the number of ordinary shares outstanding.

Maturity Date

The date on which the principal amount of a bond must be repaid.

Maturity Value

Also known as par value. The amount that an issuer agrees to repay on the maturity date.

Mean-Variance Analysis

The use of past investment returns to predict the investment's most likely future return and to quantify the risk attached to this expected return.

Median

A measure of central tendency established by the middle value within an ordered distribution containing an odd number of observed values or the arithmetic mean of the middle two values in an ordered distribution containing an even number of values.

Mezzanine Debt

Subordinated debt which is usually unsecured and provides a high return to the lender through a combination of a high coupon and equity warrants.

Minority Interest

The proportion of the profit/loss and assets/liabilities of a company's subsidiary not attributable to the company's own shareholders. Instead, this 'minority interest' is attributable to minority shareholders of that subsidiary. Also called non-controlling interest (NCI).

Mode

A measure of central tendency established by the value or values that occur most frequently within a data distribution.

Money Market

The market for the trading of short-term (maturity of less than one year) debt instruments. Includes Treasury bills, commercial paper and bankers' acceptances.

NASDAQ

The second-largest stock market in the US. NASDAQ lists certain US and international stocks and provides a screen-based quote-driven secondary market that links buyers and sellers worldwide.

National Association of Pension Funds (NAPF)

The trade body that represents the interests of the occupational pension scheme industry.

Negotiable Security

A security whose ownership can pass freely from one party to another. Negotiable securities are, therefore, tradeable.

Net Present Value (NPV)

A project or investment's net monetary contribution to the value of a company. Calculated by computing the present value of future cash flows less the initial investment.

Net Profit Margin

The ratio derived by dividing net profit by net turnover.

Net Redemption Yield (NRY)

The annual compound return from holding a bond to maturity, taking account of both the coupon payments net of income tax and the capital gain or loss to maturity.

Net Working Capital

Current assets minus current liabilities.

New Issue

A new issue of ordinary shares whether made by an offer for sale, an offer for subscription or a placing.

Nomad

Nominated adviser: firm appointed to act as adviser to a company trading on AIM, to provide advice both at the time of admission and on an ongoing basis thereafter. Nomads also provide regulatory oversight on behalf of the LSE for those companies they advise.

Nominal Value

The face or par value of a security. The nominal value is the price at which a bond is usually redeemed, though it may be issued at a discount. For equities, it is the price below which a company's ordinary shares cannot be issued.

Non-Disclosure Agreement (NDA)

Also called a confidentiality undertaking, agreement or letter. Confirmation that non-public information to be provided to facilitate a transaction will be held confidential and used only for specified purposes.

NOPAT

Net operating profit after tax.

Normal Distribution

A distribution whose values are evenly, or symmetrically, distributed about the arithmetic mean. Depicted graphically, a normal distribution is plotted as a symmetrical, continuous bell-shaped curve.

Off-balance Sheet

An asset and corresponding liability which a company has use of but which does not appear on its balance sheet.

Offer Document

In a public takeover, the document sent by the offeror (bidder) to the shareholders of the offeree (target), setting out the terms of the offer.

Offeror/Offeree

In a takeover bid, the offeror is the company making the offer and the offeree is the target company.

Open Offer

A secondary offering by a public company of new shares to its existing shareholders in proportion to their existing holdings; shareholders' entitlements are not renounceable. Often accompanied by a placing.

Operating Cycle

The average time between acquiring raw materials and being paid for the finished goods that are sold.

Operating Margin or Operating Profit Margin

The ratio derived by dividing operating profit by net turnover.

Operating Profit

Also known as EBIT. It represents trading profit plus/less income and expense from non-core business-related activities.

Option

A contract where the purchaser has the right, but not the obligation, to buy (call option) or sell (put option) a security at a specified price for a specified period of time.

Overdraft

Short-term debt facility available to a person or company by prior agreement with a bank, up to pre-agreed limits, often for working capital purposes. Repayable on demand.

Over-the-Counter Market

A securities market where trading occurs over the telephone or by computer rather than on an exchange. This facilitates trading in non-standardised units or on non-standardised terms.

Par Value

Also known as face value or nominal value. The value of a security shown on the certificate.

Pari Passu

Of equal ranking. New ordinary shares issued under a rights issue, for instance, rank *pari passu* with the company's existing ordinary shares.

Payment-in-Kind Bond (PIK) or Loan

A bond or loan where the issuer has the option to capitalise interest payments rather than make cash payments.

Payout Ratio

Proportion of net profit paid as dividends. Also known as **dividend payout ratio** or **dividend cover**.

Pension Fund

A fund that is established for investment of pensions savings and the payment of retirement benefits. Pension funds are major investors in the worldwide capital markets.

Placing

Offer of shares in a company to new, usually institutional, shareholders. Can be used on a primary or a secondary fundraising.

Population

A statistical term applied to a particular group where every member or constituent of the group is included.

Pre-Emption Group

An organisation representing the interests of investors and listed companies which publishes guidelines on the disapplication of pre-emption rights.

Pre-emption Rights

The rights accorded to ordinary shareholders under the Companies Act whereby a company must offer any new shares to be issued for cash to its existing shareholders, in proportion to their existing shareholdings, before offering them to new shareholders.

Preference Share

A class of equity that typically has limited voting rights, priority over ordinary shares, a fixed dividend rate and the right of conversion and/or redemption.

Premium Listing

Companies listed on the Main Market of the London Stock Exchange may have a premium or a standard listing. Premium listing carries greater obligations, in particular relating to transparency.

Present Value

The value of a sum of money receivable at a known future date expressed in terms of its value today. A present value is obtained by discounting the future sum by a known rate of interest.

Price Earnings Ratio (P/E Ratio)

The price per share of a company divided by its earnings per share. A measure used in company valuation.

Price to Book Ratio

The market capitalisation of a company divided by its net assets. A measure used in company valuation.

Primary Market

The market for newly issued securities (bonds or shares).

Primary Offering

Flotation or initial public offering; first admission of a company's securities to a market.

Principal

Amount of debt that must be repaid.

Private Equity

Provision of equity capital to private companies by professional investment firms, generally operating collective investment vehicles, with the view of achieving an exit of their investment in a period of 3–5 years and a return in the region of 30%.

Prospectus

Document to be published when a company seeks to issue shares to the public, or seeks admission to listing for securities on a regulated market.

Public to Private (PTP)

Private equity backed acquisition of a publicly traded company – the public company is delisted, becoming private.

Quoted (Company)

With securities traded on a stock market and with prices quoted on a regular basis. If traded on the Main Market of the London Stock Exchange, the company may also be described as 'listed'.

Ratchet

Mechanism to vary the outcome of a financial agreement or investment, depending on circumstances.

Recommended Bid

Takeover offer where the management of the offeree company are prepared to recommend that their shareholders accept the offer.

Provisional Allotment Letter (PAL)

A document sent to those shareholders who have certificated holdings and are entitled to participate in a rights issue. The letter details the shareholder's existing shareholding, their rights over the new shares allotted and the date(s) by which they must act.

Redeemable Security

A security issued with a known maturity, or redemption, date.

Redemption

The repayment of principal to the holder of a redeemable security.

Reference Rate

A benchmark interest rate (eg, LIBOR) that is used in setting the coupon on variable rate bonds.

Representations

Statements made and information provided in the context of an acquisition of a company.

Regression Analysis

A statistical technique used to establish the degree of correlation that exists between two variables.

Retail Investors

Private individuals investing in a company they are not connected with. Also known as individual investors, or private client investors.

Return on Capital Employed (ROCE)

Calculates the operating profit generated by the company as a percentage of the capital invested in it. Calculated as operating profit (EBIT) divided by total capital employed.

Return on Equity (ROE)

The ratio of net profit to total shareholders' equity. Calculated as profit attributable to ordinary shareholders divided by shareholders' funds.

Revenue Reserve

Within a company's balance sheet, it is a reserve created from the accumulation of profits. Available for distribution as dividends.

Revolving Credit Facility

Facility provided by a bank to a borrower, allowing it to draw down and repay at will a loan for a specified period of time.

Rights Issue

Offer of new ordinary shares to existing shareholders, for cash, in proportion to their existing shareholding. Entitlement is renounceable.

Risk-Free Asset

An asset (investment) where the return is known today. Typically, government securities are risk-free assets.

Risk Premium

Also called the equity risk premium. The amount by which the expected return on the equity market exceeds a risk-free return (eg, on a government security).

Running Yield

The return from a bond calculated by expressing the coupon as a percentage of the clean price. Also known as the flat yield or interest yield. It ignores any profit or loss on redemption.

Sale and Leaseback

Financing for a company. The company sells an asset to a finance house for a capital sum then leases the same asset back for regular lease payments.

Sale and Purchase Agreement (SPA)

Contract entered into between the vendor and purchaser of a target company, binding the purchaser to buy and the vendor to sell the target.

Sample

A statistical term applied to a representative subset of a particular population. Samples enable inferences to be made about the population.

Secondary Market

The market where securities are traded after having been issued in the primary market. Trading of shares on the London Stock Exchange is in the secondary market.

Secondary Offering

Offering of new shares to existing or incoming shareholders by a company already quoted on a public market.

Senior Debt

Debt where the lender has priority in terms of interest, repayment and collateral over other lenders.

Share Buyback

The redemption and cancellation by a company of a proportion of its irredeemable ordinary shares. May be carried out through on-market or off-exchange purchases.

Share Capital

The nominal value of a company's equity or ordinary shares. A company's authorised share capital is the nominal value of equity the company may issue, while issued share capital is that which the company has issued. The term 'share capital' is often extended to include a company's preference shares.

Share Split

A method by which a company can reduce the market price of its shares to make them more marketable without capitalising its reserves. A share split simply entails the company reducing the nominal value of each of its shares in issue while maintaining the overall nominal value of its share capital. A share split should have the same impact on a company's share price as a bonus issue.

Side Letter

An agreement between parties to a transaction which varies some of the agreed terms of that transaction.

Spin-Off

Divestment of a company by way of a stock market flotation.

Sponsor

Firm approved by the FCA to perform the function of advising a company on listing, share issues or major transactions. Only companies with a premium listing on the London Stock Exchange are required to appoint sponsors.

SSAP

Statements of Standard Accounting Practice: in UK GAAP, provisions which relate to the treatment of certain items in company accounts.

Standard Deviation

A measure of dispersion of a set of data from their mean, calculated as the square root of the variance.

Standard Listing

Companies listed on the main market of the London Stock Exchange may have a premium or a standard listing. Premium listing carries greater obligations, in particular relating to transparency. Standard listing requires compliance only with European Directive-minimum standards.

Statement of Cash Flows

The statement of a company's sources and uses of cash, and changes in cash reserves, over a financial period. Also known as the cash flow statement.

Statement of Comprehensive Income

The statement of a company's income and expenditure over a particular period. Also called the profit and loss account or income statement.

Statement of Financial Position

Also referred to as the balance sheet. A statement of a company's assets and liabilities as at a particular date.

Subordinated Loan Stock/Subordinated Debt

Loan stock issued by a company that ranks above its preference shares but below its unsecured creditors in the event of the company's liquidation. Debt that ranks below senior debt but above equity.

Takeover Code

Regulation for takeovers when the target is (broadly) a UK public company; stipulates timing, conduct, disclosures, tactical restrictions in bids.

Takeover Panel

Regulator for takeovers of UK public companies; publishes and enforces the Takeover Code (Blue Book).

Term Loans

Corporate loans that have a specified term.

Term to Maturity

The length of time until a bond's maturity.

Theoretical Ex-Rights Price (TERP)

The expected price per share following a rights issue, taking into account the discounted price offered in the rights issue.

Trade Sale

Sale of a company to a commercial purchaser (as opposed to an investment firm).

Transaction Value

Valuation achieved on a negotiated sale or purchase of a company.

Treasuries

Bonds with a maturity of more than one year issued by the US government.

Treasury Bills (T-Bills)

Short-term government-backed securities issued through a weekly Bank of England auction. Treasury bills do not pay coupons but are issued at a discount and redeemed at par, to provide a return for investors.

Underwriting

In a share offering – an agreement by the issuer's bank to buy any shares that remain unsold in the offering at a pre-agreed price.

UK Corporate Governance Code

The code that embodies best corporate governance practice for all companies with a premium listing on the London Stock Exchange Main Market. Formerly known as the Combined Code on Corporate Governance.

UK Listing Authority (UKLA)

The body responsible for setting and administering the listing requirements and continuing obligations for companies seeking and obtaining a full listing. The UKLA is a division of the Financial Conduct Authority (FCA).

Variability

The extent to which data points differ from each other. In finance, it is taken to indicate the degree to which returns could differ from expectations.

Variance

A measure of dispersion of a set of data from their mean. Abbreviated to σ^2 and calculated as the average of the squared deviations from the mean.

Venture Capital

Investment funds available for investment in smaller, younger companies that are perceived to have high growth prospects.

Volatility

A measure of the extent to which investment returns, asset prices and economic variables fluctuate. Volatility is measured by the standard deviation of these returns, prices and values.

Warranties

Confirmation that a particular state of affairs or a statement made is correct and complete. Found, for example, in a sale and purchase agreement.

Warrants

Negotiable securities issued by companies that confer a right on the holder to buy a certain number of the company's ordinary shares on pre-specified terms. Warrants are essentially long-dated call options but are transferable and frequently traded on a stock exchange rather than on a derivatives exchange, as they represent new capital for a company on exercise.

Weighted Average Cost of Capital (WACC)

Weighted average of a company's cost of debt and cost of equity. Calculated as ((Kd x MVd) + (Ke x MVe))/(MVd + MVe). Used as a discount rate in evaluating the company's value or its investments.

Winding-up

Termination of a company's existence through a legal process, either on an insolvency or otherwise. Requires liquidation of all assets, repayment of all liabilities, and payment of any surplus funds to shareholders.

Yield Curve

A graph that shows the yield to maturity of bonds of different maturities issued by entities with the same credit rating. The basic yield curve in the UK is based on government bond yields.

Yield to Maturity (YTM)

The annual compound return from holding a bond to maturity, taking into account both interest payments and any capital gain or loss at maturity. Also known as the **gross redemption yield (GRY)**

Zero Coupon Bonds

Bonds in which no periodic interest payments are made. Both the principal and 'implied' interest are paid at maturity in the form of a premium to the issue price.

Multiple Choice Questions

1. Mangrove plc has shareholders' funds of £120 million, including 100 million shares currently trading at 250p. It has £120 million in debt with a weighted average after-tax cost of 2.5%. Its beta coefficient is 0.8, the current risk-free rate is 2.5% and the equity market return is 7.0%. What is Mangrove's weighted average cost of capital?

    A. 5.20%

    B. 4.30%

    C. 4.93%

    D. 4.14%

2. Davis ltd has short-term debt of £11,250,000, long-term debt of £56,326,000 and shareholders' funds of £139,000,000. What is the company's debt to equity ratio?

    A. 40.52%

    B. 48.62%

    C. 52.35%

    D. 45.67%

3. Bridge financing is best defined as:

    A. Funds provided to bridge the gap between institutional equity and senior bank financing

    B. Short-term funds available by banks to bridge the gap between temporary and permanent financing

    C. Short-term funds with a bridge interest rate that is calculated as a spread over the bank rate

    D. Funds offered to smaller companies to bridge the period of time between monthly cash outflows and profitability

4. Which of the following costs is most likely to be included in the 'cost of sales' item on an income statement?

    A. Advertising costs

    B. Sales department costs

    C. Cost of raw materials

    D. Cost of company cars

5. Which of the following is not a common feature of mezzanine debt?

    A. Subordinated security

    B. Equity warrants

    C. Bullet repayment profile

    D. Zero coupon

6. A company has a current share price of 735p and EPS of 64p. What is its price earnings ratio?

    A. 8.71

    B. 9.96

    C. 11.48

    D. 12.34

7. An investor bought some shares in ABC plc when they were 220p and they are currently priced at 265p. The latest dividend payment was 18p per share plus a tax credit of 2p. What is the net dividend yield at present on the investors' holding?

   A. 6.79%

   B. 7.55%

   C. 8.18%

   D. 9.09%

8. A bond is purchased with exactly one year remaining until maturity. The bond's purchase price is £968 and its maturity value is £1,000. During the year, £15 is received in interest. What is the holding period return?

   A. 3.31%

   B. 6.20%

   C. 4.86%

   D. 1.55%

9. An investor bought 1,000 ordinary £1 shares for £2.20 each and the current share price is £1.80. What is the 'nominal value' of each share at the moment?

   A. £0.80

   B. £1.00

   C. £1.20

   D. £1.80

10. A portfolio of shares has experienced the following annual returns:

    Year 1: 3.22%;

    Year 2: (6.74%) (negative);

    Year 3: 11.56%.

    What is the variance (assume a population)?

    A. $0.5596\%^2$

    B. $0.8394\%^2$

    C. $0.3487\%^2$

    D. $0.6206\%^2$

11. A bank loan is secured by a fixed and floating charge. Which assets have been pledged as security?

    A. All of the company's current and non-current assets

    B. Specified current and non-current assets

    C. All of the company's current assets

    D. All of the company's non-current assets

12. An investment costing £10 million is expected to have the following future cash flows:

Year	1	2	3	4
Cash flows (£ million)	−1.0	1.0	4.0	8.0

The company's WACC is 6%. To the nearest two decimal points, what is the NPV of the investment?

A. −£0.36 million

B. £1.53 million

C. −£2.14 million

D. −£1.61 million

13. Which of the following rights would not generally be available to a holder of preference shares?

A. Right to a dividend

B. Right to repayment of capital

C. Right to vote

D. Right to receive the report and accounts

14. Where the profit figure shown on an income statement appears after deduction of taxation, this amount is normally described as the:

A. Total profit

B. Operating profit

C. Gross profit

D. Profit for the year

15. A company is considering investing in a project and needs to ensure it provides an adequate return. How will it calculate the internal rate of return of the project?

A. Calculate the company's cost of capital, using WACC.

B. Calculate the discount rate at which the project's NPV is 0.

C. Calculate the returns from its existing projects with the same risk profile.

D. Calculate the present value of the cash flows using the IRR of similar projects.

16. Acquirer is carrying out a DCF valuation of Target. It has estimated Target's free cash flows and discounted them using Target's WACC. What is the resultant value?

A. The equity value

B. The residual value

C. The enterprise value

D. The terminal value

17. If the provisions of a hold harmless letter are triggered, this usually means that:

    A. A sale has fallen through

    B. A loss is being indemnified

    C. A new adviser is being appointed

    D. A period of exclusivity is to apply

18. In a prospectus, the financial information on the issuer may be accompanied by:

    A. A verification report

    B. A long-form report

    C. An accountants' report

    D. A competent person's report

19. Which of the following best describes a contingent convertible bond?

    A. It can be converted into equity of the issuer, only if both holder and issuer agree

    B. It must be converted into the equity of the issuer, if the issuer wishes

    C. It must be converted into the equity of the issuer, if the holder wishes

    D. It must be converted into the equity of the issuer, if some specified event occurs

20. A company raises finance by selling some of its current assets (its trade receivables) to a specialist finance company in exchange for cash. This financing is referred to as

    A. Asset based lending

    B. Invoice factoring

    C. Sale and leaseback

    D. Finance leasing

21. A portfolio of shares has experienced the following annual returns:

    Year 1:   3.22%

    Year 2:   −6.74%

    Year 3:   11.56%

    What is the arithmetic mean return of the portfolio during the three years?

    A. 7.17%

    B. 5.23%

    C. 2.68%

    D. 4.11%

22. A company's shares are trading at 79p. There are 600 million shares in issue and it has £200 million of debt. The company has £5 million in cash and owns £65 million of securities. The bank debt has a finance cost of 6% and the securities have a return of 5%. Calculate the enterprise value for this company.

    A. £204 million

    B. £474 million

    C. £604 million

    D. £669 million

23. A company has announced a 2 for 6 rights issue at 100p. Its share price is currently 130p. What is the theoretical ex-rights price?

    A. 120p

    B. 100p

    C. 107.5

    D. 122.5p

24. When an 'indemnity clause' appears in an engagement letter, its main purpose is normally to:

    A. Indemnify the client for any liability incurred as a result of the engagement

    B. Indemnify the adviser for any liability incurred as a result of the engagement

    C. Ensure the client maintains confidentiality

    D. Ensure the adviser maintains confidentiality

25. When the offeror in a takeover bid makes the target shareholders a cash-only offer, this has the advantage of:

    A. Improving the P/E ratio of the offeror's shares

    B. Smoothing out the dividend level of the offeror's shares

    C. Avoiding a dilution in ownership interest of the offeror's shareholders

    D. Protecting the target shareholders from the effects of inflation

26. What impact would an increase in a company's tax rate have on its weighted average cost of capital?

    A. It would rise

    B. It would fall

    C. It would become more stable

    D. It would become more volatile

27. A company's gross profit is £7.2 million, profit before interest and taxation is £4.8 million, profit after taxation is £3.1 million and retained profit is £1.8 million. Assuming interest expenses of £105,000, what is the company's interest cover?

    A. 17.1

    B. 29.5

    C. 45.7

    D. 68.6

28. An exclusivity agreement can be part of which of the following documents:

    A. Information memorandum

    B. Letter of intent

    C. Comfort letter

    D. Prospectus

29. What is the main purpose of the publication of an IPO prospectus?

    A. To provide the UKLA with full information on a company coming to the market

    B. To provide potential investors with full information on a company coming to the market

    C. To provide the London Stock Exchange with full information on a company coming to the market

    D. To provide existing investors with full information on a company coming to the market

30. What is generally considered to be the best reason for merging with another company?

    A. To create a dominant market position

    B. To diversify sources of revenue and income in order to reduce the volatility of earnings

    C. To create value for the shareholders

    D. To increase the overall customer base

31. A company plans to issue ten year zero coupon bonds with a £1,000 face value. The company and its bankers have assumed that an appropriate rate of return for these bonds is 9.35%. What is the price that investors will pay for these bonds?

    A. £456.73

    B. £623.90

    C. £504.87

    D. £409.08

32. Gold Bar plc has just paid a dividend of 12.5p per share, and believes that its dividends will grow by 3.4% annually. Using the dividend discount model, what is Gold Bar's share value (based on a cost of equity of 8.23%)?

    A. 268p

    B. 259p

    C. 302p

    D. 291p

33. Linton's current assets and liabilities are as follows.

    Assets:
    - inventory £500,000;
    - receivables £450,000;
    - cash £50,000;
    - cash equivalents £100,000.

    Liabilities:
    - short-term debt £100,000;
    - current portion of long-term debt £150,000;
    - trade creditors £320,000.

    What is Linton's quick ratio (acid test)?

    A.   1.05
    B.   1.93
    C.   2.40
    D.   1.14

34. When is a sponsor required?

    A.   To advise companies on their suitability for admission to AIM or the main market of the London Stock Exchange
    B.   To advise premium and standard issuers on their access to funding under the UKLA listing regime
    C.   To provide ongoing advice and support to listed companies to ensure that they comply with their regulatory obligations
    D.   To advise main market premium issuers on specific transactions where required under the listing rules

35. Garibaldi plc owns a 22% shareholding in Raisin ltd. For the purpose of preparing Garibaldi's consolidated accounts, it must:

    A.   Include 100% of Raisin's income, expense, assets and liabilities
    B.   Include 22% of Raisin's net assets and net profit or loss
    C.   Include dividends from Raisin on the income statement, and the valuation of the holding on the balance sheet
    D.   Include 100% of Raisin's income, expense, assets and liabilities together with a non-controlling interest adjustment

36. If a company produces an information memorandum, this usually indicates that the organisation is:

    A.   Partly or wholly on sale
    B.   Planning to make a hostile bid
    C.   In the process of demerging
    D.   Applying for a stock market listing

37. What level of return would a mezzanine financier usually expect to earn on a typical buyout?

   A. 2.0% to 3.5% above LIBOR

   B. 2.0% to 3.5% above senior debt returns

   C. 15% to 20%

   D. 30% to 35%

38. In relation to a loan agreement, what is the best definition of a covenant?

   A. A confirmation by the borrower that a particular statement or data is correct

   B. A condition which must be complied with by the borrower before a loan is made

   C. A commitment by the borrower to comply with certain performance conditions over the life of the loan

   D. A commitment by the bank to advance funds as required over the life of the loan.

39. How is market capitalisation calculated?

   A. Total number of authorised shares multiplied by nominal value

   B. Fully diluted number of shares in issue multiplied by current share price

   C. Total number of shares in issue multiplied by current share price

   D. Total number of authorised shares multiplied by current share price

40. What is the best definition of 'carried interest'?

   A. In a buy-out, share of the exit proceeds attributable to the private equity investor

   B. In a buy-out, share of the exit proceeds attributable to the management team

   C. In a private equity fund, share of the portfolio proceeds attributable to the limited partners

   D. In a private equity fund, share of the portfolio proceeds attributable to the general partner

41. Which of the following assets would be depreciated in the company's accounts?

   A. Freehold land

   B. Plant and machinery

   C. Goodwill

   D. Inventory

42. In which of the following situations is an asset-based valuation most likely to be used?

   A. A large company is being valued prior to demerging into several individual subsidiaries

   B. An insolvent company is being valued for sale to a third party

   C. An overseas company is being valued prior to being floated on a foreign stock market

   D. A public limited company is being valued as part of a merger proposal

43. Free cash flow is calculated by taking net operating profit after tax plus non-cash expenses and:

    A. Deducting both capital expenditure and increase in working capital

    B. Adding both capital expenditure and increase in working capital

    C. Deducting capital expenditure and adding increase in working capital

    D. Adding capital expenditure and deducting increase in working capital

44. A company with debt of £1 million is being valued for sale. Its current year EBIT is expected to be £2 million, after a depreciation charge of £0.5 million. A similar quoted company has a current year EV/EBITDA multiple of 6x. Based on this data, what is the equity value of the company?

    A. £15 million

    B. £11 million

    C. £8 million

    D. £14 million

45. Sample plc has announced a recommended offer to acquire the shares of Target plc. Which of the following statements is true in relation to the offer document:

    A. It must be approved by the Takeover Panel

    B. It must be posted within 28 days of the announcement of the offer

    C. It must be approved by the UKLA

    D. It must be posted within 21 days of the announcement of the offer

46. Which of the following is a typical feature of value enhancing acquisitions?

    A. The acquirer possesses good industry specific knowledge

    B. The acquirer is a similar size to the target

    C. The target has a track record of increasing dividends

    D. The target is a regular supplier of the acquirer

47. Stock A and Stock B have generated the following returns:

Period	Stock A	Stock B
1	10%	5%
2	12%	6%
3	8%	5%

What is the correlation coefficient of the stocks?

    A. 0.87

    B. 0.02

    C. 2.31

    D. 0.43

48. Last year, ABC company had turnover of £1,358,000 and cost of goods sold of £606,000. It had EBIT of £359,870. What is the company's operating profit margin for the year?

    A. 22.94%

    B. 37.85%

    C. 55.38%

    D. 26.50%

49. A portfolio has three investments with the following returns:

    | Investment A | 8% |
    | Investment B | −2.5% |
    | Investment C | 6% |

    What is the standard deviation of the returns (assume a population)?

    A. 4.55%

    B. 0.21%

    C. 0.62%

    D. 5.95%

50. Which of the following is not a primary function of a company's report and accounts?

    A. To enable employees to understand directors' remuneration policies

    B. To enable shareholders to understand how directors have managed their investment

    C. To enable banks to evaluate the credit-worthiness of their customers

    D. To enable shareholders to assess the quality of the directors' corporate governance and management

Answers to Multiple Choice Questions

1.   **C**   **Chapter 3, Section 3.4**

Cost of equity is 6.1%, calculated as Rf + (beta x(Rm-Rf)), ie:

0.025 + (0.8 x (0.07–0.025))

WACC can then be calculated as:

$$\frac{(Kd \times MVd) + (Ke \times MVe)}{(MVd + MVe)}$$

$$\frac{(0.025 \times 120,000,000) + (0.061 \times 250,000,000)}{(120,000,000 + 250,000,000)} = 4.93\%$$

2.   **B**   **Chapter 2, Section 5.2.1**

Debit to equity ratio =

Total debt ÷ Shareholder equity = (11,250,000 + 56,326,000) ÷ 139,000,000 x 100 = 48.62%.

3.   **B**   **Chapter 5, Section 2.4**

Bridge finance is a form of short-term finance provided (primarily) by banks to purchasers in order to cover temporary finance requirements between agreeing deals and permanent finance becoming available.

4.   **C**   **Chapter 2, Section 3.2.2**

Cost of sales refers to the direct costs associated with the production of goods/services provided, including the purchase of raw materials. Operating expenses includes general overheads such as selling, marketing and administration.

5.   **D**   **Chapter 5, Section 2.4**

Mezzanine debt is typically bullet repayment debt that is either unsecured or has subordinated security; it commonly has equity warrants attached; and it will normally carry a relatively high coupon.

6.   **C**   **Chapter 4, Section 6.3**

The P/E ratio = share price ÷ EPS = 735 ÷ 64 = 11.48

7.   **A**   **Chapter 2, Section 5.3.4**

The net dividend yield is the net dividend (ie, excluding tax credit) divided by the current share price = 0.18 ÷ 2.65 = 6.79%.

8. **C** **Chapter 1, Section 2.2**

The holding period return includes both the coupon and any profit or loss on redemption. It is calculated here as $((1,000 - 968) + 15) \div 968 = 4.86\%$.

9. **B** **Chapter 3, Section 1.1.2**

The nominal value of a share is the original value at the time the class of shares was first created.

10. **A** **Chapter 1, Section 2.4.1**

Variance =
$[(3.22\% - 2.68\%)^2 + (-6.74\% - 2.68\%)^2 + (11.56 - 2.68)^2] \div 3 = 0.5596\%^2$.

11. **B** **Chapter 3, Section 2.2**

A fixed charge relates to specific named non-current assets, and a floating charge relates to specific classes of current asset such as inventory or trade receivables.

12. **A** **Chapter 1, Section 4.1.2**

$-10 + (-1.0/1.06^1) + (1.0/1.06^2) + (4.0/1.06^3) + (8.0/1.06^4) = -0.36$.

13. **C** **Chapter 3, Section 1.2**

Preference shares generally do not carry voting rights.

14. **D** **Chapter 2, Section 3.2.2**

Profit after tax is called the profit for the year. This profit may be used to pay dividends or retained in the business.

15. **B** **Chapter 1, Section 4.3**

The IRR is the average annual return generated on an investment by a stream of cash flows. It is calculated by establishing the discount rate at which the NPV of these investments and cash flows is zero.

16. **C** **Chapter 4, Section 7.2**

Pre-interest free cash flows (free cash flows to enterprise) are discounted using the weighted average cost of capital to calculate an enterprise value.

17. **B** **Chapter 6, Section 3.5**

Hold harmless letters are the means by which one party indemnifies another in relation to a particular loss.

18.   **C**   **Chapter 6, Section 5.1.4**

The accountant's report may be required in a prospectus or other public document to confirm that adjusted financial information provided represents a 'true and fair' view of the company's position. It may also be required where the document contains a profit forecast or pro-forma balance sheet, in which case the report states, broadly, that the information has been properly compiled on an appropriate basis.

19.   **D**   **Chapter 3, Section 2.4**

A convertible bond can be converted into equity shares at the option of the holder. A reverse convertible can be converted at the option of the issuer. A contingent convertible must be converted into equity if a specified event occurs (such as breaching a particular financial threshold).

20.   **B**   **Chapter 3, Section 2.6.1**

Invoice factoring (also known as debt factoring) involves a company selling its trade receivables to a factor, who advances (say) 80% of the value and takes on the obligation to collect the amounts due.

21.   **C**   **Chapter 1, Section 2.3.1**

Arithmetic mean = sum of all returns ÷ number of returns =

3.22 – 6.74 + 11.56 ÷ 3 = 2.68%.

22.   **C**   **Chapter 4, Sections 2 and 7.3.4**

Enterprise value = market capitalisation plus net debt. Net debt is total debt less cash and near-cash items (such as marketable securities)

Market capitalisation = 474 (600 x 79p)

Net debt = 130 (200 – 65 – 5)

Enterprise value is therefore £474 million + £130 million, ie, £604 million.

23.   **D**   **Chapter 5, Section 3.3.7**

After the rights issue, shareholders will have six shares with a pre-rights value of 130p and two new shares with a value of 100p. The theoretical ex-rights price is calculated as ((6 old shares x 130) + (2 new shares x 100)) ÷ 8 total shares.

24.   **B**   **Chapter 6, Section 2.2**

The indemnity clause is intended to indemnify the adviser for any liability incurred as a result of the engagement, other than due to its own negligence or misconduct.

25.   **C**   **Chapter 5, Section 1.6**

By solely offering cash, bidders do not dilute the ownership interests of their current shareholders.

26.   **B**   **Chapter 3, Sections 3.1 and 3.2**

The cost of debt formula includes a multiplication of (1 – t) where t = the tax rate; so the higher the tax rate, the lower the cost of debt. Cost of debt is a major constituent of WACC.

27.   **C**   **Chapter 2, Section 5.2.3**

Interest cover =

profit before interest and taxation divided by interest expenses = 4.8 million ÷ 105,000 = 45.7.

28.   **B**   **Chapter 6, Section 3.3**

An exclusivity agreement can be either a standalone document or part of a letter of intent/heads of agreement.

29.   **B**   **Chapter 6, Section 5.1**

The prospectus is a document prepared to provide potential investors with full information about a company which is proposing to issue new securities to the public, or to list on an equity market.

30.   **C**   **Chapter 5, Section 1.2**

The only widely-approved economic rationale for Western M&A deals is to create or enhance value for shareholders.

31.   **D**   **Chapter 1, Section 4.1.1**

Price = £1,000 ÷ $(1 + 0.0935)^{10}$ = £1,000 ÷ 2.4445 = £409.08.

32.   **A**   **Chapter 4, Section 5.1**

Share value = (12.5p x 1.034) ÷ (8.23% − 3.4%) = £2.68

33.   **A**   **Chapter 2, Section 5.1.5**

The quick ratio compares current assets excluding inventory, with current liabilities. The calculation is:

$$(450 + 50 + 100) ÷ (100 + 150 + 320) = 1.05$$

34.   **D**   **Chapter 5, Section 3.2.3**

A sponsor is required under the Listing Rules to advise a premium issuer on specific transactions such as rights issues, IPOs and significant transactions. AIM companies must retain a nominated adviser; standard issuers are not required to appoint a sponsor except when transferring to premium status.

35.   **B**   **Chapter 2, Section 2.1**

Raisin would be classed as an associate of Garibaldi and its earnings and assets would not be consolidated.

36.   **A**   **Chapter 6, Section 3.1**

The information memorandum is a comprehensive description of a company or division that is for sale.

37.   **C**   **Chapter 5, Section 2.3**

The typical expected return rates for mezzanine debt lies between 15% and 20%.

38.   C   Chapter 6, Section 4.2

A loan agreement contains financial covenants (financial benchmarks which must be met by the borrower) as well as non-financial covenants, such as the borrower's commitments to pay interest and capital repayments and to provide information.

39.   C   Chapter 4, Section 3.1

Market capitalisation =

Number of shares outstanding (ie, in issue) x current share price = 16,783,000 x 2.40 = £40,279,200.

40.   D   Chapter 5, Section 2.4

In a private equity fund, all proceeds (dividends, realisations, etc) are initially attributable to the limited partner until the LPs have received a return equivalent to their 'hurdle rate'. Beyond this, a 'carried interest' of around 20% of all proceeds is paid to the general partner, with the LPs receiving the balance.

41.   B   Chapter 2, Section 3.1.8

Freehold land is not depreciated; goodwill is amortised or written off, and inventory is a current asset which is not amortised.

42.   B   Chapter 4, Section 4

The most common uses of asset-based valuations are liquidations/windings-ups, valuing private companies for tax purposes and valuing asset-based businesses.

43.   A   Chapter 4, Section 7.1

EBIT less taxes equals net operating profit after tax. If non-cash expenses are added back and capital expenditure and increase in working capital is deducted, the net result is free cash flow.

44.   D   Chapter 4, Section 6.6

The company's expected EBITDA is £2.5 million. Its enterprise value is £15 million (6 x 2.5) and its equity value is £14 million (15 – 1).

45.   B   Chapter 6, Section 3.7.1

The document must be posted to all shareholders within 28 days of the 'firm' announcement. It does not need to be approved by the UKLA or the Takeover Panel.

46.   A   Chapter 5, Section 1.2.1

Value enhancing acquisitions are almost always in industries where the bidder already possesses good resident knowledge.

47. **A** **Chapter 1, Section 3.1**

The correlation coefficient is 0.87. Your formula should show:

$\Sigma A = 30$; $\Sigma B = 16$; $\Sigma AB = 162$; $\Sigma A^2 = 308$; $\Sigma B^2 = 86$.

$$\frac{\dfrac{162 - (30 \times 16)}{3}}{\dfrac{\sqrt{(308-(30^2)) \times (86-(16^2))}}{3} \quad \dfrac{}{3}}$$

48. **D** **Chapter 2, Section 5.1.2**

Operating profit margin =

Operating profit ÷ Turnover = 359,870 ÷ 1,358,000 x 100 = 26.5%.
Note that EBIT = operating profit.

49. **A** **Chapter 1, Section 2.4.2**

The mean return of the investments is: 3.83% (((8%–2.5%)+6%)/3).

The variance is: 0.21%: $[(8\% - 3.83\%)^2 + (-2.5\% - 3.83\%)^2 + (6\% - 3.83\%)^2] \div 3$.

The standard deviation is the square root of the variance, ie, $\sqrt{0.21\%} = 4.55\%$.

50. **A** **Chapter 2, Section 1.1**

The primary purpose of accounts is to provide information to shareholders and other investors.

Syllabus Learning Map

Syllabus Unit/ Element		Chapter/ Section
Element 1	**Quantitative Methods for Corporate Finance**	**Chapter 1**
1.1	**Financial Mathematics** On completion, the candidate should:	
1.1.1	understand how to measure the risk and return of investments	2
1.1.2	be able to calculate the expected return/arithmetic mean of investments	2.3
1.1.3	be able to calculate the degree of variability of investments using the variance and standard deviation of returns	2.4
1.1.4	be able to calculate the covariance of investments	3
1.1.5	understand the impact of correlation on diversification	3
1.1.6	be able to calculate the correlation of investments	3
1.2	**Discounted Cash Flows** On completion, the candidate should:	
1.2.1	be able to calculate the present value (PV) and net present value (NPV) of future multiple cash flows using the discounting formula	4.1, 4.2
1.2.2	understand the internal rate of return (IRR) for a series of multiple cash flows	4.3

Syllabus Unit/ Element		Chapter/ Section
Element 2	**Financial Statements Analysis**	**Chapter 2**
2.1	**Basic Principles** On completion, the candidate should:	
2.1.1	understand the purpose of financial statements	1
2.1.2	understand the requirements for companies and groups to prepare accounts in accordance with applicable accounting standards	1.3
2.1.3	know the purpose of and major differences between: • International Financial Reporting Standards (IFRS) • Statements of Standard Accounting Practice (SSAP) • UK Financial Reporting Standards (FRS) • US Generally Acceptable Accounting Principles (GAAP)	1.3
2.1.4	understand the differences between group accounts and company accounts and why companies are required to prepare group accounts (candidates should understand the concept of goodwill and minority interests but will not be required to calculate these)	2
2.2	**Statement of Financial Position/Balance Sheet** On completion, the candidate should:	
2.2.1	know the purpose of the statement of financial position, its format and main contents, (including off balance sheet items)	3.1
2.2.2	understand the concept of depreciation and amortisation	3.1
2.2.3	understand the difference between authorised and issued share capital, capital reserves and retained earnings	3.1
2.2.4	know how loans and indebtedness are included within a statement of financial position	3.1

Syllabus Unit/ Element		Chapter/ Section
2.3	**Statement of Comprehensive Income** On completion, the candidate should:	
2.3.1	know the purpose of the statement of comprehensive income, its format and main contents	3.2
2.3.2	understand the difference between income from ordinary activities and other items included in comprehensive income	3.2
2.3.3	understand the difference between capital and revenue expenditure	3.2
2.4	**Statement of Cash Flows** On completion, the candidate should:	
2.4.1	know the purpose of the statement of statement of cash flows; its format as set out in IAS 7	3.3
2.4.2	understand the difference between profit and cash flow and their impact on the business	3.3
2.4.3	understand the concept of free cash flow, including EBITDA and NOPAT, and the difference between enterprise cash flow and equity cash flow	4
2.4.4	understand the concept of cash available for debt servicing	4
2.5	**Financial Statements Analysis** On completion, the candidate should:	
2.5.1	understand the following key ratios: • profitability ratios (gross profit and operating profit margins) • return on capital employed • return on equity • liquidity (including quick ratio and current ratio)	5.1
2.5.2	be able to calculate the following key ratios: • gross profit • operating profit margins • return on capital employed • return on equity • liquidity (including quick ratio and current ratio)	5.1
2.5.3	understand the following financial gearing ratios: • debt to equity ratio • net debt to equity ratio • net debt to EBITDA • interest cover	5.2
2.5.4	be able to calculate the following financial gearing ratios: • debt to equity ratio • net debt to equity ratio • net debt to EBITDA • interest cover	5.2

Syllabus Unit/ Element		Chapter/ Section
2.5.5	understand the following investors' ratios: • earnings per share • diluted earnings per share • price earnings ratio (both historic and prospective) • enterprise value to EBIT • enterprise value to EBITDA • net dividend yield • net dividend cover • price to book	5.3
2.5.6	be able to calculate the following investors' ratios: • earnings per share • diluted earnings per share • price earnings ratio (both historic and prospective) • enterprise value to EBIT • enterprise value to EBITDA • net dividend yield • net dividend cover • price to book	5.3

Element 3	Capital Structure	Chapter 3
3.1	**Components of Capital Structure** On completion, the candidate should:	
3.1.1	Understand the elements of capital structure and the ranking of the various different instruments (levels of seniority for equity and debt)	2.2
3.2	**Equity Capital** On completion, the candidate should:	
3.2.1	know the typical characteristics of ordinary shares including: • voting rights • rights to dividends • rights to participate in a surplus on winding up	1.1
3.2.2	know the typical characteristics of preference shares including: • redeemable preference shares • cumulative preference shares • convertible preference shares	1.2
3.2.3	understand the meaning of the terms 'listed' and 'quoted' in relation to a company's shares	1.1
3.3	**Debt Capital** On completion, the candidate should:	
3.3.1	know the typical characteristics and differences of the main types of debt instrument including: • bank overdrafts and revolving credit facilities • loans • bonds • convertibles • zero coupon bonds • contingent convertible bonds	2, 2.4, 2.5

Syllabus Unit/ Element		Chapter/ Section
3.3.2	know the typical characteristics of the following alternative ways of debt financing: • invoice factoring • asset-based lending • finance leasing • sale and leaseback agreements	2.6
3.3.3	know the difference between fixed rate and floating rate interest	2
3.3.4	understand the difference between a fixed and a floating charge	2.2
3.3.5	understand the difference between senior and subordinated debt	2.2
3.3.6	understand the difference between par and premium redemption	2.3
3.3.7	understand the yield to maturity of loan stock	2.3
3.3.8	understand the tax treatment of interest for the issuer of debt	2
3.3.9	understand that debt can be quoted or unquoted	2
3.3.10	understand the key factors in the pricing of debt	2
3.4	**The Cost of Capital** On completion, the candidate should:	
3.4.1	understand the meaning of the weighted average cost of capital	3
3.4.2	be able to calculate the weighted average cost of capital	3
3.4.3	know that the cost of equity is equal to the expected rate of total return on shares	3.3
3.4.4	understand what beta measures in relation to equities	3.3
3.4.5	Know that the expected rate of total return on shares can be estimated using the Capital Asset Pricing Model (CAPM)	3.3
3.4.6	be able to calculate expected return using CAPM formula	3.3
3.4.7	be able to calculate the present value of a bond (three-year)	3.2.1

Element 4	Introduction to Business Valuations	Chapter 4
4.1	**Equity Value and Enterprise Value** On completion, the candidate should:	
4.1.1	understand the distinction between equity value and enterprise value	2
4.1.2	understand the use, advantages and disadvantages of enterprise value	2
4.1.3	know the differences between public and private companies with respect to the availability and reliability of company information; the typical sources of such information; and the various responsibilities of public and private companies to make information available or respond to information requests	6.2.1
4.2	**Stock Market, Transaction and Break-Up Values** On completion, the candidate should:	
4.2.1	understand the distinction between market, transaction and break-up values of a business	3
4.2.2	know how to calculate the market value of a quoted company	3
4.2.3	understand how to compare the market values of companies in similar sectors by use of multiples such as P/E ratio, EBIT and EBITDA multiples	3, 6

Syllabus Unit/ Element		Chapter/ Section
4.3	**Asset-Based Valuations** On completion, the candidate should:	
4.3.1	understand the use of asset-based valuations	4
4.3.2	know the limitations of asset-based valuations	4
4.4	**Dividend-Based Valuations** On completion, the candidate should:	
4.4.1	understand the use of dividend-based valuations	5
4.4.2	be able to calculate a valuation of a business using the dividend valuation model	5
4.4.3	understand the limitations of the dividend-based valuation	5
4.5	**Earnings-Based Valuations** On completion, the candidate should:	
4.5.1	understand the use of an earnings-based valuation	6
4.5.2	be able to calculate the equity value of a business using P/E ratio	6
4.5.3	be able to calculate the enterprise value of a business using EBIT and EBITDA multiples	6
4.6	**Cash Flow-Based Valuations** On completion, the candidate should:	
4.6.1	understand the use of cash flow-based valuations	7
4.6.2	understand the limitations of internal rate of return (IRR) and discounted cash flow (DCF)	7
4.6.3	know how to calculate: • free cash flow • NOPAT • EBITDA • EBITA • EBITD	7
4.6.4	understand the key stages that need to be followed in a cash flow-based valuation: • historical analysis • forecasting • calculating a terminal value • identifying an appropriate discount rate, using weighted average cost of capital	7
4.6.5	be able to calculate a simple cash flow-based valuation	7

Element 5	Corporate Transactions	Chapter 5
5.1	**Acquisitions and Disposals** On completion, the candidate should:	
5.1.1	know the key types of acquisition or disposal and the reasons why they happen: • listed or private • hostile or recommended • owner/manager exit • existing/continuing/new management participation	1

Syllabus Unit/ Element		Chapter/ Section
5.1.2	understand how acquisitions are typically financed and by whom	1.6
5.1.3	understand the basic tax considerations in the UK for acquisitions and disposals	1.6
5.1.4	know the key features of and differences between a trade sale and a spin-off	1.5
5.1.5	know the key features of a transaction governed by the Takeover Panel	1 & Chapter 6, 3.7
5.1.6	be able to calculate proceeds to holders of ordinary shares in a trade sale or corporate exit	1.5
5.2	**Private Equity and Debt Financed Transactions** On completion, the candidate should:	
5.2.1	know the definition of private equity	2
5.2.2	know the key features of and differences between: • a management buy-out (MBO) • a management buy-in (MBI) • a leveraged buy-out (LBO) • a leveraged buy-in (LBI) • a buy-in management buy-out (BIMBO) • an institutional buy-out (IBO) • a public to private (PTP)	2.1, 2.2
5.2.3	understand the key terms and phrases typically used in private equity and debt transactions: • debt/equity ratio • gearing/leverage ratios • capital structure, ie, types of shares and their rights (eg, dividend, liquidation preference, redemption conversion, anti-dilution, pre-emption, voting) • ratchets • investment hurdles • 'drag and tag' provisions • good leaver/bad leaver • 'pay to play' • bridge finance • burn rate • capitalise • carried interest • co-investment • mezzanine debt • down/follow-on round • founder shares	2.4

Syllabus Unit/ Element		Chapter/ Section
5.2.4	understand the types of investment and the funding components of a typical: • trade sale • MBO/MBI • PTP	2.3
5.2.5	understand the principles applied in determining the levels/ratio of equity and debt that may be available in such transactions	2.3
5.3	**Quoted Equity Transactions** On completion, the candidate should:	
5.3.1	know the main types of investor and their ability to invest in either or both of quoted and unquoted shares: • pension funds • insurance companies • collective investment schemes (including open-ended funds and closed-ended funds) • venture capital investors (including venture capital trusts in the UK) • directors/employees • private individuals • family offices	3.1
5.3.2	understand the roles of the professional advisors in an IPO: • reporting accountants • sponsor • nominated adviser (Nomad) • underwriters • lawyers • PR consultants • independent expert	3.2
5.3.3	understand why a company may choose to raise additional capital via: • a rights issue • a placing • a placing and open offer	3.3
5.3.4	understand the basic mechanics including the options available to a shareholder and role of any underwriters of: • a rights issue • a placing • a placing and open offer	3.3
5.3.5	understand pricing of secondary issues as mandated by UK relevant rules and guidelines: • Institutional Voting Information Service (IVIS) • National Association of Pension Funds • Pre-emption Group of the Financial Reporting Council • UK Listing Authority (UKLA)	3.3
5.3.6	be able to calculate the theoretical ex-rights price	3.3.7

Syllabus Unit/ Element		Chapter/ Section
5.3.7	understand the effect of clawback by qualifying shareholders under a placing and an open offer	3.3
5.3.8	understand how the book-building and pricing process works	3.2
5.3.9	understand secondary market liquidity and its importance	3.2
5.3.10	understand the consequences of equity issuance on corporate control	3.3

Element 6	Corporate Finance Documentation	Chapter 6
6.1	**General Documentation in Corporate Finance Transactions** On completion, the candidate should:	
6.1.1	understand the purpose and scope of a confidentiality letter	2.1
6.1.2	understand the purpose and scope of an engagement letter	2.2
6.1.3	understand the meaning, purpose and scope of representations, warranties and indemnities	2.3
6.1.4	understand the purpose of a disclosure letter	2.4
6.1.5	understand the use of vendor protection clauses	2.3
6.1.6	understand the purpose and scope of a shareholder's agreement	2.5
6.2	**Buying and Selling Documentation in Corporate Finance Transactions** On completion, the candidate should:	
6.2.1	understand the purpose and key contents of an information memorandum	3.1
6.2.2	understand the purpose of a letter of intent and heads of agreement	3.2
6.2.3	understand the purpose of an exclusivity agreement	3.3
6.2.4	understand the purpose of comfort letters and side letters	3.4
6.2.5	understand the purpose of a hold harmless letter	3.5
6.2.6	understand the purpose and scope of a sale and purchase agreement	3.6
6.3	**Loan and Security Documentation in Corporate Finance Transactions** On completion, the candidate should:	
6.3.1	understand the concept of taking security in the context of a corporate finance transaction	4.2
6.3.2	understand the purpose and scope of a term sheet	4.1
6.3.3	understand the purpose and scope of a loan agreement	4.2
6.3.4	understand what guarantees, indemnities and covenants are in the context of a debt transaction	4.2
6.3.5	understand the purpose, scope and limitations of loan representations and warranties	4.2
6.3.6	understand the purpose of an intercreditor agreement	4.2
6.4	**Public Company Documentation in Corporate Finance Transactions** On completion, the candidate should:	
6.4.1	understand the purpose and scope of subscription/placing agreements	5.3
6.4.2	understand the purpose and scope of underwriting agreements	5.3

Syllabus Unit/ Element		Chapter/ Section
6.4.3	understand the purpose of verification notes	5.2
6.4.4	understand the purpose and scope of a prospectus or admission document	5.1
6.4.5	understand the purpose and scope of long-form and accountants' reports	5.1
6.4.6	understand the purpose and scope of a due diligence report	5.2
6.4.7	understand the purpose and scope of a competent person's or independent expert's report	5.4
6.4.8	understand the purpose and scope of a public takeover offer document	3.7

Examination Specification

Each examination paper is constructed from a specification that determines the weightings that will be given to each unit. The specification is given below.

It is important to note that the numbers quoted may vary slightly from examination to examination as there is some flexibility to ensure that each examination has a consistent level of difficulty. However, the number of questions tested in each unit should not change by more than 2.

Element number	Element	Questions
1	Quantitative Methods for Corporate Finance	6
2	Financial Statements Analysis	10
3	Capital Structure	8
4	Introduction to Business Valuations	9
5	Corporate Transactions	10
6	Corporate Finance Documentation	7
Total		50

CISI Associate (ACSI) Membership can work for you...

Studying for a CISI qualification is hard work and we're sure you're putting in plenty of hours, but don't lose sight of your goal!

This is just the first step in your career; there is much more to achieve!

The securities and investments industry attracts ambitious and driven individuals. You're probably one yourself and that's great, but on the other hand you're almost certainly surrounded by lots of other people with similar ambitions.

So how can you stay one step ahead during these uncertain times?

Entry Criteria:

Pass in either:

- Investment Operations Certificate (IOC), IFQ, ICWIM, Capital Markets in, eg, Securities, Derivatives, Advanced Certificates; or
- one CISI Diploma/Masters in Wealth Management paper

Joining Fee: £25 or free if applying via prefilled application form   **Annual Subscription (pro rata):** £125

Using your new CISI qualification* to become an Associate (ACSI) member of the Chartered Institute for Securities & Investment could well be the next important career move you make this year, and help you maintain your competence.

Join our global network of over 40,000 financial services professionals and start enjoying both the professional and personal benefits that CISI membership offers. Once you become a member you can use the prestigious ACSI designation after your name and even work towards becoming personally chartered.

* ie, Investment Operations Certificate (IOC), IFQ, ICWIM, Capital Markets

Benefits in Summary...

- Use of the CISI CPD Scheme
- Unlimited free CPD seminars, webcasts, podcasts and online training tools
- Highly recognised designatory letters
- Unlimited free attendance at CISI Professional Forums
- CISI publications including *S&I Review* and *Change – The Regulatory Update*
- 20% discount on all CISI conferences and training courses
- Invitation to CISI Annual Lecture
- Select Benefits – our exclusive personal benefits portfolio

The ACSI designation will provide you with access to a range of member benefits, including Professional Refresher where there are currently over 60 modules available on subjects including Behavioural Finance, Cybercrime and Conduct Risk. CISI TV is also available to members, allowing you to catch up on the latest CISI events, whilst earning valuable CPD hours.

Plus many other networking opportunities which could be invaluable for your career.

Professional Refresher

Self-testing elearning modules to refresh your knowledge, meet regulatory and firm requirements, and earn CPD hours.

Professional Refresher is a training solution to help you remain up-to-date with industry developments, maintain regulatory compliance and demonstrate continuing learning.

This popular online learning tool allows self-administered refresher testing on a variety of topics, including the latest regulatory changes.

There are currently over 60 modules available which address UK and international issues. Modules are reviewed by practitioners frequently and new topics are added to the suite on a regular basis.

Benefits to firms:
- Learning and tests can form part of business T&C programme
- Learning and tests kept up-to-date and accurate by the CISI
- Relevant and useful – devised by industry practitioners
- Access to individual results available as part of management overview facility, 'Super User'
- Records of staff training can be produced for internal use and external audits
- Cost-effective – no additional charge for CISI members
- Available to non-members

Benefits to individuals:
- Comprehensive selection of topics across industry sectors
- Modules are frequently reviewed and updated by industry experts
- New topics introduced regularly
- Free for members
- Successfully passed modules are recorded in your CPD log as Active Learning
- Counts as structured learning for RDR purposes
- On completion of a module, a certificate can be printed out for your own records

The full suite of Professional Refresher modules is free to CISI members or £250 for non-members. Modules are also available individually. To view a full list of Professional Refresher modules visit:

cisi.org/refresher

If you or your firm would like to find out more contact our Client Relationship Management team:

+ 44 20 7645 0670
crm@cisi.org

For more information on our elearning products, contact our Customer Support Centre on +44 20 7645 0777, or visit our website at cisi.org/study

Professional Refresher

Top 5

Integrity & Ethics

- High Level View
- Ethical Behaviour
- An Ethical Approach
- Compliance vs Ethics

Anti-Money Laundering

- Introduction to Money Laundering
- UK Legislation and Regulation
- Money Laundering Regulations 2007
- Proceeds of Crime Act 2002
- Terrorist Financing
- Suspicious Activity Reporting
- Money Laundering Reporting Officer
- Sanctions

Financial Crime

- What is Financial Crime?
- Insider Dealing and Market Abuse Introduction, Legislation, Offences and Rules
- Money Laundering Legislation, Regulations, Financial Sanctions and Reporting Requirements
- Money Laundering and the Role of the MLRO

Information Security and Data Protection

- Information Security: The Key Issues
- Latest Cybercrime Developments
- The Lessons From High-Profile Cases
- Key Identity Issues: Know Your Customer
- Implementing the Data Protection Act 1998
- The Next Decade: Predictions For The Future

UK Bribery Act

- Background to the Act
- The Offences
- What the Offences Cover
- When Has an Offence Been Committed
- The Defences Against Charges of Bribery
- The Penalties

Compliance

Behavioural Finance

- Background to Behavioural Finance
- Biases and Heuristics
- The Regulator's Perspective
- Implications of Behavioural Finance

Conduct Risk

- What is Conduct Risk?
- Regulatory Powers
- Managing Conduct Risk
- Treating Customers Fairly
- Practical Application of Conduct Risk

Conflicts of Interest

- Introduction
- Examples of Conflicts of Interest
- Examples of Enforcement Action
- Policies and Procedures
- Tools to Manage Conflicts of Interest
- Conflict Management Process
- Good Practice

Risk (an overview)

- Definition of Risk
- Key Risk Categories
- Risk Management Process
- Risk Appetite
- Business Continuity
- Fraud and Theft
- Information Security

T&C Supervision Essentials

- Who Expects What From Supervisors?
- Techniques for Effective Routine Supervision
- Practical Skills of Guiding and Coaching
- Developing and Assessing New Advisers
- Techniques for Resolving Poor Performance

Operations

Best Execution

- What Is Best Execution?
- Achieving Best Execution
- Order Execution Policies
- Information to Clients & Client Consent
- Monitoring, the Rules, and Instructions
- Client Order Handling

Central Clearing

- Background to Central Clearing
- The Risks CCPs Mitigate
- The Events of 2007/08
- Target 2 Securities

Corporate Actions

- Corporate Structure and Finance
- Life Cycle of an Event
- Mandatory Events
- Voluntary Events

Wealth

Client Assets and Client Money

- Protecting Client Assets and Client Money
- Ring-Fencing Client Assets and Client Money
- Due Diligence of Custodians
- Reconciliations
- Records and Accounts
- CASS Oversight

Investment Principles and Risk

- Diversification
- Factfind and Risk Profiling
- Investment Management
- Modern Portfolio Theory and Investing Styles
- Direct and Indirect Investments
- Socially Responsible Investment
- Collective Investments
- Investment Trusts
- Dealing in Debt Securities and Equities

Principles of RDR

- Professionalism – Qualifications
- Professionalism – SPS
- Description of Advice – Part 1
- Description of Advice – Part 2
- Adviser Charging

Suitability of Client Investments

- Assessing Suitability
- Risk Profiling and Establishing Risk
- Obtaining Customer Information
- Suitable Questions and Answers
- Making Suitable Investment Selections
- Guidance, Reports and Record Keeping

International

Dodd-Frank Act

- Background and Purpose
- Creation of New Regulatory Bodies
- Too Big to Fail and the Volcker Rule
- Regulation of Derivatives
- Securitisation
- Credit Rating Agencies

Foreign Account Tax Compliance Act (FATCA)

- Reporting by US Taxpayers
- Reporting by Foreign Financial Institutions
- Implementation Timeline

Sovereign Wealth Funds

- Definition and History
- The Major SWFs
- Transparency Issues
- The Future
- Sources

cisi.org/refresher

Feedback to the CISI

Have you found this workbook to be a valuable aid to your studies? We would like your views, so please email us at learningresources@cisi.org with any thoughts, ideas or comments.

Accredited Training Partners

Support for examination students studying for the Chartered Institute for Securities & Investment (CISI) Qualifications is provided by several Accredited Training Partners (ATPs), including Fitch Learning and BPP. The CISI's ATPs offer a range of face-to-face training courses, distance learning programmes, their own learning resources and study packs which have been accredited by the CISI. The CISI works in close collaboration with its ATPs to ensure they are kept informed of changes to CISI examinations so they can build them into their own courses and study packs.

CISI Workbook Specialists Wanted

Workbook Authors

Experienced freelance authors with finance experience, and who have published work in their area of specialism, are sought. Responsibilities include:

*   Updating workbooks in line with new syllabuses and any industry developments
*   Ensuring that the syllabus is fully covered

Workbook Reviewers

Individuals with a high-level knowledge of the subject area are sought. Responsibilities include:

*   Highlighting any inconsistencies against the syllabus
*   Assessing the author's interpretation of the workbook

Workbook Technical Reviewers

Technical reviewers provide a detailed review of the workbook and bring the review comments to the panel. Responsibilities include:

*   Cross-checking the workbook against the syllabus
*   Ensuring sufficient coverage of each learning objective

Workbook Proofreaders

Proofreaders are needed to proof workbooks both grammatically and also in terms of the format and layout. Responsibilities include:

*   Checking for spelling and grammar mistakes
*   Checking for formatting inconsistencies

If you are interested in becoming a CISI external specialist call:
+44 20 7645 0609

or email:
externalspecialists@cisi.org

For bookings, orders, membership and general enquiries please contact our Customer Support Centre on +44 20 7645 0777, or visit our website at cisi.org